THE WATER STILL
AHEAD...

Gerard C. O'Brien

Library of Congress Control Number:
2004090361

ISBN 0-9743850-0-X

Additional copies of this book are available by mail.
Send $12.00 each (includes tax and postage) to:
Gerard C. O'Brien
115 Essex St.
Indian Orchard, MA 01151

Printed in the United States of America
by Morris Publishing
3212 E. Hwy 30
Kearney, NE 68847
800-650-7888
www.morrispublishing.com

Acknowledgments

- To my wife Eva, and children Jed, Ben, Erin and Moira for their patient listening to my tales years before I put them on paper.

- To my wife Eva and friend Art for their assistance in the designing of the front cover.

- To Art Lourenco for swashbuckling through my spelling and grammar and for his invaluable editing.

- To Art's wife Reggie, for lending him out.

- To my good friend Doug Kimball, for sharing his resources on Connecticut Valley wildlife and natural history.

- To Mr. Ron Allie of the New Hampshire Fish and Game Division, for his cooperation in securing access to search and rescue files on the Connecticut River.

- To the parents and adults who were instrumental in making our dream a reality.

- To Ray Roberge, Jr. for having the sense and foresight of bringing his camera on the trip and gracefully sharing his treasured photos.

- To Joe O'Brien III for saving his souvenir photo of the *Tom Colton Show*.

- To Joe O'Brien III, Ray Roberge, Jr., Gene DeGrandpre, Ed "Sparky" McGrath, Kevin Boulais, Dennis Riel, Jim O'Brien, Steven Kelly, Kevin Sullivan, and (in memory of) Mr. Pete Boulais for their persistent paddling and failure to quit. Thanks for the memories.

- Finally, Thanks Be To God, who makes all things possible.

"This stream may perhaps with more propriety than any other in the world be named the beautiful river. From Stuart (Stewartstown, NH) to the Sound it uniformly maintains this character. The purity, salubrity, and sweetness of its waters; the frequency and elegance of its meanders; its absolute freedom from all aquatic vegetables; the uncommon and universal beauty of its banks, here a smooth and winding beach, there covered with rich verdure, now fringed with bushes, now covered with lofty trees, and now formed by the intruding hill, the rude bluff and the shaggy mountain - are objects which no traveler can thoroughly describe."

- Timothy Dwight,
  Yale University President, 1795

Contents

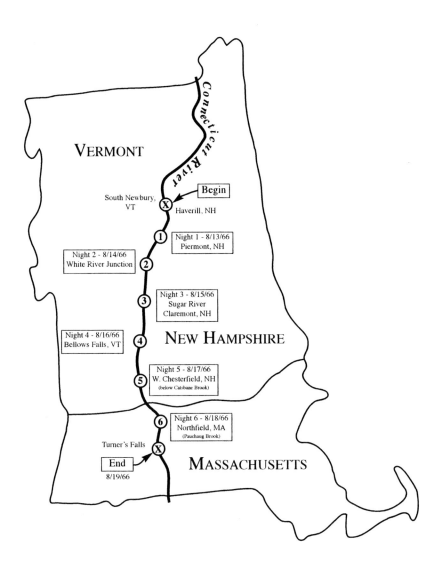

Our Itinerary

8/13/1966 through 8/19/1966

i.

Preface

The canoe trip was always in my heart and soul, and I shared it intermittently with those I chose to as I ambled through life. Too bad someone doesn't write it down, I thought sporadically as procrastination worked me over well. For better or worse, that someone was myself. Yet my sparkplug didn't ignite until August 1998, 32 years after we put down our paddles. I was returning from a Vermont vacation with my wife Eva, and daughters Erin and Moira. Coming off Route 89 South and merging onto Route 91 South, the majestic view caught my eye. The setting western sun cast its long salmon rays upon the lush emerald hills and mountains across the Connecticut River into Lebanon, NH and beyond. The beauty of the moment in that spot had me spellbound because I had never seen such a magnificent view from that height at sunset. The sky was a heavenly blue smattered generously with whipped cream clouds seemingly right out of an aerosol can. Directly below our coasting van was White River Junction, VT with the Connecticut flowing serenely towards the next town of Hartland, VT. How well I knew that in Hartland a serene river would transform into a savage one even if only for a short spell, but long enough to inflict some serious damage on anyone who dared to paddle her. This thought was fleeting as the onslaught of good times came rushing into my head once again. I've gotta write what I remembered I thought. And so I did.

There's a story in every one of us, yet for reasons too diverse for explanation many of us don't record it as a book, tape, CD, or in a laptop for that matter. Many do.

My reason was perhaps too simple for many but none the less it was mine. It was because I had a marvelously good time amidst all the risks and I wanted to share it with others. That's all.

If you're like me, I really found it an annoyance wading through the prologue, foreword, introduction or preface of any book, especially one I thought I might take a liking to. So I'll help you scuttle through this one real quick and try to finish up in the next sentence.

Now find yourself a cozy spot, in your favorite chair, perhaps by a fireplace or special window, on a rainy or wintry day and sit back and enjoy.

Introduction

Looks really are deceiving. The water quality upon putting in at South Newbury, VT appeared clean and relatively clear with low turbidity. Yet the Connecticut River's water quality was and is elusive depending on one's location. In 1966 we were basically swimming and canoeing in a polluted river but it didn't seem so. The landscape was picturesque, the atmosphere calm...so how could this water be contaminated? Simple. Communities and industries viewed the river as a toilet. Just flush our wastes away at full throttle. The river was a convenient out for mills and factories, and scant laws existed, if any, to protect waterways.

Canoeing the Connecticut in 1966 placed us six years before the 1972 Federal Clean Water Act and seven years ahead of the 1973 Endangered Species Act. There wasn't an exorbitant amount of records and classification available regarding aquatic life in the sixties, but a few things were consistently cropping up. Foul smelling air, discolored waters and belly up fish were at home in the American rivers including the Connecticut. This triad of symptoms needed no scientific laboratory to rile activists and environmentalists into action.

Farmers for their part played a positive role in that they refused to yield to pressure to sell off their land to developers and industries. They knew what the early English and Dutch settlers knew which was that the Connecticut River Valley was rich and fertile, ideally suited for farming. The native Americans had taught them well.

In 1972, the CRWC (Conn. River Watershed Council) estimated that "between 1955-1965 more than 75 sewage treatment plants were built in the valley." The river was to be clean enough for people and fish to swim in by 1974 in Connecticut and Massachusetts and by 1976 in Vermont and New Hampshire. Boy, we were swimming in that river 10 years prior! This did not seem odd at the time for the water quality presented itself as clean as we maneuvered the intervals between White River Junction, Hanover, Bellows Falls, Brattleboro and Turner's Falls. Perhaps the river is portrayed as clean since the 148 tributaries in its watershed also appear to be clean. Any high school chemistry lab offers ample demonstrations of solutions, mixtures and dilutions. The deception lies in the clear water's safe appearance which easily mirrors three drinking buddies having a good time until each discovers who's got the glass of water, the glass of vodka, or the glass of ammonia. The river and its tributaries may "look" clean but it's the chemical composition therein that gets the federal dollars. In any event, we did not drink the Connecticut. Swam it, yes. Canoed it, yes.

For our part, we were well intended to keep the river clean but our intentions perhaps didn't go far enough. You see it was a trifle impossible to lug a Sani-can with us on the trip so when nature called and it needed easing we simply ambled a few yards off shore and did our easing. What did not decompose eventually leached down and back into the water table I'm afraid, so we were a bit guilty also.

For every action there is a reaction and on the river this situation is no less. Without a doubt dam construction gave us a welcome flood control program but it also launched a metamorphosis on the Connecticut River. In Bacon's 1907 book, *The Connecticut River*, there are ample photos of the river prior to dam construction in the 19th century. Most dams were built from 1790 onward, and were short lived due to the fragility of wood. Regardless, when they gave way they were rebuilt somewhere and somehow.

The modern dams created large "lakes" which gave rise to increased boating, canoeing, and other aquatic recreation on the river. The dams we encountered, Wilder (1950), Bellows Falls (1928), Vernon (1909) and Turner's Falls (1916) slowly and stealthily transformed a wild, raging and impassable river into a calmer, lake like quick water. Without a doubt, the lack of these dams would have resulted in no canoe trip.

Yet our gratitude for a safer and more navigable river to paddle upon had encountered another drawback. Anadromous fish, salmon and shad in particular, were dealt a cruel hand by dam construction however beneficial. Man had tamed this here river but technology locked out these great fish. Atlantic salmon relying upon northern rivers to reach their spawning grounds could not arrive at this crucial spot. These fish can jump but not so high as over a dam. How short sighted was that? Very. Luckily, shad survived by spawning below the dam making the most of this man made hurdle. For this reason, salmon was last sighted on the Connecticut when George Washington was president in 1794. They returned to the sea on a one way ticket for 191 years.

Enter the fish ladder. The Holyoke, MA dam added one in 1955 which enabled salmon and shad to jump enough to migrate upstream but still in polluted water. The 1972 Clean Water Act went to bat for these fish and more ladders were erected. Our three portage dams had no fish ladders in 1966 which is why we probably saw only belly up carp. Wilder Dam had their fish ladder up in 1987, 21 years after we left. Bellows Falls had one in 1984; Vernon Dam caught on in 1981; and Turner's Falls opened theirs in 1980. Then Wildlife and Fish Biologists went to work on the salmon's comeback. This arduous program showed dividends in 1985 when an Atlantic salmon was finally spotted in a pool at White River Junction, VT.

Yes, the river has undergone quite a metamorphosis since we pulled back our paddles in 1966. Countless dollars were sunk into fish ladders while federal, state, and local conservation groups labored selflessly to bring back the Connecticut to a state that it once was. In 1997, the Connecticut River was selected nationally as one of 14 rivers designated "An American Heritage River." Now the challenge is to maintain the purity that has been reestablished by the hard work of others.

I'm indebted to those who had the vision that we could canoe this great river despite its subpar conditions in 1966. Had anyone waited to use the river until it was cleaned up, well, canoeing, kayaking, and boating just might be extinct by now. And that wouldn't be such a good thing. My hope is that everyone who uses the river for whatever purpose employs the principle that we had to live by in scouting...leave your place cleaner than when you arrived.

And by all means, wear a life jacket. Happy paddling!!

1 The Meeting

It was a typical Troop 40 Boy Scout meeting. Twenty five or more boys scampering about the damp basement hall of Saint Aloysius School on Worcester Street in Indian Orchard. I can still feel the welcome coolness of the basement air upon my face while descending the stairs for our weekly meeting. The smell of musty, canvas tents from the storage room is embedded in my mind. Those scents evoked certain memories also. The tents the scout moms sewed and labored over. The ones heavier than fifty pounds of potatoes each. The moms we never saw at work or appreciated until years later. By then, we really appreciated something new: nylon tents with mosquito netting. Those new tents were a dream. Oh, how we would miss lying down to sleep without being harassed by squadrons of mosquitoes before slumber set in. Or worse yet, the annoyance of one kamikaze mosquito at ground zero in your ear canal to test your resolve and sanity. Oh, you think you got him did you? Well, for the next week your ear lobe was mistaken for a ripe cherry tomato it was swollen so bad. Sure you got him.

The troop meeting had opened up with our recitation of the Scout Oath or Law. We had dispersed on orders and were now divided up by patrols, meeting in our respective corners of the hall. Patrols each had a given name and a flag usually centered around some wildlife critter. During my scouting tenure, I had been a member of the beaver patrol, falcon patrol, and the hawk patrol. After the canoe trip, I had the pleasure of being in a patrol with Kevin Sullivan. After patrol officers election, the members had the opportunity to retain the patrol's present name or change it. Sully wanted a new name and asked for a week's delay to dream one up. The next week most of us came back with the usual wildlife critter nominations. Not Kevin. He would have none of those "mundane mascots" again. He proposed the "Triple 'M' S Patrol". And thus, the "Merry Marvel Mutant Society" Patrol was born. He never gave us a straight answer exactly what the heck it meant or where he even got it, but we went with it because it was innovative and rendered us unique.

The time for patrol dues collection rolled around accompanied with the usual torturous groans piercing the air. It was a dreaded part of the troop meeting yet essential. That confounded little 3 by 5 manila envelope! The patrol treasurer commenced his weekly saunter, shuffling about from patrol member to patrol member. As you can imagine, we had scattered in order to avoid this "tax man".

"Got your dues?" asked Ernie DeGrandpre, agonizing internally, who was doing his six month stint as treasurer. "Yes sir," said Tommie MacKay, another patrol member, forking over his ten cent dues.

"Come on...who else? Pay up you guys or we ain't gonna have money for the campout," Ernie threatened us with bulging eyes.

Of course, most of us scoundrels were up and about fomenting minor mischief barely paying scant attention to Ernie's fiscal theatrics. I can see him now. Checking off the little boxes on the dues envelope next to our names with his whittled down microscopic pencil, acting proud with authority for six months. And all the while, himself aching to meander and fool around like the rest of us. But by virtue of his office knew he had to stay put and collect the patrol dues. Just grin and bear it. That is the way it is in scouting when boys assume some semblance of responsibility and do their best at it. That is the idea of trying to make real men from real boys. We, for our part, knew very little about this process simply because we were boys at heart. Our minds were focused elsewhere if they were focused at all.

Now Ernie finally made it around to me.

"Got your dues Gerry?" he asked out of monotonous habit. Yanking a dime out of my pants pocket I paid him. Ernie gaped at me in disbelief.

"Hey, you owe three weeks!" he blurted half serious, "Come on... you got a paper route!"

"I know but I forgot," said I, feigning the time tested image of an ignoramus.

"Sure...right," he retorted sarcastically.

"I remember you once owed four weeks Ernie," I recalled, hoping my three week debt would pale in comparison.

Ernie began to laugh, abandoning his astuteness, as we chuckled a few more seconds. And then when he turned to look for another fiscal victim to prey upon, I landed a good punch right to his outside upper arm. Direct hit right on the "vaccination spot". I bolted away. A ritual. A brotherhood punch. A forceful punch that almost felt good but really did not hurt. A punch most of us threw to the upper arm. A bonding punch. A punch that said, "I know where to land this so as not to do harm but says I like you as a person." That is the way it was for us in scouting when hugging was just too sissy of an act for boys, eleven to

2

eighteen years old. I knew Ernie would return the "favor" sometime soon, on the sly, as I landed his. One never suspects it. It just lands and jolts you. But after the punch, you reel to see your friend scampering off, laughing at you in retaliation. Now you owe him one in the near future. The bonding punch cycle never ends.

After the dues scenario, each scout found his way to a station. Stations were those dynamic mini-classes where older boy scouts instructed the younger scouts in scouting skills such as knots, lashings, first aid, Morse code, semaphore, knife and axe, or whatever. The list was endless. This was school, and the class didn't break up until everyone demonstrated at least something taught that night. Here one paid attention big time since everyone wanted to move on to the "game" portion of the meeting.

Now the game portion of each meeting was nuts. We despised variety and more often than not we battled like animals at "Steal the Bacon". Everyone was still clad in Khaki uniforms minus our neckerchiefs and slides since we were so hot and sweaty. Frantic, eager, and full of life were we.

The troop was divided in half with each scout having a partner. Both were assigned the same number and faced each other from across the hall, on opposing teams. Blood thirsty was a fair adjective to describe the guys in the course of this game. Game? War rather. In the middle, between the teams lie the bacon which was anything that could be grabbed with one hand. When a number was called out, both guys with that number would dart towards the bacon hoping to garner it first. The object is to bring the bacon home to your team's side for one point. If your partner tags you before you get back, you lose the point. Lunging, stretching, sprinting, cussing, screaming, complaining, and accusing...all for the sake of one point. This game as we played it made the World Cup Soccer Final seem wilted. The interest heightened when Roger Bedford tried to make it back over the line. Instead of scoring a point for his team, he was stopped fast by one of four iron lolly columns. Dropping the bacon, he crumpled up on the floor and moaned. We dragged him off to the side and by Jezebel that game went on.

Then, like the dreaded toll of a schoolhouse bell, our Scoutmaster, Mr. Peter Boulais, would raise the Scout sign. This international sign is made by forming a ninety degree angle with your right arm, elbow bent, while pointing the middle three fingers skyward, with the pinkie and thumb each bent under, holding each other static.

The Scout sign means quiet. It echoes authority without making a

3

peep. It commands respect. Upon seeing it, a scout freezes and becomes silent. Then in a show of solidarity each scout's duty is to make the sign himself, remain quiet, and listen intently for orders. As was the case often enough, Mr. Boulais would inevitably have to yell "freeze" with a disdained look, since without doubt a few scouts would always take their sweet time in responding to the Scout sign.

"The Scout sign is up, gentlemen!" he would snap and that did the trick.

Instinctively, we knew by ritual that usually the Scout sign was a forewarning that the troop game was over. Sure enough, Mr. Boulais positioned his arms out straight to his sides at forty five degree angles...the semicircle sign. We lamented despite our knowing it was futile, and fell in, forming a semi-circle in front of our Scoutmaster. Mr. Boulais always stood with his back towards the wall with the Scout Law painted upon it. His clipboard was with him and he was dressed impeccably in his Scoutmaster's uniform. A short man of about 5'6", Mr. Boulais was a former Green Beret. A military man who expected great things from his boy scout troop. High ideals. As a troop, he had us march in countless Veteran's Day and Memorial Day parades. We were drilled. We sang. He had us all wear that distinctive Troop 40 "Red Beret". This made us look classier than all other troops whether at summer camp or on camporees. We were the envy of other troops and often felt their vibes on camporees. It certainly was not a case of our troop regarding ourselves as better than other troops. We just tried to be better at those competitive camporees. After all, "On my honor, I will do my best" had to be lived out.

The gauntlet that was about to be cast down before us was a challenge that most of us hadn't dreamt of. The announcement would come from Mr. Boulais. We sort of tolerated the announcements part of the troop meeting since it abruptly ended our game. That really ticked us off especially if one was on the losing side. We came around though. These announcements had to be listened to at least halfheartedly since we needed to weed out which upcoming events pertained to us individually or by patrol.

But Mr. Boulais' proclamation that the troop was officially planning a canoe trip transformed that drone meeting into sheer pandemonium. At least temporarily. I can still see it now. How do you contain the joy and exhilaration of twenty five plus boys who have just been told their troop is taking a six day canoe trip? You do not. You let them vent that joy. And for a good while there was an abundance of arm

4

punching, shoving, face making, and ecstatic screams piercing the air.

Without doubt, each of us already had the notion of "I am going" etched in our minds. This was no ordinary event. No campout, hike, camporee, or even summer camp could possibly compare to it. You see those events were already in the "been there, done that" department. A canoe trip offered uncharted territory for this boy scout troop...no pun intended. Adventure like never before lie ahead...or so most of us thought.

Being much older and understanding things in a different light, I realize that the canoe trip announcement could have been nothing less than bittersweet for Mr. Boulais. He knew full well that his words would naturally bring a period of orgasmic feeling to all that heard the words "canoe trip". Yet in a few moments, Mr. Boulais would have to announce the conditions of the canoe trip eligibility after the dust settled from the present hysteria. You see, every gauntlet thrown down is a challenge. Physical, mental, emotional, spiritual or a combination of these. This gauntlet was no less even if it was tossed out before boy scouts. Mr. Boulais knew that a criteria would have to be met for those wishing to go.

In Scouting we had learned a sobering lesson. Good things, enjoyable things, great times if you will, are offered to anyone. But walking close beside is the worthiness and responsibility that encompasses them. We would learn this again and again down the road of life. All of us eventually would choose from a college education, military service, marriage, priesthood, a high paying job or whatever. Yet we would come to realize fast that our choices would demand certain responsibilities on our part. That freedom isn't really true freedom unless it is living hand in hand with responsibility and obligations.

And so it was with the mechanics of scouting. Scouting offered it's usual array of activities that all boys were free to engage in. Weekend campouts, walking hikes, bike hikes, week long summer camp were open to all regardless of rank, ability or income. These outings were filled with opportunities for a boy to socialize, have fun, and to learn scouting skills. Scouting skills were needed to advance in rank. It was necessary to move up in rank so a boy could be eligible for nomination for some patrol or troop office. This is where a boy tried, failed, succeeded and honed his leadership skills.

But this troop endeavor was different. How so? It had to be earned. The proposed canoe trip had a more serious tone to it. For Mr. Boulais it was perhaps a natural part of his military life. Being in the Special

5

Forces there must have been all sorts of rank to pull and selection processes to qualify for "Operation Whatever". So when the dust settled from our pandemonium we listened quite intently. You could hear a pin drop. We pretty much sensed inwardly that there had to be a little more to it than just "there's going to be a canoe trip".

"Gentlemen," said Mr. Boulais, in a more somber tone than usual, for he always addressed his troops as "gentlemen". "The troop committee has decided that a boy must qualify to go on this trip, so not everyone will be able to go on this trip," explained Mr. Boulais peering among us for our reactions. "This is how it will be," he stated with guarded authority. And so he spelled it out.

"Each scout who is going must be of the First Class Rank," echoed in my mind. "Good, I'm in so far," I thought to myself. Others were less optimistic. Those Tenderfoots and Second Class Scouts were already sighing and complaining under their breaths.

"Also, there are certain merit badges that need to be earned," he continued.

"Whoa," I said to myself. "Hold on Gerry, there's more to come ."

"Camping merit badge, Swimming merit badge, and First Aid merit badge need to be earned," said Mr. Boulais with a look of determination.

Then we waited ever so anxiously for the next merit badge or requirement to come along. But for a while it never did. Most of us knew right off if we were going or not. I definitely was since my rank was Star scout which is a rank beyond First Class. I earned Swimming merit badge at age 11 and it was in fact my first. Presently, I was working toward completing my First Aid and Camping merit badges. So for me, I knew there was a very viable chance of making this trip. The puzzling part was that Canoeing merit badge wasn't required to go. This situation found us murmuring amongst ourselves and scratching our heads. Some things will never make sense and this seemed to be one of them. We never received an answer as to why it wasn't required either. The issue wasn't pressed for fear of burdening ourselves with another requirement to deal with.

Then after quite a delay, Mr. Boulais sprung the second half of the gauntlet on us. The last requirement hinged on the first four. For those lucky enough to qualify first round, four weeks of canoeing instruction and testing awaited them. We had to be evaluated on how to handle a canoe and manage one in water. Fair enough. And that was it. For some the challenge was too great and gave up. Others were partly there like myself, and a select few had the requirements completed before the fact. Time and attitude were the only real threatening hurdles to clear. We would get through this by patient endurance.

That night after the meeting, I walked home with my brothers Joe and Jim. Trudging up Oak Street Hill we rambled on, guessing who would make the trip. At the top of the hill, some firemen returned a few waves to us from the firehouse window. The air still hung damp of a late March evening as the mist was settling in upon us. The street lights grew hazy but our minds were clear. Joe, Jim and I said it over and over, "I'm going," "Me too," and "I'll make it." Hammering these blurbs at each other all the way home, we attempted to prove our resolve to each other, at least in words. We simply knew the time to be had on such a trip.

We had "fire in our bellies" and no one was going to put it out but ourselves. In a few short months we would discover if our predictions rang true.

2 The Chosen

My view on life tends to be optimistic yet practical. As a teacher, being mindful of what my Dad always said about our school grades was true. That is, the teacher never gives you any grade...you give yourself the grade. Don't even think of putting the blame on others. You are graded upon the effort, study, and work put into your school work.

This was another indispensable lesson that boy scouting taught us, directly reinforcing principles learned in school. Similar to school grades, in scouting you got out of it that which you put into it. This principle was pretty much the unwritten and unspoken rule that we came to realize sooner or later. Some boys in the troop just plain didn't want to go on a canoe trip. Beats me why. Others worked hard at it but never cut the grade. A few started out strong but lost interest and gave up. But I can honestly say that I never heard anyone complain that the requirements were too stringent. You met the challenge or you did not. For younger scouts of eleven or twelve years of age, it meant aspiring to future troop scouting events.

Trying to earn a canoe trip wasn't the only goal we had in scouting. For those of us who advanced up the ladder to Eagle Scout, we knew that extra effort was critical. There was no favoritism in this troop or at least it never reared its ugly head. One advanced in rank and attained merit badges by working hard but above all, by being persistent. To advance steadily in rank one needed perseverance. Merit badge classes were open to everyone but one needed a desire to work towards the Eagle. In the depths of a scout's mind, heart, and soul, he knew if he would fly to scouting's highest rank. Luckily in our troop, I had the opportunity to witness my older brother Joe and his friend Ray Roberge, Jr. attain the Eagle Rank. At their Court of Honor, accolades were showered on them about being the first two Eagle Scouts in Troop 40 in a long time. I believe Chucky Hamel received his Eagle Scout a few years before Joe and Ray. This was a great incentive for younger scouts to witness older scouts garnering the Eagle Scout rank. For younger scouts, their struggle went beyond a mere dream to actually seeing, touching, and being in the presence of an Eagle. It made the trek more endurable and down to earth. To this day still only one in a hundred scouts earns the Eagle award.

8

Looking back now into the heart of those turbulent sixties we had a great troop. Ours was fairly large. It was blessed by the number of committed fathers made available for our scouting events. We needed dads for camping trips, merit badge classes, boards of review, and for planning events behind the scenes that we scouts hardly ever saw. Our moms got involved too. They stocked the goodies table with their baking at the Court of Honors. They made the canvas vests for us to wear. Patches earned at the district camporees were sewn on these vests. Us scouts and fathers would also give the moms a much needed quiet weekend for themselves when we went off camping.

But all in all, why one scout made the canoe trip and another didn't was left to fate. The scoutmaster, committee, and boys themselves all knew who was zeroing in on the canoe trip requirements. Extra boards of review were set up to facilitate any scout's effort to pass a badge or rank. Allow me to digress here to explain a "board of review." When a scout fulfilled his requirements for a rank such as Tenderfoot, Second Class, First Class, Star, Life, Eagle or any merit badge, he was never awarded that badge until he passed the board of review. The board was a panel of three men (dad's) who sat on one side of a table while you sat on the other side. The board then questioned you and interrogated you for any length of time they wanted. The focus was on any knowledge or skill you had to know for that badge or rank, and you had to know your stuff or you didn't pass, believe me. The pressure was intense, and I would much rather opt for any school exam in any subject than face the board of review. The stress preparing for it was enormous...I worried so.

My Dad happened to be on the troop Advancement Committee. He usually made most Boards of Review which were monthly. When my brothers Joe, Jim, and I went in for our boards of review, Dad would poke his head in the door and jokingly say, "throw the book at' em." You see, he could not sit on his sons' board of review for suspicion of favoritism when and if we passed. But I was relieved not to have him on my board since he would have been so thorough and exacting with us. Dad wanted the scouts to really know their stuff and he was a stickler on this. The importance of this was rudely driven home to me two years after the canoe trip in June 1968. My Dad was recuperating in the hospital from a heart attack, one that I had feared would take his life. My Eagle Board of Review was the next week at the Springfield City Council Chambers, and my mind was in a fog. I dwelt upon my Dad and if he would make it home. My efforts to review and study all my scouting material were superficial, if that. I failed the board. Never having failed one before didn't make for a better situation. I had forgotten a Tenderfoot knot and one of six early American flags in flag history. The more embarrassing and arduous task was when arriving at home, I had to tell Dad how I did. He was on the phone from his hospital bed. It was agonizing telling him about my performance. I had let him down. He wasn't upset. He told me not to worry and encouraged me by saying that I would pass it the second time around. He was right. I did, in August of that same year.

Anyhow, we prepared well for the boards and faced the music. Most of us passed our boards since we studied and reviewed our material just like a school exam. In fact, I can say that I studied my scouting material a little more seriously than my school work. But the opportunities were there to make the trip, and as the months wound down, the sifted sand left ten pebbles and a scoutmaster to go on this trip. The cast was now set. Mr. Boulais was a shoo in, for by virtue of his status he was going. In fact he was the only adult that would experience this escapade with us. Perhaps another adult should have come along for the ride but no one did. National BSA frowns upon that today, and in fact changed its policy in 1985 which required two adult leaders to be present on every scouting function. Ten of us would spend six days on the Connecticut River with our scoutmaster. They were Ray Roberge, Jr., age 16, Joseph O'Brien the 3rd, age 15, Ed McGrath, age 14, Dennis Riel, age 14, Gene DeGrandpre, age 14, Kevin Sullivan, age 14, Steve Kelly, age 14, Jim O'Brien, age 14, Kevin Boulais, age 13, and myself, age 13.

The contingent who earned this infamous voyage could rightfully have been dubbed the "Franco-Gaellic Connection", if one categorized our last names. Why just French and Irish Americans on this trip? You need to understand Indian Orchard. Obviously, the best understanding of any town would be to visit it and see for yourself. So if you haven't been there and you want to go, take I-291 East in Springfield to Exit 5A. The sign says "Indian Orchard". Take Page Boulevard eastward for 1.7 miles until you come to Berkshire Avenue. Take a left here and in one mile you'll be at the top of Oak Street Hill. Another left will bring you down to Main Street at the light. If you hang a right on the top of Oak Street Hill and go down three blocks to the corner of Oak and Goodwin Streets you'll come to 227 Oak Street. This is where the infamous Timothy Leary lived during his high school years. The house was his maternal grandfather's and Tim lived there for quite a while due to his own family difficulties. Indian Orchard has six churches at the present, three of them Roman Catholic.

Troop 40 had been granted a charter to operate as a Boy Scout troop from Saint Aloysius Parish in 1934, and still functions as one to this day.

Saint Aloysius Church on Main St. and Saint Matthew's Church on Pinevale Street, originally Pine Street, are about 100 yards from each other. Prior to the Civil War, a burgeoning influx of Irish and French immigrants found gainful employment in the Village of Indian Orchard. Both factions liked the area so much the whole lot of them stayed.

On March 3, 1873 the Rev. Father Louis A. Gagnier, a Canadian priest from Quebec founded Saint Aloysius Parish. This priest found no shame in picking up a spade to assist in excavating the church foundation when help was needed. Father Gagnier now had his work cut out for him in ministering to the spiritual needs of 800 souls. From Adam, Blais, Baron, Belisle, Bouchard, Clish, Dumas and Duquette, to Rickson, Riel, Roberge, and Yelle, the French names were myriad.

Now up the street and around the corner, the Irish had already built a church for their needs in 1864. After acquiring their first "holy ground", that is, any plot good enough to sink potatoes into "famine free", the Irish secured donated land from the Indian Orchard Mills to construct a church of their own.

Danny Ferris (Timothy Leary's maternal grandfather), Owen Lynch, Patrick Sullivan, and Ed Healy helped dig out the foundation with their own horses, wagons, and plows. Yet strangely, Saint Matthew's Church did not gain status as a parish until 1878. Why? In 1864, newly constructed Saint Matthew's was still only a mission church being formally aligned with Holy Name of Jesus Parish of Chicopee, MA. In 1878, the Rev. Fr. Patrick Healey of Chicopee turned over the mission church to the Rev. James F. Fitzgerald, the first pastor of the new parish of Saint Matthew's.

From Brady, Butler, Crean, Callahan, Delaney and Evans, to McCurry, McGrath, O'Brien, Quinn, Shea, and Sullivan, the Irish names were myriad, as well.

Yet both parish records list an intermix of both French and Irish names. Given the tight knit community and close proximity of both churches, marriage seems to be the logical explanation for this oddity. Perhaps either spouse in any given marriage preferred to remain in their own parish. The obliging partner conceded and probably jumped parish.

11

An O'Brien family registered at Saint Aloysius in 1875...no direct relation to my Dad's. The Riel family name was registered at Saint Aloysius in 1874; Roberge in 1898; DeGrandpre in 1953; and Boulais in 1955.

As for the Sullivan's, those guys have four columns in the phone book. The world is more replete with them than fallen leaves during a New England autumn. Kelly and O'Brien have only two columns in the phone directory. Our family registered at Saint Matthew's in June 1956 upon arriving from Ansonia, CT. The McGrath family hit the rolls in 1955. Even though Kevin Sullivan and Steve Kelly were in another parish in Sixteen Acres, their surnames were on the Saint Matthew's register early on. Well, as noted before, it was Patty Sullivan digging the foundation in 1864, and Sullivans were on the rolls in Saint Aloysius in 1906. Kellys had registered in The French-Catholic Parish in 1898. No McGrath had ever registered with Saint Aloysius according to their records.

Troop 40 had some grand days. I joined in April 1964, after reaching eleven years old in March. Assistant Scoutmaster Cliff Dumas spoke often of Troop 40 pride. He recalled for us new scouts the 1947 Troop 40 Drum and Bugle Corps that brought pride to Indian Orchard making 36 public appearances, garnering 38 trophies and one State Championship.

One can see the ethnic heritage lingering into the sixties and seventies with most Irish-Americans gravitating to Saint Matthew's and French-Americans opting for Saint Aloysius. In the nineties, with demographics shifting, the number of parishioners in both churches dwindled. Saint Matthew's and Saint Aloysius merged, shedding their names but retaining both church structures. Thus, the newly formed Saint Jude's Parish was born on Jan. 1, 1998.

And that my friend is how these canoeists happened to be either French or Irish surnamed.

3 Russell Pond

In late spring of 1966, the ten of us who had met the canoe trip requirements challenge faced a second hurdle. It was necessary for each of us to prove our skill at handling a canoe. Odd as it seemed, the Canoeing Merit Badge never emerged as a requirement for this trip. A few guys had already earned it but most like myself had not. I've surmised that the troop committee wanted to be absolutely sure that each of us possessed skill beyond the canoeing merit badge criteria.

To fulfill this endeavor we were required to attend a four week course on canoeing instruction at the Horace A. Moses Scout Reservation in Russell, MA. This reservation was home to three separate and distinct summer camps; namely, Camp Woronoak, Camp General Henry Knox, and Camp Frontier. All three camps utilized Russell Pond for their waterfront which included a swim area and a boat and canoe area. Camps Frontier and Woronoak were adjacent to each other along the southern shore. Camp Knox was set on the northern shoreline creating a scalene between the three. This reservation was tucked snugly into the foothills of the Berkshires, Punchbowl Mountain, Cobble Mountain, and Russell Mountain.

So over four weeks we canoe trip aspirants had to meet at Camp Woronoak's boat and canoe area to learn, refine, and to be evaluated on our acquired canoeing skills. Each week the camp canoe instructor took our group out on Russell Pond after supper. This was a time of great fun and one of bonding, even though we were learning canoeing skills in a serious light. Being thirteen, I, as well as others perhaps hadn't realized at the time that this period of canoe training had us learning about each other's personalities. There was a need to relearn to live together since the canoe trip would be a different situation than any of us had ever encountered. There would be different stresses, worries, and concerns. Unbeknownst to us, we were subconsciously learning each other's quirks. In the back of our minds we were toying with the inevitable choice of who we would be paired up with for six days on the Connecticut River. To keep the pressure of decision making about choosing a partner off us, we were told that the committee would decide on the pairing of partners. This was wise since clogging our minds early on with sizing each other up would have created bickering, factions, infighting and plain old hard feelings. Later on, however, we discovered that our input on partner selection would not go unheeded.

For me, the canoe instruction classes were a time of intense anticipation. Being thirteen years old, I had found no steady employment for the summer, with the exception of a Springfield Republican Sunday newspaper route that was shared with my older brother Joe. Most summer jobs required one to be at least sixteen years old. My summer days were spent doing chores around the house, baby sitting Kevin, Patty, and Bridget with my sister Mary, playing ball, or exploring the environs of Long Pond two or three hundred yards from our back door. My anticipation focused upon Dad arriving home from work on time, since Joe and a few other scout dads were our round trip ticket to Russell Pond.

I had spent two summers already at Camp Woronoak and was eagerly awaiting a third. Our troop was forever booked at the site called "Accomsick", a native American term. We had been indoctrinated with the motto, "Accomsick and Igohomewell". Get it? You will. Troop 40 was scheduled again for Accomsick so going up for the canoe training would give us another foretaste of being immersed in such an adventurous getaway. Summer camp was a fantastic place to be. A boy's dream. A place to be lost in enjoying adventure. Adventure that was good, clean, and fun.

The canoe instruction evenings are vivid. All of them were overcast and cloudy. Not one with sun and devoid of rain. The anticipation exhilarated me. I'm sure each of us had the six day trip already set up in our minds. Similar to most first time events, one naturally imprints visions of landscapes and scenarios upon the inner cranium walls. These usually evaporate as the reality of the event unfolds.

The Camp Woronoak boat and canoe area was chosen simply because we were all familiar with it. We also were being loaned five canoes from Camp Woronoak so it was best that we train with them. Russell Pond seems to me large enough to be a lake but it's called a pond. Back home in Indian Orchard, Lake Lorraine is smaller than Russell Pond and lakes are by definition larger than ponds. You figure it out.

It is a beautiful pond sinking forty feet in depth and offering pike, trout, and pickerel to name a few challenges to an avid fisherman. This pond will forever evoke warm and happy memories and one terrorizing bombshell if not for me. The week after the canoe trip our troop ventured off to Accomsick in Camp Woronoak as usual. It was quite a productive week for me if I may say so myself. Having arrived at camp

14

with some "partial credit" work already completed, I earned the rest of three merit badges in full, namely, Camping, Forestry, and Lifesaving. Additionally, I earned the Rowing and Canoeing Merit Badges in full. There was fire in my belly for the Eagle and I was in a beeline for it. To top this off, somehow I managed to earn the Mile Swim BSA. Somehow fins must have developed on my dorsal side. It's hard to imagine that I swam a mile nonstop but myself and a few others in our troop did.

Yet nothing has come close to the managed panic presented to me during the Canoeing Merit Badge episode with my brother Joe. We both had signed up for the Canoeing Merit Badge Class during the second morning period. Well, let me tell you, VCR's were a pipe dream back in 1966 but my life's "pause" and "fast forward" buttons were jammed together for what seemed an eternity one sunny morning.

As to be expected, Joe and I paddled way out to the dead center of Russell Pond to give our strokes and maneuvers a run. They were pretty much mundane by now given the fact that we spent six days using them on the Connecticut River. Our instructor was so eastward we lost sight of him. As a routine he was checking up on other class members. Joe and I became bored and paddled southward towards the Accomsick shore. We finished our jaunt and ceased paddling observing that we were still far out and in deep water.

"Hey, we gonna swamp this thing?" I asked Joe quizzically. "Of course," Joe snickered, with a narrow grin. "Hey wait!! Whoa!" I yelled, grabbing the gunwales quickly.

It was too late.

It was inevitable that we should swamp our canoe since everyone performed this ritual just for the fun of it whenever out in a canoe. In fact, back in camp you were regarded as a wuss if you hadn't garnered up the courage to topple your canoe.

Joe and I tumbled into the cool, refreshing water laughing like jackals. Down we submerged and up I resurfaced to discover our canoe belly up with the keel skyward and our paddles floundering off. Joe hadn't resurfaced yet so I swam the few yards to retrieve the paddles. Turning and swimming back towards the canoe my instincts hit me like a train. I froze and panicked as if just stung by a thousand purple hornets. Joe had taken much too long to come up. His trouble was now mine. I was a trifle scared stiff but I wasn't afraid. There's a big difference you know. Go look it up.

Like a couple of inane fools we hadn't donned life jackets either.

Again!? Somehow we had abandoned that "mentally awake" part of the Scout Oath. Fear tried to get a good hold on me but somehow I found courage. See, that "brave" part of the Scout Law stuck around. Glancing ashore we were still too remote for my help screams to be heard by anyone other than the angel of death.

My actions would only have mimicked the Tin Man screaming and moaning impotently in his field of poppies. The time to dillydally was past...which was only about five or six seconds. I immediately duplicated the surface dives that we were working on in Lifesaving Merit Badge class. Great on the job training. My deep surface dives were accompanied with one gruesome thought: "locating my drowned brother?" This can't be I mused. "Great capsize," I thought. "Super plan Joe." "You got drowned in the process?" "That's some maneuver," I pondered, delving into this aquatic nightmare. Plunging deep below and rocketing back up, I employed the breaststroke with a frogkick, initiating a desperate search and rescue mission. I knew the water was deep for with each arm pull and kick, greener and murkier realms greeted me. The willies began to invade my head a little. I shrugged off past thoughts of Joe's antics about sea monsters upon realizing that his corpse would beat out any sea monster I could conjure up. No doubt I put on a show for whatever fish were watching. They must have wondered why this fool was escalating up and down looking for what?

On two dives, I delayed and craned my neck 360 degrees attempting to spot Joe. With depleted oxygen I just resurfaced again in time for air. My imagination took me to Ratell's Funeral Home back home. Joe was laid out in a coffin in a Navy blue suit. I was trying to piece the story together for my family about how his demise occurred. "Good God," I thought, "get going and dive!" Catching my breath before what I thought would be my final dive, I calculated that Joe was a goner. The plan was that if on my return surface dive minus Joe, I'd better latch onto the canoe before I became victim number two. Well here goes, I reflected. Filling my lungs, I tucked and began the descent. My prayers were not traditional ones. Simply put I thought about God watching me, so I prayed, "Lord, you know what I'm doing...help me out a little."

After completing a full arm pull, my peripheral vision detected what appeared to be two dangling legs about six to eight feet above me. The sun reflected off them.

"How could this be?" I thought. "Did Joe's body actually resurface, and get tangled up under our capsized canoe?" Reversing my course I hied upward. Zeroing in closer were Joe's legs, by Jove! Here I debat-

16

ed if my discovery would be a grim one, revealing Joe's drowned facial expression. With thoughts of now or never I terminated my trajectory up under the canoe.

I extended both arms upward and grasped the two gunwales about three feet in front of Joe's body. Slowly I lifted my head above the water's surface like a turtle testing the sun's warmth.

I cringed inside and out, bracing myself for Joe's grotesque mask.

Well, he didn't look too bad. He was crying...with laughter that is. "You mindless wonder," I thought. Here was this brazen character clinging to a thwart and laughing himself dizzy. If the canoe wasn't there he would no doubt have drowned by hysterics.

Were there any more ambivalent feelings elsewhere? I could have killed him but was too elated with joy that my prodigal brother had been found? Actually he was never lost. This had all the similarities of Tom and Huck showing up in church at their own funeral...for me anyway. Joe duped me big time. He took clear advantage of my ignorance and naivete to put on a show for himself.

"Did ja see me?" asked Joe coughing and laughing intermittently.

"No! I kept diving! I almost drowned you fool!" I barked.

"I know, I watched you... from in here," he revealed with pride.

That made me look real good. Joe then explained how a capsized canoe has an air pocket of about 9-10 inches underneath where one could hang all day with sufficient air. It was from that lofty position that he made good sport of me. Yes sir, he duped me real good. The lone spectator of his own search and rescue operation.

"Hey, what the heck would you do if I didn't come back up from diving for you?" I threw at him.

"The same thing I guess," replied Joe with a smirk. From there onward I became a little wiser and more grateful.

Joe and I resurfaced again, and beckoned a canoe for help. We jacked our canoe up over the rescue canoe, flipped it over, and slithered it back on the pond. Heading towards the northwest shore we could hear the lunch bugle on the sound system confirming our lateness.

It would be days before I calmed down inside. There was an air of relief among us as canoe trip candidates. Feelings of pride and accomplishment embodied us since we had gotten to this threshold. Deep down most of us sensed that we would not fail the canoe skill training at Woronoak, because we had come too far. The light was there at the beginning of the tunnel and it wasn't going to slip away if we could help it.

Our mood was confident joviality yet in a guarded way. On training nights we would gulp down supper and be off to the Saint Aloysius School, where we'd pick up other scouts who needed a lift to Russell Pond.

Buzzing along the Mass Pike we would yak and yak like fools, oblivious to Dad's driving. We were going to do this and that. It's going to be like this, we schemed. Planning and dreaming and hoping and expecting. Something a little like desiring heaven. The rational was that we knew it was going to be a fun time and we had a right to dream about it in our own minds as to how it should be.

And that is exactly what we did.

4 Tippy Canoe

A canoe is a long, flat bottomed boat that curves up on the sides. Its two ends curl up. The front is the bow; the rear the stern. The left side is called the port side and the right termed the starboard. Canoes average about 16 to 18 feet in length and are 3-3+ feet wide. They are so topsy-turvy it is ridiculous. If you think you've got good balance try standing up and walking in a canoe. After you pick yourself up, you'll know instinctively that crouching and lowering your center of gravity is the only way to handle this craft.

Whether it was the Delawares or Mohawks or Nipmucs who perfected it doesn't matter. The Native Americans refined the canoe by pulling birch bark over wooden frames and gunwales. They had discovered the hard way that hollowed out logs were too heavy, slow, and cumbersome to maneuver especially when attempting a portage! The Native Americans had to adapt to survive. They needed a craft that simultaneously transported their belongings and was light enough to be quickly hoisted on their backs and shoulders for long distances. It was without a doubt their Model T and Subaru.

And so with much eagerness the eleven of us hooked our swimming "buddy tags" upon the waterfront tag board. Those little round cardboard red, white, and blue tags indicated who was in the water swimming or out in boats or canoes. This was a must regardless of a swimmer's ability. It was imperative that everyone had a buddy or you couldn't even get into the water. No exceptions. That is a BSA rule. We switched buddies over the next four weeks at Russell Pond because our canoe instructor wanted us to get used to working with different partners.

We learned right off that Woronoak's white aluminum canoes were flat bottomed; not rounded or curved. These camp canoes were the actual ones that would take us down the Connecticut River. This type of canoe was designed primarily for Class I and II water. Class I water is described as being "easy", fast moving with riffles and small waves. Hardly any obstacles or obstructions surface. Risk to an overboard swimmer is slight as one may easily rescue themselves.

Class II water is described as "novice", with straight forward rapids and wide clear channels being present. Scouting ahead and some maneuvering may be necessary. Rocks and mid-sized waves are easily missed by trained canoeists.

Our instructor emphatically stressed that canoeing on Russell Pond would not be the same as the Connecticut River. We discovered this gradually and quite abruptly on our trip later that summer. This was a concept that we pretty much listened intently upon at the time, yet our attempt to project the difference between Russell Pond and the Connecticut was quite weak if that. None of us had ever canoed the Connecticut River before and would not prior to the trip.

My experience with the Connecticut River was limited to sitting in the family car while Dad drove over the Memorial Bridge from Springfield to West Springfield. Here I entertained thoughts doubting the bridge's safety and wondered aloud what would happen if the Memorial collapsed. What do you think will happen dummy? Those encouraging childhood notions really annoyed my Mom. She scolded me not to even mention that projection again displaying abundant annoyance. Dad just chuckled.

Another cerebral photo for me was that exquisite panorama from the summit of Mount Sugarloaf State Reservation in South Deerfield, MA. After crossing the Memorial Bridge, Dad would bomb up Route 5 North. The Green Plymouth with the shift on the column was packed with five kids venturing north to Mount Sugarloaf. Mom loved the area because she couldn't get enough of Fenimore Cooper's "Last of the Mohicans". Visiting Old Deerfield Village gave us ample opportunity to relive the Deerfield Massacre as we listened to Mom and Dad recount the historic tales. I had to hand it to Dad. Anyone who could drive that Plymouth up Mt. Sugarloaf, full of screaming kids looking out the windows at the sheer cliff drops off the road's edge and make it to the top was definitely NASCAR certified in my book. Coming down was worse. I couldn't look half the time. It seemed that Dad's desire to save money on brake pads held more weight than saving our lives. Descending Sugarloaf involved quick glances out the side windows and then shutting my eyes while I recited some new Litany of the Saints for protection.

Yet the view of the Connecticut River from up top was difficult to beat in majestic terms. One looks southward into Sunderland at the beautiful Connecticut with trees neatly hemmed on either bank. Flanking these trees is rolling farmland sectioned into plots of corn or pumpkin. The cheesecloth netting that shields the tobacco fields completes this agricultural quilt. Farther south the prominence of the Mount

Holyoke Range looks down on the valley. Yet gently weaving through all this beauty the Connecticut rolls along seemingly motionless. Like a lake, this clear glassy ribbon quietly and stealthily creeps towards Saybrook, CT.

The gift shop at Sugarloaf is gone now. The ice cream cones and Sugarloaf pennants that Dad bought helped in taming us. The shop burned to the ground long ago one winter day but the memories are forever there. Well, this was my limited perception of the Connecticut River. Nothing here to be ashamed of or to apologize for, but a realization that for all of us in life, all new events are perceived by our past experiences, great or small, accurate or inaccurate.

All in all, the only way to really prepare to experience the Connecticut River for 133 miles of canoeing is to launch your canoe into it and start paddling downstream.

It may seem as a nonessential but when one is confronted with referring to canoes and paddles for six days with a partner, terminology is helpful. Our instructor demanded that we identify the front as bow and the rear as stern, the left as port and the right as starboard. We had to locate the keel and know it's function. That reinforced fin or rudder running the canoe length on the bottom kept things relatively on course. The gunwale is that top outer edge on both sides of the canoe. The thwarts are those cross braces that span the canoe width in the bow, middle, and stern. Thwarts are a God send for leaning against when paddling in the kneeling position for miles on end, believe me.

One important term we learned was freeboard. This was the amount of available space from the gunwale to the water's surface. If this was less than 6 inches your canoe was overloaded and unsafe for canoeing. One had to decide quick what kind of diet your craft was to undergo. Either that or get a lighter partner? Hey, don't ya like me?

We also needed to identify the paddle parts; grip, loom, throat, blade and tip.

It was crucial to possess some knowledge of the canoe because of communication between partners. We had to demonstrate what canoe part to grasp, hold, or transfer to when portaging. Later on that summer when the trip was over, myself and a few others came to realize that the canoe terminology we memorized was more extensive than the Canoeing Merit Badge requirements. This only verified that our instructor desired to make sure we possessed knowledge and skill beyond the merit badge guidelines.

There are two types of canoeing. Solo and tandem. Simple enough solo is canoeing alone; tandem is with a partner. Our instruction focused on tandem canoeing since that is what our trip would entail. Of primary concern was learning to launch and enter a canoe with your partner, both stern first and bow first. Here each canoeist grasps the gunwale on their side of the canoe about mid canoe, and gently they slide it into the water. Partners are facing each other as they go and place the canoe about five sixths length into the pond, stern first. The bowman, which eventually was me, braces the bow between his knees to steady the craft. Now the sternman enters the canoe crouched down, lowering his center of gravity, grasping the gunwales. The sternman crouches backwards stepping over the thwarts as he goes, ending his move in a kneeling position.

Here the sternman makes a post with his paddle, that is he puts his paddle into the water and secures it with his might against the canoe side. The paddle tip is stuck in the muck, with the loom perpendicular. The bowman now enters the canoe similarly while the sternman stabilizes the craft. The bowman ends his move slightly beyond midship. This position frees up the bow from the pond bottom. When the bow is off the bottom, the sternman paddles a few short reverse strokes backing the canoe away from the pondside. The sternman stops his paddling and holds a steady post allowing the bowman to slowly move from midship to his front position. The bowman picks up his paddle and off they go.

It is a wonderful feeling to glide away from shore in a canoe, particularly at dawn. Placid water with mist rising. The water is quiet, you are quiet, and the birds are quiet. Yes, the birds are temporarily still as they watch you. They are quiet for you have actually violated their space and it is necessary for them to decipher whether you are an actual threat or not. As you paddle away, you may hear the loud noise of the few drops dripping off your paddle and plunging back down onto the quiet glass, sending their circle of fading rings outward towards nowhere. It is then that one may come to realize that the only things not put here by God is your canoe, paddle, and yourself. But that you have invited yourself here somehow by virtue of your power. Then you realize that you are not that quiet transcending power here but God is. Now you come to know what is meant by "Be still and know that I am God."

As you advance, the pond bottom quickly descends below, deeper it grows until your vision can discern no more. At times, the wonders of being a fish, frog, or turtle had its envy. To explore life underwater was something I often dreamt about. But these pleasant, wishful thoughts fade quickly into reality when the balance of nature comes to mind. For just about every aquatic species below there lurks an enemy to devour it. Added to this is the diehard angler casting his line hour after hour hoping to catch his supper. Imagining that scenario put an end to my desires for it.

My drifting thoughts were cut short by a piercing shout.

"OK, let's go! Everyone over here!" startled me.

"Pay attention," barked the canoe instructor.

Such abruptness came sharply as a stone cast from the shore would violently plunge into calm, serene Russell Pond and rudely petrify a school of brown trout, gently swimming below surface. It was time to stop daydreaming and get to work. And that is what I did.

5 Same Strokes For All Us Folks

"Men," as the instructor addressed us, "you'll need to master a few strokes."

"Before we're done you'll learn the bow stroke, diagonal draw, pushover, reverse sweep, quarter sweep and the J stroke," explained our instructor firmly.

"You will demonstrate them paddling in the bow position for 100 yards, turning your canoe around, and return using the same strokes. So let's pay attention and do it right," he advised us.

Man this was too much like school, I thought.. For most of us this instruction was some kind of review, or so we thought. In our minds we knew it all of course but were really rather rusty. We all had some experience in canoeing at summer camp because one only needed to be classified as a swimmer to take a canoe out on the lake. There was no requirement to prove one's proficiency at demonstrating canoe strokes. Our skill was limited to the bow stroke and some version of the J stroke, fragmented as it may be.

The bow stroke is the most basic stroke designed to move a canoe forward. It's called the bow stroke because the bowman executes it from the bow position. And so in whatever kneeling position we preferred, one knee or two knees down, we learned precision bow stroke.

"Everyone, grab the grip of your paddle with one hand and hold the throat with the other."

"Show me!" "Good!" "That's it!" bellowed the instructor. "Man this guy's serious," I mused.

"Now extend that paddle tip forward out in front of you. Dip it into the water until you can't see the paddle's face and pull back!"

"Pull! Way back, extend your arms back. Pull! Keep the arms straight. Stay perpendicular to your canoe. Full arc!"

"Now take that paddle out and feather it." Feathering meant returning your paddle to the starting position using a horizontal hold rather than a vertical one. This was imperative if one is to reduce wind resistance so as to not lose momentum of the canoe. A 90 degree turn of the paddle if you will.

"Return it! Dip into and down. Full arc. Let's go!" the impassioned instructor persisted. He didn't miss a lick.

"That's the way..., Good!" his praises came.

The instructor prepared us with a no nonsense approach, yet his demeanor allowed us some room to enjoy the moment. Simply put, it was discipline immersed into a fun activity.

Next we moved on to the quarter sweep stroke. This stroke performed by the bowman is utilized to maneuver the bow away from his paddling side. The sweep commences at the same point as the bow stroke but the blade is straight up and down, perpendicular to the water's surface. The term quarter is used to signify the full stroke distance of only one quarter of a circle.

"Dip in men." "Paddle pull." "Pull out to your right side."

"Keep one side of the blade in the water, and one side barely out. Pull a circle clockwise! Stop that pull at 3:00 o'clock," barked the instructor. This guy is definitely drill sergeant material I thought, for sure.

"Feather and return your paddle."

"Repeat. Let's go. Stretch wide, stretch the muscles! Quarter turn."

This sweep ends at the paddler's kneeling position. Later on I would come to know the importance of this stroke in maneuvering around objects dead ahead on the river. The bowman must always be ready. He scans the river ahead attentively. He must be alert and vigilant. His eyes must be focused 50 to 100 yards downstream. Why? Simple. To prevent from happening to his canoe that fate which doomed the Titanic. Failure to detect a rock, log, or other obstruction rearing its ominous head on the river could spell disaster. An alert bowman has his eyes peeled even while engaged in the monotonous, arduous task of paddling.

Upon detecting an obstacle in the canoe's path, he will shout the warning, "quarter sweep". The sternman knows instantly to let up on his J stroke, slow it down, or use an alternate stroke enabling the craft to veer to the port or starboard side of the potential threat. Fortunately we hardly ever had to employ it.

As the name implies, the diagonal draw is a stroke that is pulled toward the bowman in a diagonal direction. Here the bowman reaches out, sinks his paddle into the water between one and two o'clock, which is half the distance of the quarter sweep.

Here I reach way out, dip, and pull my paddle directly to myself, pulling and drawing water directly into the starboard side and under the canoe. The draw coordinated with the sternman's quarter sweep quickly pivots the canoe on a right angle. It can also be used effectively to move the canoe laterally in the direction off the bowman's side. The diagonal draw stroke is completed by following through with the second half of the bowstroke.

It is a good stroke to fool around with also. A few times the sternman would shout out in sudden surprise as I would pull to the right side unannounced.

"Hey, what are ya doing dummy?!" came a voice from the rear.

"Fooling around, I guess," said I.

"You guess?" said Kelly, "Gee, don't you know?"

"Sorry," I faked it, knowing I would make this a truly repetitive act.

And the pure joy of repeating this act with glee just to dart the canoe sharply off course, swinging the stern abruptly to the left, and listening to the sternman's laments. Sometimes in tandem canoeing one must break the monotonous humdrum of paddling in order to ensure a fun day. After all maintaining your sanity and wit is a prerequisite to good canoeing.

Frivolous young boys will always have their own vernacular to describe anything. They will rename different oddities, and then while being taught a particular skill will look on in awe, asking themselves quietly, "Oh? Is that what that is called?" Such was the stroke that we scouts dubbed the "jerk stroke", a.k.a. the "pushover stroke". The bowman or sternman could use it to "push the canoe over" laterally to one side. A canoeist would dip his paddle right in the water, blade face right up against the canoe side. Holding the grip with the left hand and the throat with the right, the loom would be pressed against the gunwale for leverage. He then would jerk the paddle outward by yanking inward on the grip and pushing out on the throat. This motion would jerk the paddle blade outward and "pushover" the canoe. Thus the term "pushover" that we had previously dubbed the jerk. When both the sternman and bowman utilized this stroke simultaneously on the same side the result was a very powerful pushover to the opposite side of the stroke. Simple enough.

The final stroke we worked on for tandem canoeing was the reverse sweep. The bowman does not use this stroke too often since it tends to move the canoe backwards in too wide of a circular motion. It's used primarily by the sternman to back up the canoe and it's good to use when solo canoeing. The reverse sweep stroke starts off right where the bow stroke ends. One dips their blade in the water behind them with one blade side face down, the other side up. Here you must pull the paddle in a slight arc going forward toward the bow; a sort of back to front sweeping motion.

This stroke was good for canoeing along the river's shoreline. On days that we explored the river's edge, we found it necessary to back up our canoe as one canoeist may have missed something of interest such as a turtle, frog, or other natural wonder. The reverse sweep usually did the trick.

Slowing the canoe down or stopping it outright always evoked jolly memories of additional antics. Of course, the sternman could choose to crank out the "baseball bat swing" stop. This was nothing less than holding your paddle like a baseball bat and swinging it from behind you, full throttle, plunging the blade into the water at about three o'clock. This procedure would abruptly slow the canoe down and rock it, teetering left and right.

However, the bowman would curse it up blue in the face since he was sprayed with water mercilessly. The sternman is smirking no doubt and loving every second of it, as he contritely blurts out his weak apology to his soaked mate, who is struggling to see just how contrite this sternman is.

All in all, the simple procedure to stop was usually given on orders from the sternman. "Let it run" was the term used to designate a stop in paddling so as to slow the canoe momentum greatly. The sternman upon commanding stop, alerts both canoeists to pull back and finish their present stroke, pulling the loom to the gunwale and then locking the throat to the gunwale with the thumb of his lower hand. As they pull back on the grip to steady the paddle, this duo should stop the canoe pretty dead in its course.

Then after this magnificent display of teamwork halts the canoe, the bowman erupts his own reverse baseball bat swing and mercilessly soaks the living daylights out of his sternman in return payment for his free cold wet tee-shirt.

The most important stroke to learn and master in canoeing is the J stroke. Everyone had to learn this stroke and demonstrate it proficiently despite the fact that it is primarily a sternman's stroke. The reason for this is simple. If your sternman becomes ill or injured, the bowman would be automatically transformed into a solo canoeist. He would have to secure his sick or injured buddy in the middle of the canoe and paddle him to safety. So not only would it be imperative that one would paddle and transport the weight of two but one must keep the canoe on a reasonably straight course which the J stroke is designed to do.

In this stroke, the sternman dips his paddle into the water in the identical manner as the bowman initiating the bowstroke. He now executes a regular bowstroke motion until the lower arm holding the throat, just passes his body. The grip hand is pushing out and backward. Now is the critical point in the making or breaking of the J stroke. It was very awkward and difficult for me as well as for many others. It is a challenge because one must rotate and supinate the fingers and wrist of the grip hand. That is plain work for that body part. It's a motion we hardly ever use. It is uncomfortable but necessary to put up with to acquire the correct form. It must be practiced over and over the right way early on since creating a wrong J stroke is a pain to undo and teach again.

So here we changed our grip hand position from a knuckle down to a thumbs down position. The rotated hand turns the blade perpendicular to the water's surface. The grip is then pulled across the paddler's front while the throat hand pushes water out sideways from the canoe. The whole picture for you is the paddle turns outward at the end of the bowstroke to produce a letter J in the water. It's easier said than done, no doubt.

We all had to pass that J stroke test regardless. A few picked it up easy as is the case for any new skill just taught. Yet I for one did not like the stroke simply because I learned it wrong the year before. Now I had to relearn it. About half of us had to keep drilling and persisting at this stroke under our partner's watchful eye. Retest we did. Our instructor was kept busy just correcting our J stroke faults. Finally when he was satisfied with our strokes we all then paddled the 100 yards using this stroke, both solo and tandem. He had kept his word.

6 Fun, Fun, Fun

In our minds we were done with canoe skills and ready to go. What else was there to do? I mean we were now skilled at paddling and moving this craft along. Canoes weren't going to capsize for us. That circumstance happened to others. Our feeble minds would deal with swamped canoes when it occurred. Thankfully our instructor thought otherwise keeping our instruction diphasic.

So the flip side of our canoe instruction covered emergency situations and safety issues, no pun intended. Inevitably, a canoe, not being the most stable craft is bound to capsize, especially canoes manned by young boys full of vinegar. But on a more serious note, one needs to know what to do and how to respond in such precarious situations. How does one help themselves while solo or tandem canoeing and their canoe capsizes? How can canoeists assist and rescue others in a capsized canoe? These are very important issues to be dealt with since in failing to execute the proper rescue or by ignorance alone means we are now meddling with the possible loss of life.

Similar to all scouting skills we needed to tackle this situation with no less of an attitude. Whether sending out Morse Code, setting a splint on a fractured leg, containing a brush fire, or administering CPR, the domain of canoeing emergencies required seriousness. But let us not forget that we are teaching boys to act as men. We were instructed to use common sense and maintain a cool head, as well as knowing how to take command and delegate authority to those standing idle. Yet even in these safety classes in scouting the element of joking and humor always crept in. For regardless of scouting skills we were still boys, and boys will remain boys. It is a gradual process from boyhood into adulthood, yet for some it comes quicker.

There will always be teenage boys who act more mature than many full grown men. This is more of a direct result of how these boys are brought up in their respective families and what their parents expected of them or did not expect of them. That, along with the belief that God is more the father of our children than us dad's are.

But none the less, here was an activity that we looked forward to. Why? Simple. It was fun. Cool. Actually, this was great. What boy who could swim and being out in a canoe, rowboat, or sailboat would not delight in capsizing it with his buddies?

Prior to our canoeing instruction classes, I had spent two years at Camp Woronoak for one and two week sessions. These were great experiences that I will never forget. As mentioned previously, the only requirement a scout needed to take a canoe, rowboat, or Sunfish sailboat out on Russell Pond was that he be classified as a swimmer. Yes sir. We could hardly wait for the free time period each day right after siesta. Siesta was that short rest period succeeding lunch. It was outright torture because it wasn't short enough. How do a bunch of boys rest or sleep after lunch? They don't. They squirm, fidget, and get on each other's nerves waiting for free period to begin. Fun memories on Russell Pond fill my mind. The sun sparkling and glittering off the small swells, blue skies, white puffy clouds, and August sunshine warming your back. I particularly relished sailing the Sunfish. Toying with the main sheet, releasing it to snatch some wind in the mainsail, and gliding effortlessly across the pond. What a feeling. Better yet to come was keeling. The wind filling the mainsail fuller and fuller with such force that now the craft is at a 45 degree angle. The thrill of the keel. Screaming in the breeze, hair whipping, and then letting her go down, plunging into cool, dark Russell Pond. Deliberately keeling over. I loved it...we loved it. And then your partner and you grunt and groan and lean over to upright the mast and mainsail. Water flowing off the nylon sail, dripping down upon us as we struggle to become upright and sail off to repeat that glorious ritual over and over again. Such are the memories of the sweet summertime at Camp Woronoak on Russell Pond.

On our instructor's command, we swamped our canoes with immense joy. Yes siree! With both hands on the gunwales the bowman and sternman leaned slowly to one side until the canoe tips at such an angle that water pours right in. And filled it did. And down we went. Now these aluminum canoes at Camp Woronoak have a chunk of styrofoam tucked into the stern and bow. Or so we were told. For this reason the canoe did not sink to the bottom but remained swamped with water. It just floats on the surface filled to the brim with water and going nowhere fast.

Lest I forget to tell you, this drill was carried out fully clad in street clothes. Our canoes were positioned approximately 50 yards off shore. Of course the whole lot of us are laughing like bloody fools during the execution of this drill, while our instructor is ranting impassionately to regain our attention. He did.

"Now crawl back in!" bellowed our dedicated mentor. Here we tried to slowly roll back into our swamped canoes without submerging them any deeper into the evergreen water. Next we had to stow our paddles on the inside bottom of the canoe. Since the paddles were wonderfully inclined to drift away, we sat on them to contain them. This was an invaluable lesson priming us for the reality of losing our paddles if and when we would capsize. From here my partner and I paddled from the sitting position. And with our fannies right over the middle keel and with legs spread out in a "V" position, we discovered this position stabilized the canoe best.

Working together we discovered by trial and error that it was necessary to synchronize our arm movements in the water to cover maximum distance. You see, our arms were improvised as the paddles that would propel us safely to shore. We did not employ an alternate arm pattern as in the front crawl stroke but moved them as a butterflier or breaststroker. This provided the quickest impetus and sustained momentum the best.

To steer our canoes left or right the sternman would command the bowman to mimic him, paddling on the left to veer right and vice versa. This was a strange but enjoyable experience. This adaptable craft would not sink despite containing 98 per cent water with the additional cargo of two scouts sitting on their single blade paddles and making a go of it. "Wicked cool" as they say. This kind of ride any amusement park could set up and operate while raking in a few dollars doing it. Eventually this hydro excursion terminated much to our dismay. Upon reaching the halfway mark to shore, about 25 yards, the order came forth.

"Now roll out again!"

Here we were instructed to disrobe and tie our clothes to the thwarts as best we could. We now would tackle tugging this cumbrous baby ashore. Subsequently this skill entailed the bowman swimming in the water at the bow, tugging the canoe toward shore with one hand while the other arm is utilizing the sidestroke or lifesaving arm pull to swim. The sternman is pushing the canoe from the stern with one hand and using a one arm breaststroke to assist in the effort.

Now the sternman initiated great fun for himself during this episode by hanging on to the stern as a ride, at the expense of the bowman rapidly exhausting himself. Needless to say it did not take the bowman long to catch onto the fact that something was amiss as his energy was depleting fast. Intermittently the bowman would rotate his head, peering back to check out the rear situation. Of course he surmised the sternman was slacking off. The trick was to catch the sternman in the act of shirking his duties. The sternman would always recover his arm stroke in time, failing to be detected, displaying that innocent, quizzical look, "What's the matter?"

"Come on! You know darn well what's the matter!" quipped myself. Both knew the ritual.

The sternman loved it since he had the advantage of stealthily watching the bowman at his arduous task. He had just enough view, and relished watching the bowman struggling at tugging both him and the canoe ashore. What a scene. The sternman without doubt is toiling to prevent his drowning by laughter. This terminates comfortably in jest as the bowman is so peeved and ornery that he has deserted his labors and is hanging on the gunwales to rest himself. Reality sets in as the sternman knows they are going nowhere fast. And so sensibility wins over the moment as the buddies cooperate once again to pursue their quest for shore.

On first thought, one tends to chuckle at the notion of uprighting a swamped canoe and draining it of water only to be used again to scoot around the pond. But that was exactly the task set before us if we were to pass this training course. This idea certainly intrigued me as to how this feat would be accomplished. Most of us scoffed under our breaths at this task and blurted "no way" in claiming this to be nearly impossible.

"Buddy up by canoes and paddle out to the middle of the pond," commanded our confident instructor.

The six canoes quietly slipped out into the approaching dusk of Russell Pond.

I remember Steve Kelly and I as canoeing partners on this final night of training. We easily complied with orders and swamped our canoe eagerly. Following this act our partner canoe approached us who were treading water and hanging onto our canoe. Under the instructor's directives, Steve and I turned the canoe over belly up. Now one end of our canoe was positioned right at the middle of the rescue canoe along the gunwales. I then swam to the opposite gunwale of the rescue canoe, holding the gunwales with two hands to stabilize the craft. Steve is now at the far end of the canoe, pushing it downward toward the pond's bottom. This motion lifts the end of our overturned canoe just enough to enable the two rescuers to lean over and lift our canoe end up onto their canoe gunwales. While they steady the canoe, Steve moves to my side and both of us hold and stabilize the rescue canoe. On the signal "go", the rescuers pull our canoe slowly inward and towards themselves across their gunwales. Presto! Soon our canoe is lying across the rescue canoe's gunwales upside down.

Steve and I now swim to opposite ends of the canoe and hold on. On the command "flip" the four canoeists, two rescuers on the sides, and Steve and I on the ends gently flip our canoe over. Our canoe bottom is now resting upon the rescue canoe gunwales, emptied of all water and steadied to be guided back onto the pond for canoeing.

Since a canoe is long and awkward to maneuver by oneself, it seems that one could not be emptied and made upright in the middle of a pond unless perhaps by the services of a helicopter? Actually one can "rock" the water from a swamped canoe while treading water but we never practiced this manuever. Yet leverage, listening, and that indispensable concept of teamwork made this task seem almost easy yet challenging. This was another example of scouts working together in action to accomplish a goal that others may not even attempt.

After this feat, we all felt confident and good about ourselves which is vitally important to any boy. Little things such as flipping over a swamped canoe, climbing a mountain, keeping warm and dry in a tent when it's snowy and 2 below zero overnight, cooking a meal on white hot coals without utensils were lessons no book could teach us. We had to see it being done. We needed to be exhorted by scout leaders and older scouts that most things were possible to those who would believe. And we learned that. With each feat in scouting one learned that obstacles were to be faced and surmounted. My self confidence was bolstered as a result of success in acquiring skills and overcoming challenges. Conditions such as these are what all boys need. Give me the ideals, the skills, the morals and virtues of the Scout Oath and Law...and give me a chance.

Scouting has always possessed the best after school and weekend program to keep boys off the streets and crime free. It was and still is available to all boys regardless of race, color, creed, ethnicity, and religion. It has withstood a barrage of critics and only recently won a Supreme Court challenge defending their right to adhere to a higher moral standard than some would like.

Unfortunately many parents were not looking down the right road and let their sons meander into inappropriate groups or no group at all.

Many fathers did not see the value in scouting. This is not to say that all fathers shirked their duty in their sons upbringing. Many did a fine job in their own way despite scouting. But in scouting a boy receives so many valuable lessons and challenges that he must solve using his own judgment, or in cooperation with others. Scouting offers to quench the thirst boys have for goodness, fairness, and duty to the One God. This ideal seems to have been lost in the public school system yet has been retained in scouting. It would bode well for the school systems to recoup that duty to God and country, to teach right and wrong..., a morality that is conducive to all.

And so the four week canoeing session was drawing to a close. Overcast and cloudy skies prevailed as we brought our canoes out of the water. The task of lying them on the racks to dry had just been completed when a curve ball came flying at us. As a group, our understanding was that the troop committee would pair us scouts as partners for the canoe trip. This did not happen. The choice was given to us on the drop of a hat. Nor did we ever find out who made the decision for us to decide, troop committee, scoutmaster or both.

Regardless, we heard that command that delegated the choice in selecting our partner to us. Mr. Boulais stated it clearly.

"Gentlemen, you need to pick your partner for the canoe trip right now."

Boy. We scampered about, darting here and there like mice searching for an escape route. This scenario would have been ideal for a psychologist delving into the reasons that friends choose friends, husbands and wives select each, and the subconscious attractions we use to choose companions.

There was zero time to poll each other. Before one knew it, one or two pairs were already set. I found myself next to Steve Kelly whom I had paddled with that evening. Steve was a very nonthreatening and pleasant sort of guy. I recall his braces bright and shiny when he smiled. Brighter still when he laughed. I regarded him as more intellectual than myself for he seemed to be always discussing some heady issue with Kevin Sullivan. Oh well. We sort of just gravitated to each other when I asked him.

"Do you want to canoe with me?"

He flashed that metallic grin and said, "Sure." And that was that.

This entire selection lasted all of thirty seconds or less if that. When the partner picking was near complete all of us became aware of Dennis Riel and Kevin Boulais still searching for a partner. Perhaps they were too selective or too slow in choosing but regardless of the reason, it was pretty clear that neither was left with a choice. Instinctively they knew each had become the other's partner. This seemed a bit unfair as all eyes were upon them. Everyone was cognizant that their choice was gone. Their awkwardness was only momentary as we all quickly shifted our concern to foolish antics and gibberish about the trip ahead.

Mr. Boulais let it be known that he would be the odd man out, rotating to one of the five canoes each day of the trip. He would be the third man in a different canoe each day but never made it to canoe with Steve and me.

And so it was complete. Our challenge just to become qualified closed its chapter. The added canoe instruction was behind us. No one failed and we felt proud. Right here my feelings went awry for a spell. Although my heart was joyful and eager, I began to feel for the remaining boys in our troop and other scouts that wouldn't be going on a canoe trip. I now realized how lucky we all were to have earned a trip of this magnitude. Deep inside my wishes were that all boys experience a canoe trip.

"Let's go, Gerry!" startled me, as someone yelled, breaking up my stupor. The walk along the narrow path was about 150 feet back to the paved road. I had been moping along wishing others would participate in this trip. It was really never meant to be. The cloudy sky on this summer night was growing cloudier. Dusk was settling in. Our skin was clammy with the dew.

Hearing my name, I bolted along the trail toward the parked cars on the road, the damp leaves caressing my flailing arms. My feelings returned as my brothers came into view. The incessant shoving, arm slapping, and general nonsense of the nine other scouts brought me back down to earth.

Dad was already in the car.

"You'd better get in guys...it's a long walk home," he deadpanned, with his dry Irish wit. You think he was kidding? Before we knew it the car caravan was buzzing along Birch Hill Road hugging the shoreline of Russell Pond. We descended the long, steep General Knox Road which always had me wondering if the car brakes would give out.

Route 23 to Route 20 hitched us up with the Mass Pike. The eastbound trek home into Indian Orchard was a blur. We floundered about in expectation. In a few short weeks, the event would confront us. Our minds painted scenarios of what it would be like up there. We rambled on foolishly. We were the cast of a spectacular event that none of us could describe. The imagination of young teenage boys has great promise amidst the ordinary events of life. But what was to transpire for six days of canoeing 168 miles from our little Indian Orchard was near impossible to project.

The plan was to drive northwards into upper central Vermont and canoe back down the Connecticut River 133 miles, hopefully reaching Turner's Falls Dam in Turner's Falls, MA. That is a big chunk to chew on for young teenage boys. So we didn't chew it. We simply dreamt again. We all entertained our imaginations until that eventful day would bring us northward into South Newbury, VT to begin the trek down the Connecticut River. What else could we do? We were half crazy with excitement as it was. Anything else would have taken us over the top.

7 A Lemon Cake Day

The canoe trip departure date had arrived and it was not without an emotional price. I was tired because the night before minimal sleep was acquired. At least at our house it was. Joe and Jim, my older brothers by two and one year and I cackled on for hours before succumbing to slumber. Our bedroom was a good sized 10' x 21' with beaver board walls and ceilings. It was on the third floor of a ten room house. We slept there quite comfortably.

Our talk was filled with excitement and intense expectations of what lie ahead for us on this historic trip. Historic trip? Well, for us and Troop 40 it was. Our ignorance of the area and environs made the wait unbearable.

"OK, boys..., let's get the lights out," commanded Dad with his near nocturnal ritual, from the bottom of the third floor stairs.

He would stand there in silence until those lights clicked off, and then reply, "That's better."

We could see him clearly in our mind's eye wearing his Chesire cat grin, even though it was pitch dark.

But continue to talk we did. Lying there in the dark, our underwear sticking to the sheets on those hot, humid August nights, rambling on about the trip. Actually Joe and I were the oddballs in our family of nine. The heat and humidity never fazed us. We always watched other family members wilt and suffer from the heat of summer, but Joe and I carried on as usual. The third floor was the best. All the house heat rose anyway and Jim said to open the window wide to let in more hot air. We didn't see a fan until our college days.

"OK boys..., let's knock off the yakking and go to sleep," came Dad's startling voice in the dark. Our conversation was at such a din we hadn't detected Dad's footsteps approaching the bottom of the stairs. This was one of two or three warnings from Dad to quiet us down. Heaven knows he tried. In retrospect, it seemed that Mom and Dad appeared aloof to our boyhood roller coaster antics and emotions. It took becoming a parent to realize that they knew all along we were running around headless at times.

The time to sleep crept up late during the night. We gave in unwillingly and unknowingly. The last one awake sensed that eerie feeling which we all go through. That was the awareness of talking to yourself simply because your two brothers haven't uttered a word for five or ten minutes.

"Hey Joe?...Jim?..Anyone?" said I. Silence.

Oops. I guess it's time to cease babbling because these guys are zonked out and doing soliloquies isn't something I cherish at the moment.

Saturday, August 13 was sunny and not particularly humid when we gave our gear a final check. The U. S. Weather Bureau at the Springfield Armory Station recorded a high temperature of 78°F and a low of 59°F with a trace of rain somewhere in the vicinity. The ten of us plus parents met in the school yard of Saint Aloysius School, our regular troop meeting place. The parents and dads who would drive us were conversing in their secluded huddle, ironing out last minute details and plans. Directions given. Lead car. Trail car. What to do if our retinue became separated. Where to stop for lunch.

As teenage boys it was difficult to imagine the concern and responsibility of our parents and scout dads in an event like this. We took it for granted the scout dads would be there for every event. As scouts we felt their place was to be away from us, in the huddle. Adults discussing what the kids can and cannot do. We even had it set in our myopic minds that these men were old fogies! Good heavens, my Dad and most of the men helping out were in their early forties! We felt they were all washed up and over the hill. As time moves along, I realize how youthful they were. That we were so darn lucky to have our parents and adult scouters present was a blessing. A blessing that few of us could see or appreciate at the moment.

The canoes for our trip had to be picked up at the Horace A. Moses Scout Reservation in Russell. Administration was lending us five white aluminum canoes, with paddles and life jackets included. These canoes were the ones we had trained with for four weeks at Camp Woronoak on Russell Pond, so we certainly had a familiar craft to move along in.

Cliff Dumas was our pickup man. He drove an old pink Rambler with a small beat up trailer hitched to it. Cliff carted just about everything for us scouts on campouts and other scout excursions. Today was no less of a challenge. It always looked like both car and trailer would collapse at any given moment, but it never happened. Cliff somehow got hold of a larger trailer and rigged up those five canoes as good as any rigger could.

Cliff was always there for us scouts. He never had a son but treated us all like we were. A big, burly Frenchman was he. A balding man of about six foot and then some. He habitually pushed his spectacles further up on the bridge of his nose with his middle finger, then rubbed his hands together as if to warm them when he meant to get down to business. Cliff also referred to us as gentlemen. He loved recounting stories about Troop 40 when he was a scout. The troop had a Drum and Bugle Corps in the forties and Cliff was so proud to be in it. He was very amiable but direct with us, but if anyone of us crossed him enough, boy the room would freeze over with just one look at his face.

I can't recall a campout without Cliff breaking out "Chicken in a Biskit" snack crackers. He just had to have them. Cliff was the expert Cooking merit badge counselor for our troop. Your beef stew had to have dumplings in it or you didn't pass. In February 1966, my brother Jim and I went to Cliff's house on a Saturday morning. We built our fireplace with rocks and kept it going while whipping up beef stew with dumplings from scratch and chocolate pudding. He let us do the dishes in his wife's kitchen. We passed the badge.

In any event, Cliff was to pickup the canoes and then rendezvous with the rest of us in West Springfield where the Mass Pike (Route 90) intersects with Interstate 91 North. After departing, our caravan headed west over the Memorial Bridge into West Springfield. Cliff arrived with the canoes in tow by the Mass Pike entrance, then we re-routed up 91 North to our anticipated destination, South Newbury, VT.

Ray Roberge, Sr. teamed up with Norm Kelly, Steve's dad in helping to drive us guys north. My Dad helped cart some of the boys along in his 64 Ford Wagon. And Gene DeGrandpre, Sr. assisted by driving his gray Ford Van in lugging the rest.

The ride northward was pretty uneventful if you can relate to a teenager enduring a three hour vacation ride. Sometime in the early afternoon about one or two o'clock, our entourage of cars and canoes puttered to a halt somewhere for lunch. Each of us had brown bagged it which was typical for scouts on field trips at the time.

There is no better way to put the clamp on a bunch of yakking scouts than to put good food in front of them. Any group of kids for that matter. And if the kids are really hungry the food doesn't necessarily have to be that good. It just needs to be food.

I do not recall any other available dessert offered for the group at lunch time but my Mom had baked a lemon cake for the canoe trip departure trip. She had worked all day Friday at home which was her custom with seven kids. Any feminist who claimed she wasn't working had better step aside. She baked this cake after dark about nine o'clock. Watching her complete it I remembered her words to me, "This cake is always better the day after." Well, let me tell you, it was better the day after but it didn't last.

Dad retrieved the cake from the back seat of the station wagon and proceeded to slice it up for the boys. It was in a 10" x 15" flat cake pan. A sheet cake. Its rapid disappearance could have set a time record. As the first few pieces were distributed everyone meandered over to see what goodies were being doled out. No one knew that this lemon cake was different. It had different forms of lemon in it and boy was it good. In fact, it was beyond good. From here it went so quickly, it was hardly believable. I sensed a bunch of ravenous animals. This cake had a moistness through it and was so tangy with just enough sweetness to make it delectable. This intense situation was accompanied by many grunts and groans, and oohs and ahhs. Having knocked off my first piece, I noticed the guys hovering about the cake pan again. Some dads were attempting to secure their first piece of cake and were having trouble at it. Fat chance amigo.

Wriggling in and out, elbowing here and there I somehow maneuvered in to grasp my second piece of cake. It was a small square and one of a few left, so I was lucky. Shuffling away one could hear the complaints of those who lost out. The guys then verbally pounded me with my mealtime name, "piggish one!" I had earned the dubbing by eating nonstop on campouts. "Hey, leave me alone!" I retorted, "my Mother made it!" which pretty much dispelled all opposition thereafter. I was amazed and annoyed in garnering only two pieces. I felt it was owed to me to have more since Mom did make it. Not so. Further pondering convinced me that I was actually lucky to get two pieces given the scavengers that Troop 40 harbored.

The juices that are poured over and into the cake actually soak in and permeate overnight. This creates a very drenched and succulent cake. A sort of "get out of my way cake" which has you returning for more and more. The lemon cake lingered on in more ways than one. On most campouts thereafter, the guys were always asking if a lemon cake came along. And so lest I forget, here is the recipe so you may enjoy it yourself. My assumption is that you do like lemon.

Mrs. O'Brien's Canoe Trip Lemon Cake

Cake

- One package of lemon cake mix
- 3/4 cup of oil
- 1 cup of water
- 1 3 oz. pkg. of lemon jello
- 4 eggs
- 1/2 teaspoon salt
- 1/2 teaspoon of lemon extract

Grease bottom and sides of 13" x 9" x 2" pan (Mom used a larger one). Combine all ingredients and beat 5 minutes with a mixer on medium speed. Bake 30 - 40 minutes at 350 degrees.

Icing

- 1 1/2 cups powdered sugar plus 6 tablespoons of lemon juice.
- Mix sugar and juice.
- Remove cake from oven and immediately punch holes in the top with a long tined cooking fork, reaching the bottom of the pan.
- Pour the icing over the hot cake
- The icing will soak downward permeating throughout the cake. The lemon icing and cake combine to form a truly scrumptious assault on one's palate. Let the cake cool and set. It's best served the next day..., if you can wait.

And so after the lemon cake demolition we re-filled the vehicles with bodies and continued the trek northward. Traveling up 91 North was pretty monotonous. We loved joking about Cliff's trailer with the five canoes in tow being the lead car. Bets were on and off as to whether those canoes were to finish the trailer ride to South Newbury, VT. Why the way they swayed left and right we were sure they'd slide off at any given moment.

The ride north took a more interesting and scenic turn on behalf of the interstate highway construction. As of August 1966 Interstate 91 was completed only as far north as Windsor, VT. The section from Windsor to White River Junction, VT was still under construction, forcing our caravan onto Exit 9 and bringing us into the town of Hartland, VT.

Here someone in the car shouted, "Hey, this is the town. The Hartland rapids are around here somewhere!" Certainly we could not stop and delay the trip to locate these infamous rapids. Believe me, we would encounter them soon enough, my friend. Now we were chugging along Route 5 North which presented more of a nightmare watching Cliff's canoe trailer from behind. The serpentine Route 5 hugged the Connecticut River shoreline creating a slinkier road versus the straight and unobstructed 91.

Cliff Dumas kept right on moving being accustomed to the highway speeds...or so it seemed. He probably decelerated from 65 MPH to 45-50 MPH but it seemed faster. To watch those canoes shift laterally at that speed was both funny and frightening. Initially, we regarded this as a laughing matter until a few oncoming cars approached. Certain that the trailer's tail end would swerve to the far left across that double yellow median strip into oncoming cars, we froze. Coasting behind Cliff's trailer we could easily follow his Rambler, shifting right or left at each curve in the road. This was nerve wracking because as the Rambler shifted sideways the momentum of the trailer was still headed forward for what seemed like too long of a second or so. It appeared that the trailer would remain on its course and smack head-on into each oncoming car. Trying to ascertain which car would get smacked kept our nerves on edge. Of course, at the precise moment the trailer hitch would transfer the canoes keeping them on the right side of the road.

"Whoa! Look out!" we yelled, as if Cliff could really hear us.

"He just missed that truck! Oh, my God!" we screamed. This scenario persisted for the next 40-50 miles right into South Newbury. It provided us with fun and heart stopping suspense on an otherwise boring 3 1/2 hour ride. It must have been nerve wracking for my Dad who was driving because those canoes easily could have swerved too far left and struck a car or simply dislodged and fell off. Watching the canoes, I remembered Cliff's knowledge of knots. He knew many above and beyond the required scout knots and passed many hours on campouts showing us scouts how to tie them. In any event, I was somewhat relieved that we arrived at our destination with the canoes intact. I really can't recall the knot Cliff used to secure the canoes but I'm glad it wasn't a slip knot.

The view is quite scenic along Route 5 North. Lazy, rolling green hills and pastures dotted with brown and black spotted cows. Marriages of red barns and protruding silos with white farmhouses nestled besides. The quiet Quiet. Both Vermont highway and back roads driving subtly reveals a uniqueness about this beautiful landscape, and that is the absence of advertising billboards by law. This is quite relaxing on the eyes. It is only as one gets closer to the cities that billboards begin to raise their commercial heads.

Our put in spot at South Newbury, VT. This is the new bridge built in November, 1971. (7/99 Photo)

Momentarily our entourage slowed and hung a sharp right onto Newbury Crossing Road. This abrupt harbinger startled us as we babbled and fooled around in the back seat. Having abandoned our hobby of watching the swaying canoes, we had lost our sense of where we were. Rumbling eastward toward the river's shore we reoriented our focus. For all intents and purposes our arrival was imminent.

Moving at a much slower pace now, our retinue crawled to a stop then trundled across the rails of the Boston and Maine. The autos edged along the left side of the road and came to our long awaited point of departure, rolling to a stop on the sandy shoulder. We had arrived.

The Newbury Crossing Bridge lie before us. This 2-Thru Pratt Truss structure spans 330 feet from South Newbury, VT into Haverhill, NH. Engineer John W. Storrs designed it and United Construction Co.

erected it on Dec. 1, 1913. That was 53 years prior to our arrival and the pale green iron beam bridge showed those years with generous smatterings of rust, speckled about. A July 22, 1942 inspection revealed the general condition as "fair". In 1944 it was painted aluminum. We would never see her again as a new bridge came to life in November 1971 after John Storrs' was dismantled being deemed unsafe years before. In 1913 the maximum water depth here was one foot plus a fathom, and was probably the same when we arrived. Regardless, the car doors shut solidly into a silent vacuum. A few birds could be heard chirping perhaps discussing our pretentious arrival. So this was it. So peaceful...so anticlimactic. Henceforth, our pre-trip imaginations would dissipate minute by minute into reality.

Like fools we descended the embankment in a clamor, shouting excitedly. Brushing aside over extended branches ready to whip into our faces, we halted abruptly at the river's edge, almost plopping in. The surface was calm; similar to a lake. Yet, crumpled yellow leaves riding softly southward dashed any notions of a stagnant river.

"Let's go! Get up here and unload your canoes!" bellowed a few of the dads, piercing our few moments of wondered awe. Back up the embankment we bolted. A few of the guys were already unloading their canoes and gear and returning to the river for departure.

Steve Kelly and I lugged our canoe down the embankment, swaying like mad and laughing most of the way. Mr. DeGrandpre assisted us by carrying our gear down the hill. Steve and I slid the canoe onto the surface then we steadied it. I crouched and entered first being the bowman. Mr. DeGrandpre tossed in our gear and helped me to hold ship while Steve gently and cautiously stepped in.

We knelt and peered downstream only to notice a couple of canoes already downstream a few hundred feet. It was a frenzied effort not to be last with each duo and their canoe out for themselves.

We shoved off.

8 BonVoyage

There are three indispensable principles for a successful canoe trip, especially in tandem canoeing.
- Get along with your partner.
- Get along with your canoe.
- Get along with your paddle.

Steve Kelly was about as amiable as a guy could get. Why we ever gravitated to each as partners after canoe training, I defer to the consulting psychologists. I hope my trip comportment conveyed the same amiability towards Steve as he did for me. We got along and had fun, too.

There was a dual responsibility for us in overseeing the welfare of our canoe. This baby was going to be our home, transportation, and recreation while on this here river for six days. While it wasn't a terribly arduous feat in protecting and caring for our canoe, any amount of inattentiveness could invite trouble.

This was especially true if encountering fast moving water, rapids, and strainers. One just never knows what's out there or under there for that matter. To lose respect for or detract from the importance of canoe safety on our part would be a brazen abuse of responsibility. Luckily we knew that.

The paddle was our "A" Number One essential tool. There is only one thing worse than being upstream without a paddle, and that is being downstream without a paddle, which is where we were headed. Our paddles were plastic, metal, and buoyant. If our paddles went astray then luck was with us as they would be retrievable. Conditions would regress instantly from good to torturous if one lost or broke a paddle since we hadn't brought replacements. Imagine Steve with his paddle and I pulling water with the front crawl stroke with my chest stuck on the gunwale up front. Beautiful. Going nowhere fast. One would enjoy the trip more if their food and personal belongings were gone rather than their paddle. Heavens!

And so we instinctively heeded those three principles and moved on down.

The Connecticut River is 410 miles long. This great river commences at the Fourth Connecticut Lake about three hundred yards south of the United States/Canada border. You may access it by traveling to the U.S. Customs House on Route 3 at the Quebec/New Hampshire border.

Actually, this lake forms when it rains. In a hollow surrounded by spruce and fir trees the lake manifests itself with the normal fall of rain and snow in the region. It spans 120 yards and wildlife abounds. Beaver, red-tailed hawk, otters, mergansers, ducks, loons, deer, black bear, and moose all make their home in this natural habitat.

The Fourth Connecticut Lake empties into the Third Connecticut Lake only a half mile below. Continuing on the Third Connecticut Lake pours into the Second Connecticut Lake, four miles south. The Second Connecticut Lake gushes along for two more miles prior to flowing into the First Connecticut Lake. Finally, the last link of these four lakes is the Saint Francis which is deluged with the contents of the previous three. Due to the elevation in this locale the river's water between each successive lake is quite turbulent. The drop in one stretch, three miles from the Second Lake to the First Lake, is 200-300 feet! Running the river here should not be attempted except by expert canoeists and kayakers.

Historically, the first recorded trip attempted from the Fourth Connecticut Lake to the Connecticut River's mouth in Old Saybrook, CT was by Dr. Joseph G. Davidson, President of the Connecticut River Watershed Council, and Mrs. Davidson in 1959.

The Davidsons' were leading a group to impress upon the public the reality of a dirty, neglected, and polluted river. Dr. Davidson immersed a jar into the Fourth Connecticut Lake and filled it with clear, cold water. His entourage drank of it, and were reminded that "this is the last drink we'll take from the Connecticut."

Dr. Davidson's group completed the trip to Old Saybrook, CT in seven days, chugging along by way of canoe, powerboat, and automobile. Negotiating the Hartland Rapids in VT/NH (Sumner Falls), in a turbojet-propelled boat, the Davidson's party hit a submerged rock. The river excursion ended abruptly no doubt and fortunately left everyone unscathed.

These same rapids challenged Major Rogers and his Rangers with similar difficulties while traveling this waterway from Saint Francis, Quebec to Fort #4 in Charlestown, NH in 1759.

Perhaps for no other limitation except time, our canoe trip was to be only 133 miles on this great river. From South Newbury, VT we would paddle and portage south for six days, terminating our adventure at the dam in Turner's Falls, MA.

And so, gliding gently away from shore the Newbury Crossing Bridge towered before us. It seemed to challenge us, daring us to coast under her. Having drifted only about 75 feet from shore, Steve and I found ourselves beneath her massive steel beams, exposing more under carriage rust than her upper tiers. This structural leviathan allowed us to pass under her without incident, as I breathed a sigh of relief that she hadn't toppled upon us.

"Good luck! See you on Friday," shouted Mr. DeGrandpre. Taking my eyes off the river before me, I glanced back quickly and gave him a wave. Mr. "D" as we called him, my Dad, Norm Kelly, Cliff Dumas and Ray Roberge, Sr. were waving from the shore and shrinking by the second. As we paddled downstream I craned my neck to see them fade into specks.

Our mobilization was completed without any fanfare or pretentious send offs. Just get in your canoe and move out. And that is how we commenced this momentous canoe trip of ours.

I felt a relief and a particular calmness with the river. Here the water appears dormant, almost asleep but it is not. Although this section of the Connecticut is categorized as Class I "flat water", its movement is slow but steadfast. What briefly caught my attention was the early foliage in the region. A few birches had turned yellow already.

A magnificent afternoon in August, 1966.

These serene flat waters in Newbury provided many a crumpled brown and yellow leaf a great medium for a floating downstream race. They coasted along side, competing with us. I asked myself who would reach Turner's Falls first? "Why, us!" I concluded, since it is difficult for floating leaves to make three portages!

South Newbury is picturesque. We were leaving our little world behind and chancing the great unknown for six days. At least unknown to us by experience. Presently our minds were preoccupied with fun and adventure. We were here on faith. Nothing was certain but three things. The sky above us...the river below us...and our movement southward. What was to come was sheer speculation.

The waters of the Connecticut here in South Newbury are quite calming to one's spirit. The river geographically divides Vermont and New Hampshire wearing the hat of east/west border. The terrain on both sides of the river is near identical and then some. Small sloping embankments with lush green rolling pastures. Erect cornfields, 6-7 feet high, ready for harvest. Red barns, silos, and farm houses seem more prevalent on the Vermont side. New Hampshire begins its farm-land also but more quickly gives way to its granite and towering White Mountains.

Birds fluttering low enough to scoop bugs from the river's surface. The intermittent "Con-ka-ree" of the Red Winged Black-bird pierced the quiet surroundings along the banks. This familiar song mimicked the same refrain of Long Pond's identical species back home in Indian Orchard. I loved to watch them take off from the cattail marsh accompanied by the rapid fire flicking of their red, contrasting with the black as they flew.

Wooden fence posts harnessed by barbed wire between them. And cows. Cows? Oh yes. We were no doubt under the watchful stare of many a Vermont cow. Actually they had a right to stare since it was our "canoe confederation" that had intruded upon their peaceful grazing grounds. We after all had disturbed the peaceful atmosphere of their "dairy world".

Canoeing almost allows one to see the world from ground level. Kneeling down, a canoeist is able to peer ahead from a 2-3 foot height similar to bobbing around like a swan or an egret. Canoeing is therapeutic because it is relatively quiet. To dip your paddle in, down, out, and return only to hear a few drops trickling back onto the waters surface awakens your senses. Hearing yourself breathe. Feeling your muscles flex and extend; pull and release. Glancing over your shoulder, watching the ripples fading behind you, created by a submerged and surging keel.

In the mid afternoon sun all five canoes have gone their way leaving just enough distance between each to keep within view. At this point we are all pretty much filled with excitement and exhilaration. It is a time for absorbing the river. A time to acclimate to her surroundings and vastness. This is not Russell Pond. Her width was greater than I had anticipated. How so much different than peering down from a car on some bridge. The divine spark in me jumped a little nudging my senses to a higher level of fear and respect for this great wonder.

Most of us envisioned a queer sight looming the river's width downstream. About a quarter mile on the horizon there appeared to be a pine tree of gargantuan proportions spanning the entire width of the river. Could there be a tree that tall that had fallen in the river? I thought. No. Not around here anyway. As we paddled closer, our mirage of a fallen tree turned out to be none other than the infamous Bedell Covered Bridge. One of the few remaining covered bridges on the Connecticut River grew larger and became more focused as we paddled on down.

"Wow, look how long it is?" proclaimed Steve, a bit awestruck.

Our entire entourage ebbed to a stop, ceased paddling, then drifted with the current beneath the Bedell. Her massive wooden beams shouted out in silence. My thoughts briefly jumped back in time and pondered life far removed when this teeming hulk was constructed. Did the Bedell ask herself? "Would anyone go over me or under me when I'm 100 years old?" Regardless, yes they would and yes we did.

Little did we know at the time that she was in fact exactly 100 years old having been constructed in 1866. This 396 foot baby from South Newbury, VT to Haverill, NH was the fifth such bridge built on site, the first being erected in 1805 to replace a ferry at Toll House Road in New Hampshire. This bridge fell victim to the elements as did the ensuing three bridges prior to the Bedell's tenure.

"Can we go up and run through it?", my brother Jim yelled across the water to Mr. Boulais.

"We've got to check and see if it's open to traffic," responded the Scoutmaster.

Up ahead, someone already discovered the discouraging news.

"It's closed. We can see the traffic barriers from here."

"Don't get discouraged," Mr. Boulais cautioned us, "there's another covered bridge downstream."

With obvious reluctance and minor discouragement, we begrudgingly commenced paddling again, stifling our desire to climb onto that bridge and run through it from end to end, stomping along its "wooden road."

The Bedell was closed to traffic in 1958 after a discovery of weakened arches on the Vermont side. A 1973 flood further weakened the bridge and the New Hampshire side arches were deemed unsafe for traffic. A scheduled demolition never came to pass. Supporters on both sides of the river rallied to her rescue.

A state contract mandated stabilization against further deterioration by May 15, 1974, and a return to vehicular traffic by November 11, 1976.

Milton Graton, an expert in covered bridge repair and construction was given the green light to bring the Bedell back. His crews worked doggedly with local donations, but soon the project was delayed as expected federal funds did not arrive. Sound familiar? Now the Federal government may well make anyone and everyone wait but it will never succeed in delaying Mother Nature. She generously shared her mild and harsh weather with all including the Bedell.

It is precisely because Mother Nature usually gets her way that we would never set eyes upon her again. On September 14, 1979 a violent windstorm leveled her, leaving the wooden wreckage in the river bed to be dragged a bit further downstream by rising flood waters.

The Bedell has never been rebuilt or attempted. I am happy just to have seen her, drifting about under her mammoth wooden frame. What scant remains there are lie sleeping on the river's bottom awaiting another curious scuba diver's meticulous scrutiny.

In July 1999, a visit to the Bedell Bridge State Park in Haverill, NH offered the stark reality of what Mother Nature rendered. Picnic tables, a boat ramp, and two stone abutments that supported this bridge is all that remains aside of memories. An engraved granite marker about four feet high tells the tale:

The Bedell Bridge

"The last of five 19th century bridges which existed at this location was erected in 1866 by local entrepreneur, Moody Bedell, who operated a ferry service here prior to the first bridge in 1805. The 396 foot structure was the largest surviving example of a two span covered bridge utilizing Burr truss and timber arch design. Following several years of human effort which corrected decades of deterioration, the newly restored landmark reopened on July 22, 1979, and was destroyed by a violent windstorm on Sept. 14, 1979."

The Bedell Covered Bridge on 8/13/66. She collapsed on 9/14/79.

We had to move on despite our petulant mood. I for my part felt frustration as if forbidden to open a Christmas present despite having knowledge of its content. Somehow we let the Bedell go. We offered it up, if you will. Perhaps the allurement of six adventurous days before us softened our mood. That and the idea that another covered bridge awaited us helped us shrug her off.

An hour or so passed. Steve and I managed to pick up speed a bit. How we knew that I'll never know because we hadn't anything to measure it by. An urgency arose to share our excitement and feelings with the others, so we decided to churn it a bit faster. As we paddled towards the others a sense of closeness came over me. The time seemed ripe to return to the group. We needed to be sure everyone was safe and we wanted to be safe if our circumstances somehow turned sour.

"Hey! Wait up!" I screamed to the others.

"Slow down!" yelled Steve, who chortled a bit realizing the futility of our out distanced outbursts.

Gradually the canoes appear to merge closer and closer. We are converging on each other mid point on the river.

In a few moments my brother Joe and Ray Roberge, Jr. slithered up along side our canoe. Joe and Ray were the senior leaders in the troop and are only 15 1/2 years and 16 years old respectively on this trip. These guys were chums, attending Cathedral High School together in the same class. I always regarded them as the more intellectual type. They lived up to it too because achieving the honor roll became a habit for them both. Each pursued and eventually rounded out productive careers in the scientific fields.

Joe and Ray were good senior leaders as well as good role models. I can't recall when either one lost their cool with us younger scouts. Both possessed a calm disposition as their trademark. It was good to see them in a more relaxed role on the canoe trip. Presently they were laughing over something.

"How's it going?", Joe inquired, matter of factly to Steve and me.

"Pretty good," replied Steve Kelly, with his metallic grin.

"Well, they're gonna get better," said Joe with humorous caution, "cause we don't have the life jackets now."

"What?!" I replied pensively with stark realization.

"Oh yeah,"... my voice trailed off.

"Where are they?" inquired Steve with a puzzled look.

"On the way back home," answered Ray informatively. Momentarily it dawned on us that amidst all the hype and confusion of shoving off at the bridge everyone forgot to break out the lifejackets.

"How did we forget those?" I asked Joe incredulously.

"We didn't,'" remarked Joe, "Mr. Boulais decided at the last minute that we probably wouldn't need them."

"Gee...I hope he's right," replied Ray.

And off we paddled downstream into the setting sun entertaining sporadic thoughts of just how perilous this trip might be.

****

We paddled on for an hour or so more. The weather was ideal. Sunny, mild to warm. A low of 58 degrees and a high of about 74 degrees. Early that morning in Newbury there was a rainfall around 8:00 AM of only 0.25 of an inch. The day prior, the 12th of August, saw a 1.48 inches of precipitation. But on August 11, just two days before we arrived, the South Newbury Weather Station had reported "high winds, rain, thunder, a lightening bolt at 4:22 PM and hail!" Now that would have proven beautiful conditions in which to commence a canoe trip. Needless to say, we simply lucked out by evading that ominous forecast.

As we coasted and glided along the river each winding bend revealed a panorama of repetitious beauty. The peaceful coexistence of the Vermont and New Hampshire landscapes flooded our senses. On our initial day of canoeing, the itinerary was from South Newbury Crossing Bridge to a sandy New Hampshire riverbank in lower Piermont. This distance was about 13-15 miles, give or take a few miles depending on where one stopped.

A good stretch of the Connecticut here appeared murky and brown-ish offering poor visibility. Despite these conditions intermittent spots of clear water broke through downstream. This allowed us to peer directly to the bottom. Moving slowly across stream from a Vermont farm, we approached the New Hampshire shore about 50 feet away. The water's depth seemed 6-8 feet down. Suddenly Steve and I were startled.

"Whoa, look at that down there, Steve!" I alerted my sternman.

Hunkered down below lie an old jalopy. It appeared to be an antique Ford or Chevy still all intact. It slept there on its side covered with a fine layer of powdery rust undisturbed from years of hibernation. We hovered briefly to check it out, but then moved out quickly since it gave us the "willies" just staring at it. Imaginations are great aren't they?

"I wonder how it got there?" we ruminated aloud to each other.

Our discussion for a few good nautical miles centered on how that jalopy ended up in its Connecticut river grave.

"It could have been a frozen river and someone tried to drive it across," I offered.

"That would take brains," replied Steve.

"How about a flood?" Steve pitched in.

"Who knows?" said I. "Maybe it was stolen and some guys rolled it into the river," I speculated further.

As we paddled into the setting sun, it cast its long warm tentacles towards us resisting every effort to slip behind the Green Mountains of Vermont.

Our first day on the Connecticut was winding down. The five canoes already bypassed Bradford, VT and the confluence of the Waits

River. Paddling began to evolve into quite the humdrum activity. The visual effects were pretty much identical on both sides of the river. Sandwiched between the White Mountains and the Green Mountains we pined for new sights and novel adventure. You see, beauty even if continually in one's presence develops a tendency to be taken for granted, sad as that may seem. It is not appreciated as it should be especially when viewed by high school boys.

The riverbanks here seem to climb 8-10 feet above eye-level so that one hardly sees the real world going by on either shoreline. We drifted down in a world of our own if you will. Kneeling at water level for six days would not allow us to know the happenings on either Route 10 in New Hampshire or Route 5 in Vermont. Cornfields flourished. We came to expect the sight of them early on. Following the sun's descent which was always westward on the Vermont side, the river rolled lazily to the right toward Fairlee.

The sun had gone to bed by now. "Tucked down behind the purple hills," as Thornton Burgess would say. Dampness is setting in. Like a sheer veil, a soft dew settles down and transforms my dry shirt into a cool, moist one. It clings and hangs heavier on my frame than an hour ago.

The mosquitoes make their presence known. Landing on our arms their demise by smashing is imminent lest they fly off quickly. Off they depart to the water's surface hovering about. Barn swallows mimicked dive bombers at Midway. Emerging from nowhere these birds chased mosquitoes at every geometric angle possible, gobbling them up in flight. Mosquitoes above the water's surface found no refuge either. The swallows swooped down along the river's face, darting here and there, flitting about, devouring the winged insects. No pun intended but I wondered, "is this the reason they are named 'swallows'?" Mr. Boulais was up ahead with my brother Joe and Ray Roberge, Jr. They were discussing where to turn in for the night.

"I'm hungry," said Steve in a tired voice.

"We'll be stopping soon," I replied to Steve, "they're starting to pull up on the New Hampshire side." And so it was.

The group followed suit and trickled in canoe by canoe, beaching our crafts on a sandy shore in lower Piermont, NH. You'd never know it but this was designated as a town camping area. There was plenty of meadow followed by cornfields on the horizon to greet us.

"We'll settle here for the night," stated Mr. Boulais. Steve and I beached our canoe by lugging it about 20 feet off the sand and plopped it on the grass. We all turned our canoes belly up to protect our gear from possible rain.

A feeling of closeness began to overcome me. I sense that the knit is tightening between us all and a sense of family is emerging. The beach campsite was a lonesome place. None of us are familiar with it here. A sandy shore, a grassy swath of meadow about 100 feet at the foot of a massive cornfield was to be our bedroom tonight.

"Hey, who owns this place?" quipped Gene DeGrandpre in his amusing way.

"Who knows? Who cares?", half of us rambled and teased him with.

The game plan for camping overnight was to occupy a desolate spot and preferably public. Hopefully we would not encounter any belligerent landowners, eager to kick us off "their" property. As far as we were concerned the beach had to be public or at least a portion of the way inland did.

While we gathered our personal gear and sleeping bags, a few guys built a campfire on the sandy shore. Its warmth emanated a good feeling on our skin. Even in August, the nights harbor a cool dampness that needs to be dispelled. Our little campfire did the trick preserving an enjoyable campout along this clammy waterway.

After supper, we enjoyed hot chocolate, shared stories and acted foolish in the twilight. We stood motionless and gawked into the fire's orange flames. I wondered about home and appreciated it a little more. Before realizing it, dusk had slunk away and night's cloak of utter darkness shrouded us. Back home on campouts we were always near some house lights or street lights, but here there wasn't a light in sight. This situation lent us the rare opportunity of peering upward into the heavens to gaze the bright stars like never before. Absent were the city lights that normally impede and block the true view of constellations and stars under clear celestial conditions.

Slowly we groped our way up onto the grassy field between the sandy beach and the cornfield. Our sleeping bags were laid out and awaiting us complete with a fine layer of dew. Some of us mulled the idea of fetching our ponchos to cover the bags but most of us were so darn tired the notion went nowhere. As we snuggled into our sleeping bags the retrieval of ponchos became a chucked idea. Besides, the sky was so clear that we forecast the weather on our own. We projected that no rain would fall that night. It was crisp and clear with an overnight temperature of 47°F but we would sleep like rocks.

Fixated upon the heavens from our sleeping bags, we were awestruck at the vast multitude of stars hovering there.

"Hey look! Cassiopeia is right there," shouted Dennis Riel, pointing out the "lady in the chair" resembling the letter "W". Soon we found ourselves attempting to outdo each other in locating the constellations of the summer sky. This skill was a requirement for all of us to earn our First Class Scout award. We had to locate and identify five constellations in either the summer or winter sky.

"Big Dipper!" screamed my brother Jimmy, with added antics.

"North Star!" bellowed another.

We were venting our excitement and yelling out because of our happiness. Any troubles we had were left behind at home and now we were poised for adventure.

"Hey, no one can hear us out here," said Ed "Sparky" McGrath, in his soft mellow tone. And so we screamed like fools again.

"There's Orion the Hunter!"

"The Little Dipper!"...Yeah!

A few of the guys were able to locate and identify Leo, the Lion, Ursa Major, the larger Bear and Ursa Minor, the little Bear. These constellations always seemed too elusive for me in tracking them down.

I believe it was my brother Joe who sent out the first war cry alerting us to a shooting star darting from one end of the sky to the other. Sure enough, August is the month for meteor showers and we were witnessing the notorious "Perseides Meteor" showers which appear during the second week annually. These showers originate in the constellation Perseus located in the Northern Hemisphere near the constellations Andromeda and Auriga. In Greek mythology, Perseus was the son of Zeus and Danae who put Medusa to death and rescued Andromeda.

The sky tonight provided perfect viewing. Lying supine, with diligent patience we peered heavenward hoping to be the next one to spot a shooting star. Those streaking stars seem to have come and gone in three or four minute intervals. This entertained us for quite a spell despite being so tired that we lacked the sense to close our eyes.

Inevitably it grew quieter and quieter in our grassy bedroom. Eleven cocoons were lying adjacent to each other with eyes gazing heavenward. After tiring of tracking shooting stars someone suggested guessing the number of stars in the universe. Needless to say that notion had a quick funeral.

"Gentlemen, try to get some sleep," advised Mr. Boulais, "we've got to rise, make breakfast, and paddle into Orford for Sunday Mass," was the last thing I remember, as the gentle arm of slumber finally put me asunder.

✕9 Enter the Dragonfly?

I woke by daylight which is my usual way. Disorientation veered me about as I visually groped for the beaverboard walls of my third floor bedroom by habit. Still snuggled in my sleeping bag, I shifted my eyes about and verified our weather forecast from the night before. It hadn't rained but the dew was thick. The river's surface was sheer calm. Breezes had not roused any visible ripples or waves yet.

Peaceful and serene is the world by any waters' edge in the wee hours prior to sunrise, and no less here. It was misty. However, the dense fog was definitely losing it's battle with the sun's rays. Minute by minute the fog dissipated into thin air as the "light" infantry (no pun intended) of burning rays multiplied above the field of cornstalks. It felt good knowing we wouldn't be paddling in the rain.

Joe and Ray were up and seemed to be discussing something with Mr. Boulais by the canoes. Before long everyone had rolled out of the sack. Excitement was escalating since this was our first wakeup on the river.

Our culinary needs on the trip were met by Chuck Wagon Foods. This outfit was a freeze dried, de-hydrated food company which prepared foods especially for special trips like ours. Campouts, canoe trips, or hikes of long duration gave rise to the necessity of quick, non-perishable, lightweight foods. Most Chuck Wagon breakfast menus included powdered eggs, powdered juice similar to Tang, instant oatmeal, dried mixed fruit which was resurrected in boiling water, and instant pancake mix. Chuck Wagon also created an instant jelly for breakfast which was also given life by adding water and mixing it up right in its plastic bag. The trouble here was the same flavor emerged at breakfast on six mornings: pineapple. Oh boy...can't wait.

Now besides the regular Chuck Wagon menu selections there was made available to us a delectable biscuit called "Bolton Biscuit". Now Bolton Biscuits were for the taking at every meal and for snacks...if you desired. But you see, not many of us desired them which is probably why they were always so plentiful! Bolton Biscuits were little brown square biscuits about 1 1/2" x 1 1/2", and were in all probability the closest facsimile to hardtack used in the Civil War. These biscuits were so hard to bite into that the mere idea would make any dentist cringe.

Many a tooth neared its breaking point when biting into a Bolton Biscuit. It tasted like cardboard a few days shy of petrification. Smeared pineapple jelly on them helped a bit, but not much. Their memory is etched well into my mind and will accompany me to the grave.

So what could be more appropo than to compose a ballad surrounding the realities of a Bolton Biscuit. When paddling became unbearable this rendition could be heard being belted out by two balladeers in some lonesome canoe:

"I like Bolton Biscuits,"

"Yes, good old Bolton Biscuits,"

"I like mine cause they break my teeth,"

"Yes, I like Bolton Biscuits."

And following melodious suit, the next canoe would pick up the refrain and add a new stanza of their own. Hang on:

"I like Bolton Biscuits,"

"Yes, good old Bolton Biscuits,"

"I like mine cause they're brown and hard,"

"Yes, I like Bolton Biscuits."

Yes sir, good old Bolton Biscuits were the rage that week. And how ironic that hard tack is also called "ship biscuit" and "pilot bread." Hmmm?? Conspiracy.

With breakfast behind us, we slid our canoes back onto the Connecticut. The sun continued its ascent and it seemed it would remain a sunny day. It did. Conditions proved ideal as the forecast remained sunny with no wind and a high of 77°F.

We pressed our paddles at an even clip. Our goal was to make it to Sunday Mass in the 9:00-10:00 AM range. We had been making good time when Joe startled us.

"Yikes! Look at the size of that!" yelled Joe, pointing to a huge granite precipice bulging off the west side of Route 5. Our group had just discovered the Palisades, although we didn't know its name at the time. This massive granite cliff rises some 200-300 feet towering over all in the area. This gigantic slab imposing itself upon us must have a name.

"What a cliff!" Joe blurted out.

"Let's give it a name!" shot back Kevin Sullivan.

"Hey...it's Cliff's Cliff," declared Joe, with obvious reference to Cliff Dumas, our beloved "Cliffy" who had lugged our canoes into Vermont and who forever held a secure place in our hearts.

Kevin Sullivan and Ed "Sparky" McGrath paddle towards the Palisades in Orford, a.k.a. "Cliff's Cliff."

The Palisades, a.k.a. "Cliff's Cliff." (7/99 Photo)

The entire group cracked up with laughter over the re-naming of the Palisades. Mr. Boulais loved it also. And so it was. We proceeded to send the name "Cliff's Cliff" to each other by screaming like fools from canoe to canoe.

"Hey!! It's Cliff's Cliff," resounded across the water over and over again. "It's Cliff's Cliff!" Talk about redundancy.

In retrospect, it was very much like Cliff Dumas after all. That intuitive old fox, Joe.

Large, massive frame, omnipresent, a sign of stability. Someone that could be counted on. Relied upon. The essence of stability and loyalty. That was Cliff.

Having arrived in time we beached our canoes and disembarked. The riverbend hugged Route 10 in Orford. About 100 yards across a field of waist high grass was Our Lady Queen of Peace Roman Catholic Church, a small yellow wooden structure. Our Lady Queen of Peace was a summer mission church of Saint Dennis' Parish in nearby Hanover, NH. The morning sun clashing with the yellow paint created a lucency that squinted my eyes. We snuck in the back door of the just completed basement chapel in the nick of time for Mass.

After Mass, I recalled many of the worshipers, especially the elderly ladies, bidding us adieu at the riverbank. Good heavens...some of them were actually waving their hankies at us. Boy, I felt a bit embarrassed to say the least. Mr. Boulais chatted with the pastor and no doubt was sharing the whole canoe trip inside and out by the stretch of time we waited.

For the second time that day we shoved off. The morning sun seemed unusually bright and high for the time of day. Drifting and paddling away I glanced back with a sense of pride. These worshipers were our first contact with the real world on this trip. They delighted in our extravaganza down the Connecticut. Perhaps it was the notion that even though these folks had always heard about canoe trips on this river yet the chance probably never presented itself to actually meet those canoeists moving lazily along.

It never entered my mind that Our Lady Queen of Peace Church would ever change. But change it did. Years far removed the Diocese of Manchester, NH closed this mission outpost of Saint Dennis and sold it. Her pews found refuge elsewhere and a country store offered antiques for sale where once many frequented the Sacraments. Presently, it occupies a small card company indeed if that endeavor hasn't changed yet.

Change...so quick. Side by side a river that hardly ever does.

As is more often the case than not, youngsters as well as adults possess a certain degree of ignorance of historical facts. This situation proved no less for myself and my comrades drifting downstream. Life rambles on identical to the sluggish current of the Connecticut. With age I discovered intermittently that places we had visited were replete with great historical figures and events. At thirteen I was ripe with ignorance about these events as we paddled through each locale.

Such was the unappreciated section of the Connecticut River from Fairlee, VT directly across from Orford, NH. At least unappreciated by us.

In West Fairlee lies Lake Morey named after inventor Sam Morey. Now the history books will unanimously proclaim Robert Fulton as the inventor of the steamboat, but the story veils a hidden twist.

In 1790 Sam Morey tinkered with the steam engine hoping to improve the propulsion of it's side paddle wheel. With a paddle wheel in the bow, Morey probably peaked at 4 miles an hour rather than his proclaimed 7-8 miles per hour on the Connecticut River.

In 1797 Sam contacted Chancellor Robert Livingston, drew an interest in him, and then took Sir Bob for a ride in his steamboat on the Connecticut. Livingston promised Sam Morey a "considerable sum" if he could crank up the boat to 8 miles an hour. Sir Robert even offered Morey $7,000.00 for the right to use his invention on the Hudson River. Sam declined.

In 1801 Livingston met Robert Fulton in Paris. The two collaborated and were granted a monopoly on steam navigation in New York State. Fulton and Livingston eventually made a steam-boat design and in 1807 Fulton's steamboat made that historic voyage up the Hudson River, propelled by side paddle wheels, identical to Morey's.

But since Morey did not patent the rights to his "contraption" in 1797, he lost out. Fulton patented his rights in 1811 and Morey could not legally use them thereafter...the very invention he developed himself!

And so it was. Cruising by Orford and Fairlee we had no inkling of this great historic undertaking right there on the Connecticut River. What tales lie dormant in rivers, lakes, and seas waiting to be told.

****

Traversing along this particular day found us raring to explore and eager to absorb the great unknown with a pulsating zest. Being teenage boys the wait for Mass to end was penance itself. The afternoon sun danced off the three inch waves which lapped the bows of our canoes at a cadence that led to slumber.

Today we were witnessing the trip as our first full day from sun up to sun down. We paddled vigorously. Cognizant that we would encounter portage number one hours away we maintained a steady pace. From the morning campsite to Wilder Dam was a distance of about 25 miles, so it was necessary to high tail it and not dawdle. Actually the "lake" behind the Wilder Dam commences about 1.5 miles below Howard Island. This is the spot that flat water begins to take hold as a lake, a distance of 35 plus miles from Wilder Dam.

Somewhere in the vicinity south of East Thetford, VT and Lyme, NH a quick lunch break was taken. The river became serpentine. With a few shallow sand bars and droopy willow trees hovering about my senses told me I was in a Louisiana bayou. A quick noon time repaste would seem remiss without our beloved Bolton Biscuits. Despite smearing them liberally with peanut butter and pineapple jelly to render them edible there were quite a few to spare. Wonder why?

"Hey, what are you guys doing?!" Mr. Boulais snapped at a few of us who were skimming biscuits out across the water. Sheepishly none of us could really talk ourselves out of the fact that we were caught red-handed skimming Bolton Biscuits from our riverside bistro.

"Put them back in the box. We'll run out by Friday if we waste them." Mr. Boulais continued in a softer tone. Actually that was the general idea...to waste them on something else other than ourselves. They were great little skimmers that skipped the surface 4 or 5 times before dying out. I thought of them eventually sinking to the bottom of the river absorbing and swelling with water as they descended. That is if they could absorb water. Well, I shouldn't paint such a bleak picture of these notorious delectables for none of us ever broke out with pellagra during the six days. Perhaps some commercial baker doubled up the niacin no doubt.

We skimmed one more biscuit concealed in our hand as Mr. Boulais reprimanded us. Dropping the other biscuits into the box, we turned to ready our canoes for departure.

Pushing offshore and embarking again the river gave us a glimpse of tranquillity so unperturbed as to snare one's attention with pleasure. Being Sunday the atmosphere possessed an edifying stillness. Sunshine and limpid blue skies crafted a lazy, lazy, lazy day on this here river.

Dormant farm machinery that only yesterday belched noise and fumes lent the necessary prescript for such placidity.

Once again I observed the river, this time with a keener awareness, for it never ceases to intrigue me to this day. The breezes blew elsewhere. Coasting along the riverbank the purple Loosestrifes held their position of attention for us. This spiked flower waited for us each day with heights of up to five feet. Its magenta to purple spectrum dotted the riverbank keeping monotony at bay with welcome refreshing hues. When the breezes returned, she would graciously bow to us repeatedly as we paraded on by.

The serenity was overpowering especially in these flat water sections where one may be easily deceived into assuming that a lack of water power exists here.

My thoughts reverted homeward as I pondered my Mom's singing while she ironed, hoping to empty a basket of clothes. Emma sang with the Philharmonic Club at Hope High School in Providence, RI and successfully retained that melodious disposition throughout life. We were blessed were we not (?) as she crooned us to sleep for a nap we never wanted to take. Or just to soothe our nerves perhaps. Tis true what she sang...and Mom loved to sing that song, "Old Man River", right out of "Showboat."

> *Old Man River, The Old Man River,*
> *He don't plant cotton, He don't plant taters,*
> *But them that does it are soon forgotten,*
> *Yeah Old Man River, he don't do nothing,*
> *He just keeps rolling along.*

Yes sir, that's exactly the scenario here. However, the crop is corn rather than cotton up in these here parts, but the truth cannot be evaded about this river or any river. Despite man's assault on the river it "keeps on rolling along". For ages many have underestimated a river's power. Quite often these miscalculations proved fatal. Man challenged rivers by damming them up, but mastery of them remains elusive if not absurd. As long as north and south peacefully co-exist with gravity and water, rivers will trickle south regardless of man's effort. Rivers may be dammed and held temporarily at bay but they must be free to flow or they will emancipate themselves by their own inherent power.

"Now how wide do you think it is across this river?" I quizzed Steve Kelly.

We both glanced from side to side in an effort to "guesstimate" the span stretching shore to shore.

"I don't know," said Steve, with an air of simple honesty. After exchanging a few wild and bizarre guesses, we agreed upon a distance of about a quarter mile.

Next came our math calculations.

"Hey," said Steve in his thinking cap mode, "for swimming merit badge we had to swim 150 yards...that's 450 feet. From out here it seems a lot further than 150 yards to shore."

"It looks a long way in. We'll probably just make it to shore if we ever swamp and try to swim in from out here," I answered Steve, calculating our survival or demise.

"Well, let's not even try," replied Steve tongue in cheek, "we'll just hang on to the canoe and pull it to shore."

"And hope the sea monsters don't get us!!" I screamed out.

"What?!" blurted Steve, looking perplexed as ever.

"The sea monsters!" I iterated, laughing like a ninny, "Joe says that all the time when he swims in dark, unknown waters."

"Be quiet and paddle," Steve half commanded with a stare of disbelief, "you guys are crazy."

In retrospect, our guesstimate was a trifle off. On the Vermont-NH section of the Connecticut the average span extends only about 600-800 feet across. The quarter mile width that we projected wouldn't materialize until downstream in the Longmeadow, MA section where it would reach 2100 feet, it's widest stretch. Regardless, it still would have been more comforting and reassuring while paddling about had we donned a lifejacket. Oh well.

****

The August afternoon sun performed it's duty upon us, as our skin glowed with the pinkish orange of a sunburn. The projected late afternoon portage at Wilder Dam seemed remote. Similarly, yesterday, our departure day now seemed distant. It's funny how age tinkers with one's perception of time. At thirteen, my first portage was a mere 3-4 hours away. Yet in my carefree mind it loomed way off in obscurity perhaps due to the onslaught of adventures coming at us.

Steve and I trudged on. The day was warm. A sufficient cool breeze off the river preserved us from cantankerousness. I began to realize the capaciousness of the Connecticut with each passing hour. The expanse between its banks, the strength of its diverse currents, water depth, combined with my general ignorance about strange water, gradually created a more formidable respect in me for that which flowed beneath us. This river was not the Russell Pond where we had trained for the canoe trip. More and more a fearful respect for this great river seeped into my consciousness. And I'm glad it did.

My thoughts relapsed back home. The Chicopee River was the "big" river up to this point in our lives. Since it carves out Indian Orchard's northern border we spent quite a few memorable times there. It's tributaries spring from three sources, namely the east branch of the Swift River draining from the Quabbin Reservoir, the Ware River, and the Quabog River. These rivers all merge into one at the Three Rivers section of Palmer, MA giving birth to the Chicopee River.

As youngsters we were forbidden to go near the Chicopee River, especially near the West Street bridge, a.k.a. "the Singing Bridge". I'm sad to say we disobeyed. The bridge had an iron mesh road that would sing when cars and trucks raced over it. Believe it or not we would hang from the pipes under the bridge while our legs dangled in mid air with nothing below us but the rocks and boulders of the Chicopee. Such choice lunatics were we. Here the river's width is approximately 150-200 feet which helped enable my brothers and me to chuck stones from Indian Orchard onto the Ludlow riverbank.

Yet Steve and I agreed this Connecticut made the Chicopee piddle in comparison even though it is the largest tributary in the Connecticut River's 410 mile basin.

The breeze was northerly. The sun's glare was relentless, coming at us incessantly, glittering each whitecap, when the monotony of the moment was pierced with screaming voices.

"Over here! Come over here!" someone screamed from a canoe about 75 yards off the port side and downstream a bit.

Steve and I paddled a bit faster and visualized that it was my brother Jim and Gene DeGrandpre gesticulating wildly from their canoe. They were situated alongside another canoe containing my brother Joe, Ray Roberge, and Mr. Boulais. Steve Kelly and I churned frantically towards the group hoping to discover the nature of their urgent summons. Also converging on the scene was Kevin Boulais and Dennis Riel in their canoe.

"What's going on?" Dennis inquired with a strong quizzical expression.

"Mr. Boulais says you can eat a dragonfly," retorted my brother Jim with a challenging and unbelieving doubt.

"Yeah sure," most of us blurted out sarcastically.

I sighed with relief. Paddling over to this scene conjured up serious thoughts as to what could be so urgent. Having ruled out drowning by everyone's obvious presence, I surmised that perhaps one canoe had somehow managed to over tilt, thereby dumping our edibles overboard. Not so. This frantic warning was all about a dragonfly?

Now what was imminently unfolding here was unlikely to be seen or repeated in science classes or survival classes for years to come. At least in my small mind it wouldn't. So with our eyes riveted upon our beloved Scoutmaster we hung on every word of his brief lecture.

"Men, when you're out on your own and become lost, you must survive," Mr. Boulais commenced, with a serious expression.

"One must not only eat edible wild plants but you can also eat bugs and insects," he continued with a persuasive air.

"AUGGH!!" reverberated our collective gasp, "No way!"

"I'll starve first!" vowed Gene DeGrandpre sitting in the stern of his canoe, donned in his red Robin Hood hat.

"Just watch...I'll show you how," our determined leader offered.

And with all the finesse of a "special forces" gourmet Mr. Boulais did just that. Presently, up to this point in the lecture Mr. Boulais did indeed employ a secure but delicate grasp on some unfortunate dragonfly. This creature was light brown with greenish hues accentuated beautifully in the sunlight. We found ourselves checking each other out by glancing quickly from canoe to canoe observing our reactions. It seemed to me that we all gave the impression that this was a splendid hoax. Yet our fearless leader held the dragonfly much too daintily for us to disbelieve him.

"You see...right here are the head and middle parts," said Mr. Boulais, referring to the anatomical structures of head and thorax.

"Right here, below the wings is the long part or the belly," continued the scoutmaster pointing to the anatomical part known as the abdomen.

"You just bite off the long belly part below the wings and throw away the head, middle and wings," Mr. Boulais instructed, matter of factly.

"No way!!" echoed our doubtful group in unison, "AUGGH!" However, expanding in my head was the crescendo notion that this man was true to his word. He was edging closer to the real thing. *"Ipso facto"* was upon us.

"It's full of protein, and considered an edible insect," divulged our scoutmaster, regarding his words as a crucial selling point.

"So nutritious," blurted out Kevin Boulais from the rear. Mr. Boulais was a book salesman by profession. Well, needless to say there probably wasn't a book anywhere that would convince any of us to chomp on a dragonfly, even with his sales pitch.

And now with this poor, doomed dragonfly writhing and wriggling to escape, it's death knoll beckoning him home, Mr. Boulais slowly drew it to himself and opened his jowls for the kill..., and lunch? Oh, I forgot, lunch was over. Snack perhaps?

No doubt we were squeamish. At this pinnacle most of us are in stupefied awe expecting the "big crunch" to materialize. And materialize it did.

The bite seemed ever so natural for Mr. Boulais. His incisors came down and dissected the dragonfly exactly where he had prophesied, between the thorax and abdomen. He released the wings and remaining torso, head and thorax. It fluttered momentarily then careened downward onto the water's surface instantaneously commencing it's drift with the current to the ocean.

This emancipated yet semi-mangled species would in all probability become the next meal for the most proximal fish in this locale. This most unfortunate dragonfly would never imagine that he would play the dual role of being on the menu for both man and fish. Long live the food chain and the balance of nature!

"AUGGH!! GROSS!!" revolted our squirmish lot. Mr. Boulais grinned while he chewed on the dragonfly, making quite the effort to restrain his chortle from full blown laughter. I can't recall what our scoutmaster said from that point on for we were all too busy adjourning our secluded rendezvous.

Dipping my paddle in and down, I looked over and caught sight of my brother Joe who was bowman in his canoe with Mr. Boulais sitting pretty in the middle. Joe's eyes were half squinted and his face discombobulated. He seemed disgusted and was gabbling to Ray Roberge, shaking his head in disbelief.

"Let's go," Joe muttered to Ray with revulsion. The two commenced paddling with Mr. Boulais kneeling between them, who mirthfully savored the moment.

The group quickly followed suit transforming our inert canoes into motion, paddling silently and dazed for a bit, and wondering if what we just witnessed might be true.

10 Wilder or Bust

It was all history now and truly a crass act at that. How could it fail to be? When one watches another bite, chew and swallow a four winged insect, you tend to remember. And he performed so adroitly did he. Well, the whole affair is freshly engraved somewhere in the granite portion of my cerebrum for better or worse.

The event didn't diffuse for a while either. Boredom was itching to creep into our afternoon but its hopes were dashed with the dragonfly incident. Based on a few overheard conversations it was easily understood why someone's lunch might curdle in their gut.

Canoeing relentlessly for the next few hours we barely stopped for a break. Only for a few moments did we delay to observe a fish or bird or some new peculiarity. As we drifted south, Steve and I continued to ruminate about the dragonfly.

"You know it seemed really gross how Mr. Boulais ate half of that dragonfly," mused Steve from behind me.

"But...if you were starving and knew that pretty soon you might die, then you would have to eat it," my sternman reasoned non-chalantly, "wouldn't you?"

"Of course you would," I said irrevocably. "But most people would probably just eat edible wild plants and forget the bugs!" I added emphatically.

"Yeah...you're right!" affirmed Steve. "I had to make tea from the Staghorn sumac shrub last year. It was really red and bitter like lemon. We had to add sugar to it. I served it with wild blueberries and raspberries," he recounted to me.

"Oh man, last year Ray Roberge passed me on edible wild plants for First Class. I had to go out and find a cattail plant at Long Pond, dig down in the muck and pull up the long root. Then I had to wash it, wrap it in foil and bake it on the coals just like a baked potato. The handbook says it's a tuber and a starch just like potatoes," I reminisced.

"How'd it taste?" Steve asked.

"They are more yellow and grainy than potatoes," I replied. "But we baked them with butter and salt and pepper so they weren't too bad," I explained.

Our paddling became a bit tiresome and tedious. The desire to continue conversation wanes even amongst canoeing buddies after a few hours of babble.

The goal today was to safely portage the Wilder Dam and then pitch camp somewhere for the night.

Amidst the ensuing quietude my reflections lapsed back to Mr. Boulais and his dragonfly. On the surface, dining on dragonfly does come across quite repugnantly. The species does not occupy a spot on most dinner menus. Gee, if any of us had thought quickly enough we could have used that pineapple jelly to mask things over for the taste buds. But we didn't did we? As a group we performed our expected disdainful response with perhaps some exaggeration of disgust when Mr. Boulais bit into that insect also.

I began to focus beyond the mechanics of chomping on a dragonfly. The larger picture unclouded and evolved translucent. With all grossness aside, the issue simply was survival. None of us, including Mr. Boulais, had a crystal ball on life. We knew not what the future held and could easily find ourselves lost in some dubious situation someday. Then prudence and discernment would definitely need the upper hand.

Mr. Boulais often came across as an extremist. Unorthodox. Yet he was bringing into scouting the skills and knowledge from his experiences in the special forces. His foresight was that life would be tough on us and so he challenged the whole lot of us. We had achieved First Class scout and it embodied only a superficial knowledge of edible wild plants. He knew this but his modus operandi was to go one up and give us the added edge in knowledge. Sure...eating dragonflies would always be deemed radical and somewhat inordinate. But then again being lost and hungry and peering upward at vultures could be described as a radical predicament whose remedy might require radical and drastic measures to solve. Thus the dragonfly.

****

Steve and I were positioned somewhere in the middle of the canoe caravan which easily stretched a mile or so on any given day. I was so immersed in the day's events that the sun imperceptibly eluded me. The sky was gray and overcast and it appeared precipitation was hedging its way in.

We had slipped quietly by Hanover, NH without even realizing it. Here the prestigious Ivy League college, Dartmouth is located. Being summer we would miss the crew teams practicing for their collegiate regattas.

We trudged on.

Our excitement escalated as we paddled on and then observed the others up ahead veering toward the New Hampshire shore. Then it came into view. Our first formidable foe was before us...the Wilder Dam. Her wall stretched out 2900 feet long and rose 59 feet high challenging us with her vast expanse. She was only 16 years old. Her fish ladder would not be constructed for another 21 years, opening up in 1987.

And so, with an obvious maneuver off the port side, we opted not to challenge her but would peacefully side step her, embarking upon portage number one.

****

South side of the Wilder Dam from the New Hampshire side. (7/99 Photo)

Finally we had come to the wall that held back the "longest lake in New England." The Wilder Dam is that wall and its headwaters back up about 43 miles north, at Cow Meadow Flat near the famous Placey Farm in Newbury, VT. We had canoed approximately 34.5 miles of that lake commencing at the Newbury/Haverill Bridge linking Route 5 and 10.

71

A portage as defined by the American Heritage dictionary is "...the carrying of boats and supplies overland between two waterways." There was a little more involved with ten scouts and Mr. Boulais leading us. Wilder Dam is built on the site of the former Olcutt Falls. These are the infamous falls that put Rogers' Rangers asunder in 1759. Their first raft was destroyed on the rocks of Olcutt as they returned from an attack on the Saint Francis Indians.

It was prudent to beach our canoes a good quarter mile from the barrel buoy to avoid being drawn too close to the dam. Heavens forbid.

"Gentlemen," as we were usually called, instructed Mr. Boulais with guarded concern. "We need to go over the guardrail and down the road," he continued, referring to a dirt road running parallel to Route 10.

"Just keep moving along it and then down the steep embankment of stone steps," he cautioned us.

"It'll level off at the bottom of these steps before we go down a second set of steps," he warned us. "So be careful."

"Follow one another and go slow," he finalized.

"Sure...," I thought, "we'll all go slow. Nice and slow."

We were all real dolts as we set out. About a quarter mile had to be traversed for this portage and without doubt we couldn't do it sanely. It had to be executed our way.

"Lift up your end!!" was echoed time and again from each canoe, as we all started out.

"You ain't lifting so I ain't lifting!" Dennis Riel barked at Kevin Boulais.

"COME ON!!".... "MOVE!!".... "$#!!&%!!@!"

Steve and I hoisted our packs onto our backs to shift our lifting load. It worked somewhat. Some guys attempted to lug their canoe with all the gear inside but it just didn't pan out.

"Whadaya think you're Hercules...put your pack on dummy!" I overheard someone command critically.

A few guys flipped the canoe over and placed the gunwales on their shoulders with their heads buried inside. Steve and I jacked our canoe up and braced the bottom on our shoulders, proceeding cautiously no doubt.

A quick glance ahead caught Gene DeGrandpre snickering and chuckling at my brother Jim's efforts to maintain his balance. Jim was ticked off and frustrated as things were so wobbly but when he saw Gene, he laughed himself silly. In his fit of laughter, Jim let his end go without warning Gene, just to torque him off.

BAM!! smashed the bow end onto the ground.

"Hey!! Come on!!".... "&!#%+#!!@," yelled Gene half laughing. "What the?!!"

"TOO BAD!" bellowed Jim with a pugnacious sneer, and simultaneously erupted with an outlandish laugh like a hyena.

Meanwhile, Sparky McGrath and Kevin Sullivan caught up to Steve and me. Their struggle was evident also as they shuffled and hobbled along, mumbling under their breaths.

"We should have all just paddled over the dam...it's much quicker," Kevin quipped in his dry Irish wit.

Steve laughed and blurted in jest,"You clown, Sully."

Steve and Kevin were buddies from the go. They lived diagonally across from each other on Ravenwood Street in Springfield, and joined the troop together. Each was part of only a handful of scouts who joined the troop from outside of Indian Orchard. I'm glad they signed on because their contributions to the troop's good times were irreplaceable. Their understanding was intact. Steve could call Sully a clown and get away unscathed since Kevin took it in stride. That was the exact nature of the guys in the troop. There was malice toward none and this was essential for any scout troop to function in the spirit of Baden Powell.

Now if any of you have ever moved furniture, needless to say is that descending a staircase is usually worse than ascending one. The slope's descent was steep and involved steps creating a double whammy. Steepness and gravity tugged every canoe and each guy contemplated his steps to avoid tragedy.

And so we trudged, lumbered, waddled, and slogged along breaking for rest or perhaps when it was critical to prevent disaster both to ourselves and our canoe. After a cumbersome hurdle over the guardrail and arriving at the pinnacle of the steep embankment a sense of cooperation somehow set in.

Our demeanor still mirrored that of a bunch of lugheads, but a keener awareness of danger came over us prior to descending the hill. To bobble things up here would prove calamitous. Two scouts could easily lose momentum shambling downhill with an awkward canoe. The situation of a pair of scouts dropping a runaway canoe downhill would almost certainly result in a punctured canoe bottom. In that event minus a repair kit, the trip would most likely terminate for those unlucky ones.

And so with reason prevailing and our goofy spirits temporarily on hold, we portaged safely on the New Hampshire side at a put in spot clearly out of danger below the Wilder Dam.

11 Sleep Tight

From Our Lady Queen of Peace Church that morning to the Wilder Dam we had ballparked a rigorous 23 miles. I might add that we did not cover nautical miles which is reserved for sea and air navigation and measures 1852 meters or about 6076 feet per mile. Our average daily mileage had to be 22.2 miles in order to cover the 133 miles in six days. We were languid. This was the end of the day's paddling. Or so we thought. As was the case more often than not most of us hadn't a clue as to where we would pitch camp for the night.

With overcast and threatening skies it seemed evident that we would utilize our ponchos for shelter. As scouts this wasn't particularly novel as we had improvised them before in setting up personal lean-tos on many hikes and campouts.

The day was middle aged and then some. A 1.5 mile jaunt downstream lie before us ending at White River Junction, VT.

"We've only got a mile or so to reach White River," said Mr. Boulais proudly. "When we get to the river we'll turn in there to check the banks for campsites. There's a high level of pollution so things might not be so good," he warned us.

Steve, I and the rest of us put into the water quickly not wanting to be the last ones to arrive. The water below the dam took on the dark, evergreen hues of the tall pines along the shore. The sprint to White River Junction evolved into an undeclared race despite our obvious fatigue. We ached to lay these paddles down. None of us had ever paddled 23 plus miles in one day before. In that 1-2 miles to White River Junction the "light at the tunnel's end" brightened for us.

Soon the Route 4 Bridge cropped up before us. This connector links White River Junction, VT with West Lebanon, NH. It didn't faze us to stop as our eagerness egged us on toward our cherished respite... wherever that may be.

As we moved across the mild turbulence at the White River's mouth, the water gradually grew shallower and appeared somewhat clearer. Heading upstream we narrowly escaped scraping bottom. The banks were quite muddy and rocky. The size of the rocks? Let's just say both sides of the river seemed to be lined with thousands of chocolate covered cream filled donuts. There was less than scant space for camping.

Then came that odoriferous pummel on our nostrils. Wow. So this is the point that Dr. Davidson was trying to make in 1959 in exposing increased levels of pollution along the 410 mile Connecticut. Here reality set in about dirty rivers. White River Junction was our first urban setting since departing at Newbury. Upstream on the Connecticut at Hanover, NH we failed to notice any unpleasant odors. True, Hanover is not an industrial town but it also had its disposal plant up and operating in early 1964. The White River is the second largest tributary of the Connecticut and many of its sawmills dumped their slash and sawdust directly into the river. The paper mills added their contaminants also.

According to Mike Lavalle of the Hartford, VT Pollution Control Dept., White River Junction didn't hitch up with the area waste water treatment plant until April 1, 1978. Why? That's when it was built!

"White River Junction was no less different than other New England cities awaiting federal monies to clean up their rivers," according to former Town Manager Ralph Lehman in 1966. He applied for those grants. I met Ralph on an August 1999 visit to WRJ. He was coming out of a diner when I decided to inquire about some area landmarks. Route 91 was completed now as well as the Route 89 interchange. In '66 neither were there.

There are still sections of the Connecticut River that contain high levels of bacteria after heavy rains. It seemed strange to us that the river looked clean but emitted a foul odor. We were coasting through waters that hadn't seen a salmon jump and swim since George Washington's Presidency! It would be 19 years before this river would finally welcome such a species upstream in a White River Junction pool in 1985.

Our entourage pulled hard off the starboard side and eventually beached just before the Bridge Street bridge. Joe and Ray had already disembarked and were conferring with Mr. Boulais about the conditions.

"Well, there doesn't seem to be any suitable spots for camping," claimed our concerned scoutmaster. "I'm going up into town to find out about a place to stay," he concluded as he darted up the embankment that supported the bridge.

I began to wonder if we were going to paddle again. Good heavens I thought, we'll be paddling by the light of the moon or the fireflies if the moon fails to glow.

With that said, no sooner was he gone. There wasn't a heck of a lot to do. We were all dog tired. Fortunately some grass provided a spot to recline and rest a spell. Unearthing muddy rocks from the muck and chucking them into the White River was the temporary pastime until Mr. Boulais returned.

Before we knew it our dedicated scoutmaster had reported back to us somewhat out of breath.

"Gentlemen, it doesn't look like we'll be camping in this area tonight because of the rocks and mud," said Mr. Boulais with a concerned expression.

"But we've got the OK to sleep over in the town fire station," revealed Mr. Boulais supporting his wide grin.

"WHAT?!" sounded off half the group in disbelief.

"Come on...stop kidding," offered a few others.

"This area isn't suitable for camping and the firemen are allowing us to sleep at the station tonight," Mr. Boulais iterated more vigorously.

I observed him more keenly. I waited, anticipating his loss of composure, hoping to reveal his concealed ploy. Surprisingly it never arrived.

"Let's get these canoes up further by the bridge," our leader summoned us as he walked toward his canoe.

Before I knew it everyone was hauling in their canoes and grabbing their personal gear and sleeping bags. Following everyone else up the embankment I harbored a sense of disbelief. The fire station was the last place that any of us would have thought of while paddling down Wilder Lake all day. But here we were enroute to the fire station? I delighted in it. Once upon the bridge we shuffled southward down Bridge Street. Coming over the bridge we stopped and waited outside the Old Fire Station on the right side of the street. Mr. Boulais was already inside gabbing with a few firemen rotating about in swivel chairs. We filed into the hallway of the fire station, waving and nodding sheepishly, as the firemen shared their friendly hellos. The sense of imposing ourselves upon the firemen quickly dissipated as their warm welcomes reached us. We ambled alongside a red fire truck and down the back inside stairs before finding ourselves standing in the basement.

Little did we know at the time that this station was 100 years old, being erected in 1866. In 1893 an addition was put on. Fifty four years later an extension for a new hook and ladder was completed in 1947. In August 1999 my visit revealed that the station was not in service for fire fighting but had been designated an historical landmark being replaced by a new station in 1989.

White River Junction Fire Station that we slept in. (7/99 Photo)

"Hey, where's the bunks?!" a few of us blurted with guarded expectancy.

"Right here," replied Mr. Boulais, "we're standing on them. Throw your bags down here because we're going to sleep on this floor," he revealed.

Boy did that surprise us. We seemed a bit duped.

"I'd rather sleep in the canoe," dead panned Gene DeGrandpre standing there with his trademark red Robin Hood hat.

He knew full well that we wouldn't be sleeping anywhere else so he quickly joined the rest of us in attempting to secure a spot on the floor. The room was about 20 feet by 20 feet with quite a few choice solid iron lolly columns. It was miraculous that no one ever collided into one of those stalwart beams. The floor we slept on was comprised of only the finest in slumber land material: solid concrete finished off with a shiny layer of top grade pink and gray 8" x 8" linoleum tiles. Beautiful. Sleep tight.

Securing our personal sleeping quarters was a debacle. We converted the time and conditions into a virtual wrestling match over the best sleeping spots. As if there were any. We whipped sleeping bags here and there immediately after someone claimed a space. Pushing, shoving, and good fun heck raising reigned over the next few minutes. Our raucous actions mirrored dementia.

Back home the Indian Orchard Fire Station on Oak Street possessed all the storybook features of a typical firehouse. Firemen sleeping upstairs in comfortable beds awakened by clanging alarms would spring into pants and boots, sprint to the long brass pole, simultaneously clinging and sliding it to the ground floor, racing to save time enroute to a fire. And wondering just how perilous this fire would be to them.

Mr. Lloyd Fairbanks, a fireman at the Indian Orchard Station and an active scouter himself showed me the firehouse in March 1966 as part of a tour while earning the Firemanship Merit Badge. It was so cool watching him demonstrate sliding down that brass pole. Yet, could any of us identify with the hazards entailed in his profession? Not many.

We never witnessed this at the White River station simply because the trucks were located upstairs and our confinement was to the basement.

Customarily one does not sleep too well anywhere the first night somewhere unfamiliar. No less here. Add to this the excellent rock hard basement floor. You know the saying, "Beggars can't be choosers." But they sure can complain like them. We had decided not to take air mattresses on the trip in order to reduce portage weight. Boy could we use one now.

The big treat that night was that pizza would replace Chuck Wagon foods since we hadn't a place to cook. Gee, someone's prayer petition at Mass was answered no doubt. I forget whether we picked it up or it was delivered but it's consumption was a blur.

Finally we turned in. Before sleep the rituals of tossing and turning and fooling around prevailed. Eventually everyone konked out as exhaustion won out over excitement. Intermittent background noise from upstairs roused a few of us from our slumber. Being a light sleeper by nature I woke briefly a couple of times and noticed snoring canoeists. It was a challenge acquiring a comfortable position hoping to induce sleep again on such a hard surface.

I don't recall the precise time in dozing off again but it didn't matter. What did matter was that my sporadic sleep was rudely terminated at 3:20 A.M. AUGGH!

The deafening alarm bell upstairs cut through all of us to the bone. Those of us who managed to roll to one side gazed at each other with a simple question in our eyes: "Was this delusion or delirium?" Probably both. As I jerked up my head, the muffle of emitted groans could be heard escaping from most sleeping bags.

Round two assaulted us with the rumbling tremors from the fire engine's ignition. The fire truck literally shook the building as it high idled...its walls vibrating in perfect unison. What symphony. Mingled gingerly with all this was the loud unintelligible rhetoric of the crew scampering about prior to jumping on the truck.

Shifting into first gear from neutral the truck kicked the deafening noise up a notch during acceleration. Could things get louder? You bet. As it lumbered out of the station the truck's siren commenced its piercing wail.

I prayed a quick Hail Mary for those at the fire and those on the truck. This was a habit taught to me by Sister Roland Marie at Saint Matthew's catechism class. She told us to pray a Hail Mary in the event of hearing a siren or a plane flying overhead. Not a bad idea.

This rude wakeup call rankled most of us to say the least. Joe never did appreciate any manner of abrupt arousings. As I peered across the room from my sleeping bag, I caught sight of him. He had just rolled over and was slightly hunched up resting on his elbows. His eyes were half open but you'd never know it, and his blond crewcut hair still managed to mimic a dry mop. Appearing half upset and half disgusted, he barely audibly moaned "God", and then slowly rolled over again. Could you blame him? Without doubt I could easily guess his choice of words now being mumbled in his sleeping bag.

Mr. Boulais tried to tone down the outbursts of rude comments from the gallery.

"Calm down," he advised assuredly, "try to go back to sleep."

Looking over to the middle of the room, Dennis Riel lie supine staring straight up at the ceiling.

"Sure," he wisecracked.... "Go to sleep....How?"

Sleep somehow dragged me back to its nebulous world. In a few hours I was awakened for good by the light of day and the bustle of guys rolling up their sleeping bags.

Our first full day was behind us, but no doubt its effect would linger with us with a night of sleep like that.

12 Is Ignorance Bliss?

Overcast conditions lingered into the morning as the fog struggled to dissipate. We extended our thanks to the firemen while departing yet not a word was uttered about the 3:20 A.M. "5 Alarm Chili" wakeup call simply because our hotel charge was on them. We were upbeat and glad to move on. As we returned over the bridge thunder rumbled in the distance. About a half inch of rain fell during the night ending just before morning. The pavement's concrete was partially dried displaying contours of cream and gray.

Today is August 15th, the Feast of the Assumption of the Blessed Virgin Mary, a holy day of obligation for Roman Catholics. In 1966, the obligation was still present even though we had attended Mass the day before on Sunday.

On Sunday afternoon my mind began to mull over how we were going to fulfill that obligation on Monday. Twice while paddling I had planned to remind Mr. Boulais of our obligation the next day. No doubt the confusion and distraction at White River Junction over where we would sleep caused me to forget this until Monday.

My parents had indoctrinated my brothers and sisters well on Mass attendance. Once I missed Sunday Mass when I was about 9 years old due to some illness. Mom had insisted that I stay home despite my not feeling too bad. I felt guilty when my family returned from Mass because I really felt I had the strength to attend Mass even though I was deemed ill.

Holy Days were no different. Everyone in our family went to Mass without questioning or challenging the practice. Well, at least outward expressions of resistance never surfaced. At thirteen, this practice was still etched indelibly in my psyche.

"Hey, Mr. Boulais, today we've got to go to Mass. It's the Assumption," I informed our scoutmaster matter of factly.

"O.K., we'll see what happens," he answered half interested, marching over the bridge.

I let it go and decided not to bring up the subject again giving him time to resolve the issue.

No sooner than arriving at the White River, we launched our canoes embarking on our third day on the water. Our group crossed the con-

81

fluence again merging with the Connecticut and headed south in search of a clearing to fix breakfast. With only a few minutes whittled away, we stopped at a spot on the New Hampshire side sparsely dotted with some small swamp maples.

The scene was a typical boy scout breakfast preparation in full swing. Some of us scoured the underbrush for deadwood to be used in the cooking fire. Our water supply had been topped off at WRJ. The group huddled around the fire watching the water come to a boil. The seething pot would soon be converted into a thick porridge that would stick to our ribs until lunch time. Off to one side dried mixed fruit was coming to life in a small pot of boiling water also. Yum-Yum.

Pete Boulais (l) and Joe O'Brien (r) cook breakfast(?) as Dennis Riel and Ed "Sparky" McGrath look on. (8/66)

Some of us were enjoying breakfast and some were bearing with it when Mr. Boulais jolted us with his remarks.

"This is it, men. This morning we'll reach the Hartland Rapids," revealed our leader supporting a smile, and cracking the relative quiet mood at breakfast.

I immediately glanced over to Jim and Gene. They were gawking at each other with bulging eyes and seemed a bit amused. As if they had a reason.

Shifting my glance to Steve, I found him staring at me expressionless. At first, I tried to discern whether he had oatmeal lodged in his throat or not, but momentarily his gulp dispelled that notion.

"Whoa," said Sparky McGrath, "whoa."

Sauntering away from the fire, I edged closer to the river bank and peered out through the vegetation. It was still cloudy. The temperature would only hit 78°F guaranteeing a relatively mild day. I thought to myself, "I hope nothing happens," and in particular, "Where are those life jackets?" Of course, I knew where they were. Addressing rhetorical questions to myself was a weak attempt to deal with the anxiety over our imminent approach of the rapids. The matter became a chronic nag on my mind.

I obsessed with this cursed section of the Connecticut. So why would I allow these impending rapids to nag me? Never before had we set eyes upon them or viewed photos of them for that matter. What had we to fear? The unknown; that's what. The unknown preserved that persistent nag. We possessed minimal knowledge of the rapids or none at all which gave birth to our uneasy feelings. Rumors only fueled the embers of our imaginations. Grandiose images reigned.

Had the troop committee adequate knowledge of the Hartland Rapids? Who knows? Did Mr. Boulais have any pertinent knowledge of these rapids? Ditto. Had anyone scouted these falls prior to our trip? Did anyone delve into that arena? How about the literature?

The AMC (Appalachian Mountain Club) publishes an excellent river guide which includes the Connecticut River. I was fortunate enough to track down the 1966 edition at the Connecticut River Watershed Council Office in Easthampton, MA. Gee, it's only 34 years later, but I sensed it might be interesting prying the pages.

Page 17, "...the Hartland Falls are difficult and dangerous, the scene of several drownings, and probably the most perilous stretch on the entire river." Lovely.

Further, "...Hartland Falls is considered unnavigable at all times." Certainly that's nice to know. Keep reading? Should I? "...A warning sign is posted on the Vermont side 2,000 yards above the falls." Where? None of us noticed a trace. Some shyster or prankster no doubt had made sport of that sign.

"...Warning is also given of these rapids by several huge boulders that emerge from the New Hampshire bank about three quarters of a mile above them. The roar can be heard a considerable distance if the water is high, but in low water it is possible to come into the rapids unknowingly." Were we asking for trouble? Inadvertently affirmative.

In conclusion, "...Lives have been lost by several trying to run these rapids, and they should be attempted only by experienced fast-water canoeists, and they should not attempt it under any circumstances in high water." Umm?

Good lordie, "...only by experienced fast-water canoeists?" Well, let's see. Skill wise we were all about four light years removed from that level and then some. After reading the 1966 river guide we should have never ventured through these rapids if we held any respect for these forewarnings. I'm going to assume that we had scant knowledge of these rapids and under-estimated their treachery to boot.

Customarily rivers seldom transform. When they do it's usually the direct result of man's intervention such as dam construction, irrigation projects, etc.

However, 23 years later the 1989 revised AMC river guide advised the following warning regarding the Hartland Rapids:

> **<u>CAUTION</u>: These rapids should not be attempted at anywater level! Portage on the right, on the unmarked path that is 1/4 mile long, ending at the picnic area at the foot of the rapids. At low water, expert paddlers <u>might</u> run these rapids, but should check with the Wilder Dam beforehand to check the release schedule!**

This message was similarly as dire as the 1966 warning attesting to little if any change in the river's fury. An additional 1989 warning to check the dam release schedule would be helpful but in 1966 the power company did not post release schedules. Talk about the 3 R's. "River Russian Roulette."

Well, in retrospect of what I've now read in 2000 perhaps none of us would have opted to shoot the rapids. On second thought we would have probably jumped at the chance being teenagers and immortal if you will. Our parents and the committee may have recommended the rapids as portage #4. Who knows? It's pure hindsight now.

Yet my thirst for the truth surrounding the precariousness of these notorious falls required slaking. Just how dangerous were they? Why their notoriety? Not desiring to risk rumor for fact I decided to dispel the former for the latter.

In September 1999 I telephoned the Hartland, VT town hall searching for facts. Being referred to the manager's office left me empty handed. No one recorded injuries or fatalities specifically on the Hartland Rapids area. My next call went over the river to Plainfield, NH the opposite shore containing the rapids. Eliciting an identical response from the town hall secretary I grew disheartened. Not to be deterred, my next inquiry elevated my pulse up to speed.

"Well, who keeps records on the fatalities on the Connecticut River?" I asked inquisitively.

The answer was somewhat ambiguous. The manager's office couldn't vouch for fatalities but informed me that all search and rescue missions on the river were conducted by the New Hampshire Fish and Game Dept., Law Enforcement Division. This was so due to court rulings that granted New Hampshire jurisdiction over all Connecticut River bridges due to the state line stretching more toward the low water mark on the Vermont side of the river. Regardless of other reasons, Vermont was out of the picture concerning water mishaps on the river.

In late September, my telephone trek led me to the Office of Colonel Ron Allie, head of the Law Enforcement Division, at the NH Fish and Game Dept. in Concord, NH. Lisa, his secretary, was quite accommodating. My request for information about search and rescue fatalities would require some formal approval. Lisa's returned calls in October and November presented a few hitches, one of which was locating records back as far as August 1966 and beyond if any existed at all.

The telephone tag game ended on Feb. 3, 2000 and somewhat of a dilemma evolved. Under the Freedom of Information Act anyone had a legal right to search and rescue records. The down point was that an April 1984 fire at the old Fish and Game Headquarters destroyed all records prior to 1970. In addition the fire had consumed the records of 1979 and 1980. Was I still interested? Certainly. What had I to lose? Even if records before 1970 were gone I might still unveil the treacherous conditions of the rapids if any. The other side of the coin was that I was given the painstaking task of poring over each search and rescue mission file year by year to compile the evidence of injuries and fatalities. Why? It had never been compiled into an up to date record by anyone.

With a February school vacation a little over two weeks away I made arrangements to begin my investigation on Feb. 22, 2000, the real George Washington's birthday. The Fish and Game Office was only open 8:00 AM to 4:30 PM so I had to finish my research in one day to save a return trip the next.

Exiting Route 93 off the Louden Road ramp, I headed up to 2 Hazen Drive about 9:10 AM. After a few minutes wait, Lisa called me to her office and introduced me to Officer Todd Szewczyk. Todd had been assigned to be my aide for the day by Colonel Allie. Officer Szewczyk and I ventured over to a locked storage building a few hundred feet away to locate the boxes of files. We climbed up some rough pine stairs and looked through shelf after shelf of cardboard boxes. It was colder inside than out and I sensed immediately that my project was going to be laborious. I was correct.

Juggling through the boxes, we finally hauled out about six or seven 18 inch containers, after identifying the correct year on the side. Loading up my blue '86 Volvo, I transported them back to an in between building that was heated. That was nice. Then it was through a maintenance garage to a small office that I would work out of.

Officer Todd then left me to myself to commence the drudgery of poring over the "sleeping" records.

True enough...there was a fire. The files were bound together by large rubber bands some of which were ready to break with age. The 1970's file was singed about the edges. The burnt outer edges of the reports crumbled carbon remnants onto my lap. Was this proof positive that a fire had occurred or what? More importantly I now realized that these remaining files sat on the brink of oblivion saved only by some diligent firemen.

I set out to work, brushing burnt carbon particles off my lap every few minutes, hoping the floor wouldn't be noticeably dirty. Here's what I found.

In 30 years, ranging from 1970-1999, 44 people drowned on the Connecticut River. This figure reflects only the section of Vermont and New Hampshire both of which share the same aqueous border. Connecticut and Massachusetts hold their own fatality rates. The Connecticut River must have claimed far greater than this cold figure of 44 given the fact that the years of 1979 and 1980 were lost in the fire as well as pre-1970 files.

This river feigns as a lost neighborhood cat that is selective of its prey but in reality is a sleeping lion that usually devours anything in its reach at the precise moment.

This drowning rate claims 1.46 victims a year. These distressing files stirred up a melancholic mood within me almost instantaneously. By the afternoon my spirits were in a slump. My heart and mind back pedalled transposing feelings to another time as the anguish of families struck home. It could have been anyone of us on the trip including my brothers or I.

In another twist each case revealed a disturbing but almost expectant trend. Human error and misjudgment consistently rang through every incident.

****

In June 1970, a 30 year old fisherman wearing a leg brace decided to retrieve his hat in the water above the Wilder Dam. I don't know if he got the hat but the river got them both.

In August 1971, a 25 year old fisherman drowned in Woodsville, NH.

In 1972, two victims were claimed by the river. A 19 year old man drowned at West Chesterfield, NH in September, and a 20 year old Dartmouth College student who had been drinking, drowned at Hanover, NH in June.

In 1973, there was one drowning and nearly another. Four college students got lucky while canoeing out of Lebanon, NH in May. Two were from Connecticut, one from Massachusetts, and one from New York. Heading south to Springfield, MA they capsized and were all rescued. Not so lucky was a man who drowned in April at the Hinsdale, NH and Vernon, NH border.

In April 1974, a 21 year old went canoeing on the Hartland Rapids and drowned. The month sheds its own story with the river being perhaps the most gorged and turbulent due to the spring thaw. Make sense?

1975 was a down year with four perishing on the river. In June, a drowning occurred at Colebrook, NH, two September drownings took a 23 year old at Haverhill, NH and another man at Lake Francis, NH and a November drowning at West Stewardson, NH kept the Fish and Game Dept. hopping.

In 1976, a June boating accident at Claremont, NH took a life as did an August suicide drowning in West Chesterfield, NH.

1977 saw much tragedy on the river as six victims became fatalities. In March, a man jumped from the bridge at West Lebanon, NH; in May, a car plunged into the river at North Walpole, NH costing 4 people their lives including a 3 year old and a 5 year old, and in July a fisherman drowned in West Chesterfield, NH.

In 1978, three people died. In January, a 13 year old got off his school bus and began playing by the Oliverian Brook in Haverhill, NH.

He slipped in by the mouth at the Connecticut River and drowned. In July one man drowned above the Moore Reservoir in NH, and in December a man drowned after his canoe overturned in Piermont, NH.

1979 & 1980 - Lost Records

In May 1981, one man drowned in a boating accident in Charlestown, NH.

In July 1982, another man drowned above the Wilder Dam in Hartford, VT.

In 1983, no casualties - Thanks be to God.

In 1984, two people drowned at and near the Hartland Rapids. In May, a 33 year old fisherman drowned above the Hartland Rapids. In June, a boyfriend picked up his 23 year old girlfriend above Sumner Falls in his canoe. Neither wore life jackets and she was a non-swimmer. The canoe capsized at the rapids with the girl drowning while the boyfriend makes it to shore.

In 1985 - no casualties - Thanks be to God.

In 1986, on August 13th, 20 years to the day that our trip commenced, a 48 year old man took his nephew canoeing on Sumner Falls. The canoe capsized on the Hartland Rapids and the uncle drowned. The nephew survived by wearing a life jacket; the uncle did not.

In 1987, two victims drowned. In May, Dr. Kenneth Kaplan was fishing with his brother at Sumner Falls. Both were wearing waders. Wilder Dam released its water and downstream the water level rose too quickly. Dr. Kaplan was swept away and pulled under due to the weight of water filled waders and drowned. His brother survived, barely making it to shore. The family filed a $7 million lawsuit claiming that the Wilder Dam should have had a warning system for boaters and anglers.

In June, a little girl was fishing with her dad above Moore Reservoir. Dad drowned without a life jacket but the daughter who wore one survived.

In 1988, the 4th of July turned tragic as a 14 year old boy drowned in Walpole, NH.

In 1989, a 35 year old fisherman fell into the river in April, drowning at Westminister, NH.

In 1990, three victims drowned. In May, an 18 year old canoeist drowned on the First Connecticut Lake in NH, in June a second man, a 24 year old fisherman drowned at Cornish, NH, and in July 64 year old fisherman Ralph Cormier drowned below the Wilder Dam while fly fishing, again a result of the water level rising too quickly from the dam release.

In 1991, October claimed two river victims. One student from Dartmouth College drowned after drinking too much at Hanover, NH; another canoe trip turned sour when three canoeists started out from Bradford, VT enroute to Putney, VT. Two of the three were brothers visiting from Italy. The three canoeists set up camp at Sumner Falls and unloaded their canoe. They then ran the canoe down the Hartland Rapids for a test run. After capsizing in the rapids, the two brothers made it to shore while the third man drowned. No life jackets.

In 1992 - In May, a 42 year old man drowned fooling around in a canoe by the Soule Farm in Stratford, VT.

In 1993, two more drownings. One in May took the life of a man at Lake Francis, the other in September claimed a man at Bellows Falls, VT.

In 1994 two more men drowned. In May, 41 year old Joe James Zaccaro was a bit over daring to say the least. Joe slipped into his kayak at the Vilas Bridge in Bellows Falls, VT without a life jacket but donning a helmet no less. His wife claims Joe insisted on taking their daughter for a ride with him. His wife refused. Joe went alone. Shooting the Bellows Falls? Yup. He never survived and came up downstream the next day.

In June, a man was drinking beer and decided to swim to a nearby island at Bath, NH. It wasn't near enough as he didn't make it and drowned.

In 1995 tragedy struck a double blow in June as two 19 year old men drowned at Stratford, NH.

In 1996 on my birthday, March 14th, a 43 year old man drowned by suicide at Hinsdale, NH. I turned 43 also. Eerie.

In 1997, a July drowning took the short life of a 15 year old boy at Hanover, NH.

In 1998 & 1999 - No casualties - Thanks be to God.

Enough?

I'll stop.

****

Well, whether or not you wanted it, there you have it. Could these figures be any starker or more morose? Hardly. Only if the numbers were elevated I suppose. So 44 people perished over 30 years on this section of the Connecticut alone. Only heaven knows how many additional victims were lost prior to the 1970 records. For that matter the number must be up in the clouds when we contemplate the decades and hundreds of years devoid of record keeping.

Figuratively, this is 1.46 victims per year on average. Did anyone ever meet 0.46 of a person? Never mind.

Need I mention that one victim over thirty years is excessive when one calculates the sorrow, loss, and heartache of a particular family?

Extrapolating these river figures more geographically to the Hartland Rapids vicinity, I discovered six drownings in the years 1974, 84, 86, 87, and 92, and then some. By "then some" I mean there were drownings here prior to filing records by virtue of common sense and the law of averages.

The rapids were, and are, treacherous indeed. And with a little bit of perilousness and perfidiousness heaped on for good measure your dendrites were sure to keep your myelin sheaths jumping for a spell. As if we needed it.

The rumors we heard about Hartland rang true. And here we were sitting pretty in our canoes minus life jackets no less and having a grand time, will you. Clueless? Somewhat.

The fabric of one's life often becomes unraveled by the loosening of a single thread. Seldom does it matter which thread. Anyone will do. The same runs true in our daily life. Whether the element of your thread is stupidity, ignorance, arrogance, naivete, presumption, or recklessness doesn't matter. What matters is that they all roll off the spool of human error.

And yet this river scornfully scoffs at each thread and gobbles them up regardless. Raging waters, dashing the boulders could care less. And so it performs its duty whatever that may be without an inkling of a presage to you.

One's duty is to know or suffer the consequences of not knowing and hope that fate doesn't catch you asleep. It would be years before we realized that we were our own worst enemy.

$\smile$13 The Harrowing Hartland

Yes sir, grandiose images reigned. The general mood shifted from a jovial tone to a somber one with Mr. Boulais' abrupt broadcast. We carried out the mundane duties of cleanup and secured all the equipment in our canoes. Sporadic light humor could not dispel the quiet atmosphere of breaking camp. We all knew our destination and none of us could control a thing. That was the uneasy part.

The landscape was subdued. The river bank and the birds hunkered down to a still beat as the water grew placid.

"O.K., let's move out," snapped Mr. Boulais with his commanding air, bringing me back to reality.

"Keep calm and just paddle with the current," he advised. "Remember, if anyone capsizes, hold on to your canoe and try to swim diagonally toward the opposite shore. Don't fight the rapids...go with them," he capped his lecture, as the group advanced slowly to the shore.

Before I knew it Steve was shoving us off as I sat in the bow awaiting another day on the Connecticut River. As we drifted from shore, those words softly resounded in my ears, "If anyone capsizes, hold onto your canoe...." For me, that was the understatement of my life. I had already made it clear to myself that if this canoe went under and I was rescued dead or alive it would probably require a jackhammer to chip my knuckles from the thwarts. I didn't relish the unsettling notion that I could be tossed and bobbed along the rapids like a runaway cork from a wine bottle, bopping my cranium against the rocks, as a side show for a few cackling crows perched on a river bank tree limb.

The imaginings were ponderous. For months before the trip we had heard many tales and descriptions of the Hartland Rapids, also known as Sumner Falls. We tried to ignore them but each time the rumors resurfaced, our imaginations rekindled. None of us had seen the rapids, so our minds naturally exaggerated their power and size. One rumor surfaced that a person had even drowned in the rapids, but to be quite honest most of us regarded this revelation as a scare tactic. What we had evaded for months had returned scare tactic or not.

Within the hour our curiosity would be punched out. Paddling the canoe that morning seemed tiresome...the paddles somewhat heavy. Perhaps this was due to the erratic sleep acquired the night before at the fire station.

A quiet eerieness hovered over us that morning. Indeed it seemed to hover over the river itself. Was she waiting for us? Can a river stalk its prey? Somewhat. Her traps are already laid out for you. You become the victim by virtue of the degree of human error that you have chosen for yourself, and hope that fate doesn't catch you dozing.

Our senses were keener and more alert. Or were they? We seemed to become more aware of every move, every chirp, every splash, and every flutter, observing like hungry hawks. It seemed like we were living the Scout Motto, "Be Prepared" in Mach 1 overdrive. Prepared we were but didn't necessarily know for what. But, oh those lifejackets, oh those lifejackets! Where were they now? "Forget the spilt milk," I thought, and paddled on.

Steve and I chatted lightly as we coasted downstream.

"Gee, I wonder what they look like?" queried my sternman rhetorically out loud about the rapids.

I dragged a chuckle and said, "Not big, I hope." We laughed hoping to rid ourselves of our nervous inner dread. With each impending river bend coming up empty of the rapids, our expectations rose and fell. We perceived them to be further downstream than previously anticipated.

Dipping our paddles in the water for the better part of the next hour didn't mollify our worried minds.

We moved on cautiously passing the Mascoma River from the east. It didn't faze us. Similarly our attitude hadn't changed as we idled by Johnston Island, Bloods Brook from the east, Burnaps Island and the Ottauquechee River from the west. Our attention was riveted on locating the Hartland Rapids and satiating our curiosity.

****

The canoe caravan was scattered about as usual with a few hundred feet between each craft when the warning rang out. Mr. Boulais, who was in the canoe with Jim and Gene for the day, bellowed out, "Rapids ahead...get ready!" They were approximately 75 feet ahead of Steve and me. Kevin Boulais and Dennis Riel were dead last in line right behind us. It seemed that Kevin Sullivan and Sparky McGrath would be the first down the rapids with Joe and Ray following them in second place.

Visual effects on the river can be deceiving. Glancing downstream upon Mr. Boulais' announcement, the rapids appeared about half a mile away. Yet kneeling in a canoe, our height was only about three feet. To view an object downstream from a trajectory of a half a mile away from a three foot height plays tricks on your visuals. Things may seem farther away since our normal viewing height is about five or six feet.

As we approached them, the notion sunk in that these rapids were coming at us much sooner than anticipated. Our adrenalin escalated.

Thoughts came at me like lightning bolts. I needed to control them or they would distract me from executing the right moves or edge me closer to panic.

The river difficulty classes of water from White River Junction to Sumner Falls (Hartland Rapids) ranges from I - IV according to the **Complete Boating Guide to the Connecticut River** (1990, CRWC). We had cruised through Class I, "...easy water, fast moving water with ripples and small waves...", and Class II, "...novice, straight forward rapids with wide clear channels, which are evident without scouting. Rocks and medium-sized waves are easily missed by trained paddlers...." Easily missed? Gee, in a few minutes hit the rewind and we'll see if we easily missed them on re-play.

Evidently, at the moment we were paddling in Class II waters. Class III, intermediate rapids lie immediately before the Hartland Rapids, and Class IV, advanced, would be plunging head on into Sumner Falls themselves.

Class III rapids are "...rapids with moderate, irregular waves which may be difficult to avoid and may swamp an open canoe. Strong eddies and powerful currents can be found especially on large volume rivers...."

Steve and I paddled slowly but steadily trying not to rush the impending scenario. From our riverside breakfast nook to the rapids was about a five mile stretch but boy did it seem a lot more.

Peering directly down below the waters surface, the depth appeared to grow shallower but insufficient enough for us to scrap bottom. The depth seemed about a foot and a half to two feet. The rocks came into view so clearly that I was deceived into thinking that the water was shallower than it actually was. Clear water gradually transformed into a brownish tone. Football sized stones now dotted the riverbed seemingly tiled and abutted perfectly with those much smaller.

With each stroke the current's speed surreptitiously increased like a quickening drum roll revving up our nerves for the drama.

Steve tried to reassure me from the stern.

"Just take it easy."

"Yeah," I managed to reply in a petrified tone. Thinking to myself, "Gee, how else are we going to take it? Here we are ready to wager our lives away. We better take it easy."

We managed to slow down our paddling to a point where if it was any slower *rigor mortis* would have set in.

Then it came. The river then introduced us to Class III water. The water evolved quickly into moderate, irregular waves with the current employing even more speed. Larger rocks made their presence known; the kind that move for no one. Rocky shoals threatened us on both sides. Instinctively, Steve and I accelerated our paddling rate to gain better control of our canoe. I used a few wider sweeps to avoid disaster with a couple of boulders and surprised myself. It was all coming at us like a runaway freight train. Attempts to stop now would surely be laughed at by Mother Nature. Events were burgeoning at such a rate that our choices narrowed to two: cooperate with the water or don't. There was no trammeling this river or these rapids so we had to spurn her fury by out witting her.

Portaging here was out of the question. If you jumped out now to stop your canoe you might as well regard it as a coffin. Broaching the subject of portaging Hartland never surfaced. A portage in the face of this challenge would be the equivalent of a defeat especially with our group. Never would we have lived it down; forever asking and second-guessing ourselves to the grave if we could have shot those rapids. Invincible were we with no room at all for wimping out.

The quickening water adopted more streaks of white as we began our tremulous cascade down through this uncontrolled cauldron of foaming root beer. A few more jarring scrapes along the canoe's sides against some jutting rocks helped to trigger a couple extra mortal fears in my half frazzled mind.

With the more turbulent Class IV water only seconds away it was inevitable that I would contemplate the real possibility of a punctured hole in our canoe's bottom. Yet there was no time for this dreadful concept to linger. The imminent drop in the river and spuming rapids told me instinctively that surviving them was the more portentous matter.

And so we moved on, like the shutter by shutter frames of a 16mm film, into what we could physically see and sense but could not project it's final effect upon us. That was the anxiety of it all. The rumors we heard in early summer now focused on a quality of blossoming reality. The low, dull rushing of white water hurtled down our ear canals. The

94

river spurted her anger at us.

Were we scared? Silly question. More the matter of just how scared were we? Perhaps as scared as hell on judgment day because in a few minutes this just might be judgment day for some of us. Scared yes...but not one of us would show a lick of it. Perhaps too much pride plus a frightening lack of gray matter to say the least. Who knows? We were hell-bent on going through this toll booth whatever the cost. But like fools we put the cost thing temporarily on the back burner.

My last thought before hitting the rough water was this: "I'm scared allright but I'm not going to panic!" I remember thinking that I could not control the river but I could keep a lid on my panic and still remain scared. I would take whatever came. The only sure way to muddle this up was to panic, sure and simple. From there on in I tried to keep my cool.

Class IV advanced, in river difficulty is described as "...intense, powerful but predictable rapids that require precise boat handling in turbulent water. A fast reliable, eddy turn may be needed to initiate maneuvers, scout rapids, or rest. Risk of injury to swimmers is moderate to high. Water conditions may make self-rescue difficult. Group assistance for rescue is often essential but requires practice skills." (CRWC 1991).

Oh boy. The amount of training on Russell Pond was paltry when stacked against what was necessary to handle this water. Simply put, we were flat water canoeists busy at hoping and praying for the best.

A mid July 1999 re-visit to the Hartland Rapids demonstrated to me the dire consequences of meddling in these waters. Thirty three years had clouded the lens of my memory regarding the size and length of these rapids. After crossing a field of high grass and plunging down a steep tree lined ravine on the New Hampshire shore, I stood awed on the banks of these notorious rapids once again. It didn't seem possible that we would have gone over them at 13 and 14 years of age minus life jackets. Its length seemed twice as long. My lower jowl didn't want to come up.

The rock formations at the river's center is called Ledge Island. Now 1/2 mile before shooting these rapids there stands erect a large 4'x 8' fluorescent orange sign on the Vermont side of the river warning inexperienced boaters to exit for portage. It's so obvious one can see it from Montreal. On both shorelines are signs warning of the sudden rise in the water depth and quick turbulence increase due to water releases from the Wilder Dam eight miles north. In 1966 there were no such

95

Hartland Rapids from the Plainfield, NH side. (7/99)

*Kayakers shoot the Hartland Rapids in July 1999.
Plainfield, NH side.*

signs, but even if there were we probably would have scoffed at them and paddled right on.

During my July re-visit, 10 or 12 kayakers were riding the turbulence of the rapids. Facing upstream, these dare devils sat stationary, combining their paddling force with the equal force of the rapids, going nowhere. A funny looking idle if you will. All the kayakers had donned life jackets and helmets.

During a lull in kayaking, I conversed with two kayakers resting on the New Hampshire shore. Both young men affirmed that no one usually attempts these falls without a lifejacket and helmets since the risks are just too great.

I shared my 1966 experience in canoeing these rapids at 13 years old with other scouts minus lifejackets and helmets. Shaking their heads, they spoke their minds and claimed that we were lucky to have survived. They had watched in horror as one canoeist shot the rapids without a lifejacket and helmet. He capsized quickly and struggled to gain shore, succeeding after a very difficult challenge.

"The world is full of nuts," one said to me.

"I know," I countered. "I was there."

****

Ledge Island has outcroppings of rocks toward the Vermont side of the river. A few hundred feet downstream are sporadic smaller, descending layers of flat rock formations also. From upstream, a quick survey revealed we had two or three fairly frightening challenges to maneuver through in these rapids.

As we encountered the first stages of turbulent water, not a sound was heard perhaps in awed anticipation and concentration of the grave situation before us. Maneuvering and hedging toward the New Hampshire shoreline we managed to skirt through some rough white water without capsizing. Our feelings of relief and success were quickly forgotten in facing the most dangerous section of the Hartland Rapids a mere few feet away.

Jim and Gene were posed directly ahead of Steve and me. Mr. Boulais was the third man in their canoe paddling from the middle position. As their canoe approached the first channel towards the NH shore, yipping and yelling became frequent and high pitched from the rest of us. They worked to pilot their craft through the 15 foot wide gap between the rocks.

Ray Roberge snaps a shot prior to descending the Hartland Rapids.
Kevin Sullivan and Ed "Sparky" McGrath wait below. (8/15/66)

Below the Hartland Rapids on the New Hampshire side. (8/15/66)

This first channel is thought to have too much of a drop for loaded canoes according to the AMC river guide. A little late now wouldn't you say?

The second channel in mid river starts out with a 30 foot width and shrinks to a 7 foot wide passageway at the bottom of the initial pitch. Large rocks at the bottom of this treacherous point must be avoided to escape disaster. Trailing Jim, Gene and Mr. Boulais by about 25 feet, Steve and I guided our craft dead ahead down the roughest part of the rapids. The yipes grew louder and more piercing behind us. We pretty much were all screeching like dutiful banshees. Hot on our tail was the last canoe of Kevin Boulais, bowman, and Dennis Riel in the stern. Our frenzied yelps quickly upgraded towards a cacophony of panicked screams and confused yelling. Kevin Sullivan and Sparky McGrath were the first brave souls to shoot the rapids followed by our two loyal leaders, Joe and Ray. Ray Roberge even found the nerve and composure to snapshot the rapids a few shrinking feet before he hit them! Heavens.

It was here. We were sliding right down the scupper like it or not. Steve and I were managing to steady our canoe no doubt with a little divine intervention, hoping and praying that this white aluminum craft would successfully rumba through this next hydro-dance. I mustered enough eye shutter speed to part a few fleeting glances ahead to Jim, Gene, and Mr. Boulais while deciding when and where to place my paddle tip.

Despite the temptations, neither Steve nor I looked back when we heard the confusion and screams resounding from our rear. Kevin Boulais was screaming like the rest of us over the undecipherable commands of Dennis Riel from the stern. Then I heard that wail. The kind that cuts one through to the bone. The type that indicates trouble. Double distress big time. An "I'll take any kinda help now," cry.

Now Jim, Gene, and Mr. Boulais had just about slithered their canoe down through the channel and were situated near the bottom when Jim heard it also. He panicked as his first thought was that it was mine. His imagination performed a yeoman's job in convincing him that I had capsized and was struggling for my life in the rapids.

He naturally halted his paddling and instinctively averted his attention behind him to see what had transpired. No sooner had Jim spun around to look when Mr. Boulais was right on his tail about paddling.

"Pay attention!!" he blared, "you're bowman!!"

Mr. Boulais took his paddle and jabbed at Jim's shoulder blades mimicking a lacrosse defenseman harassing a midfielder cradling the ball, stinging him good. This was nothing less than Mr. Boulais' attempt to have Jim revert to his paddling so their canoe would not capsize, thus avoiding a double calamity in the rapids.

Their tussle grew caustic as Jim became riled about being poked with a paddle. Fortunately, he reluctantly turned back to his charge upon discovering that I was still intact on board my canoe. Gene was probably relieved no doubt.

With round one of that bout over, Mr. Boulais took a peek behind himself also. Steve and I had just about caught up with Jim and Gene, when Mr. Boulais began barking commands to his son Kevin, and Dennis.

Amidst the pandemonium, Dennis advised Kevin to slow down his paddling so they could ride the rapids more easily. However, Kevin's easy paddling quickly evolved into a wider and faster bow stroke which shifted the canoe into a broadside position. With this, Kevin panicked and prior to descending the channel broadside, commenced screaming at the blustering fume awaiting him and Dennis. The canoe embraced a dreadful roll and began to capsize with Kevin jumping out before it did in an effort to right it. A good plan that never saw its day. He plunged headlong into the jaws of the foaming drink and managed to miraculously cling to the nearest rock in a most precarious way. Dennis, meanwhile was getting some rude scuba training minus the necessary gear. He suddenly discovered himself in this "Connecticut cauldron", and his feet simply wouldn't touch the bottom. Feeling a bit ominous with this sinking sensation, he instinctively grabbed the canoe for dear life...and saved it. His life that is, as well as the canoe. It bobbed under a bit more down the treacherous chute but he hung on.

"Hold on to the canoe!" bellowed Mr. Boulais, "Hold on!" Steve and I had our work cut out as did the others in keeping our canoes afloat. We cascaded on down and gratefully eased into calmer class III waters, surpassing Jim, Gene and Mr. Boulais who had delayed to look back.

Now Kevin Sullivan and Sparky, since they were the first ones down, watched the whole scenario from the bottom of the rapids. They were now paddling back a bit in an effort to help out with the rescue. Kevin Sullivan got within reach of Kevin Boulais with his extended paddle tip and led him to safety. Meanwhile, Mr. Boulais had jumped into the rapids, believe it or not, and assisted Dennis in lugging his canoe to shore and to assist Kevin Sullivan and Sparky in their heroic efforts.

For Dennis and Kevin their past lives must have been on re-wind in a fast-forward mode? I'd say. Perhaps with a few rapid fire Act of Contritions thrown in for insurance also.

No sooner out of imminent danger, Steve and I lulled our paddles and peered back.

Mr. Boulais sprang from his canoe into Hartland's spume lunging out for the half submerged craft. Why? He had to. The spur was that his son and companion were about to drown and he would gallantly go down with them rather than watch them perish alone. One's drowning becomes much less painful than a lifetime's nagging conscience reminding us of our failure to employ the third and tenth part of the Scout Law.

And so with Divine Providence no doubt, the three made good at holding on and bobbed right along compliments of the power of the Hartland Rapids. And using the principle of not resisting the current, they worked with it and edged portly to the New Hampshire shore. The flotsam was nil since everything was pretty much tied in. Thank God the mishap was not fatal or even resulted without serious injuries.

Finally, everyone had shot the rapids and gravitated towards the New Hampshire shore.

I don't know if fate caught Kevin, Dennis or any of us dozing but this episode was too close. Not only did they not drown but narrowly absconded skeletal re-arrangement amidst the rocks.

After helping these river rats ashore, we naturally beached our canoes and lodged our fannies into the sandy bank for a well deserved respite. Surveying the river and replaying the near catastrophic event that evaded us I mentally poked myself to affirm my existence. My take was that we were all doing this but had too much macho in our machismo to share it. We were lucky to be alive and knew it well. The reality had to sink in. Why else would we sit there mesmerized in a cold stupor? You can bet we weren't thinking about buying new school clothes.

The weather remained unchanged from early morning retaining cloudy and overcast conditions. No rain yet.

For our psychological well being, we needed to re-group after enduring such a hazardous situation. Mr. Boulais suggested we do an early lunch right there on the sandy bank and no one argued.

With the task of beaching all canoes complete most of us began scouring the banks for dry wood. I cannot recall who fixed up lunch or built the cooking fire but Kevin, Dennis, and Mr. Boulais needed dry-ing out. We forced some dry tree branches into the sand near the fire and hung up a few of their shirts on them to dry.

For all intents and purposes, we walked around in a semi-stupor. Shuffling about in the sand, going through the motions of our chores, we were lost in thought. The rapids event had been quite a catharsis for us all. I stood on the New Hampshire shore with a few of the guys and stared upstream. The length of the rapids and their force combined with the jagged rocks held me spellbound and a bit awed. The time spent now contemplating their fury was something we hadn't done before shooting them. Gee, we didn't even pull along the riverside beforehand to plan our strategy and get ready to approach them.

I mulled over the thought of how good it was to be on land as I peered into the bubbling foam. None of us had conjured up the magnitude of these rapids. To scout them ahead of time most likely would have filled our minds with fear and doubt. This situation would most likely have created "chickens" out of a few of us, perhaps sabotaging this part of the trip out of sheer terror.

In these later years, I believe that our ignorance was probably a disguised ally. What we did not know as teenagers may actually have helped us to forge ahead unhindered.

"LUNCH!" was the word that cracked the air, which meant that "eat" was the verb that drew us near.

Huddled about the cooking fire, we felt good. The chicken soup warmed us in more ways than one as our sense of family and belonging grew. It was a great feeling that we were alive and didn't have to spend this time searching the river for cadavers. Thank goodness the rapids were behind us. Well, literally they were but not in actuality. How so?

"Get the canoe!" hollered Mr. Boulais, shifting everyone's glance to the shoreline.

Somehow one of the canoes had dislodged and was edging its way backwards right into the river.

"Someone move!!" commanded our leader with increased annoyance.

Well, everyone was so comfortable and smug around the fire that not a soul wanted to move. At first I was inclined to believe everyone was just waiting for the next guy to go. But peering over the fire I noticed a lot of smirks being exchanged.

I got the picture fast.

"You're going, not me," was the general idea.

Dennis Riel bolted to the shore just in time to rescue the canoe. Otherwise, it would have drifted downstream in a flash. On his way back to the fire, he looked up at us proudly.

No sooner had Dennis returned to the huddled group when yet another canoe loosened and was being lured ominously downstream a second time.

"Another one's going!!" some guys yelled out in disbelief. Kevin Sullivan and Ed'Sparky' McGrath darted down to save this one.

There would be no reprieve today from this here river. I began to sense something sinister about this spot. Did these rapids have a repugnance for us now that we had escaped her jaws moments before? Were some souls of drowned victims still lurking about jealous at our luck? It seemed outright appalling that this river could still manage its tentacles to cast misfortunes upon us by usurping our canoes! Hey!!

Mr. Boulais put my thoughts to rest quick, being first to notice the rise in the river's water level.

"Hurry! Pull them all in...quick!" shouted Mr. Boulais with alarm, as he nearly dropped his cup of soup.

"The dam's released water!" revealed our darting scoutmaster, "pull in your canoes! Let's move!"

This time we all bolted. Steve and I grabbed the gunwales and yanked our canoe up and inland. Mr. Boulais wisely insisted that all canoes had to be totally out of the water preventing their drifting away again.

And looking northward, we came to realize what Mr. Boulais had just discovered himself. The rapids grew more engorged and turbulent... the river more fierce. We gaped at the slow disappearance of rocks being smothered by the rising rushing white water.

It now dawned on me that we had just shot the Hartland Rapids at a moderate water depth which no doubt produced a fairly challenging ride. Had we slept an extra hour or departed an hour later that morning we would have have been riding the rapids right now. Oh boy! Did we luck out? Our arrival over Sumner Falls could not have been more opportune.

Now with the water release from Wilder the river was spilling over bringing a quick, violent rise to the shoreline. Judging from the rapids at lunchtime that day it's easy to say that most of us probably would not have kept our canoes afloat. Drownings and injuries? You speculate, not me.

My analogy is this. As a youngster, my department store turtle, usually no larger than a half dollar in diameter, survived but a couple of days in the family bathtub. Funeral services generally were backyard burials or a quick flush down the toilet. To shoot Hartland after a dam release enraged it fully engorged and turgid would be to identify with that turtle hurtling down that porcelain toilet. Only the turtle was better off for he was dead before the ride. The "turtle hurtle"? Oh no.

Today signs indicating a sudden rise in the water volume and velocity warn boaters and shore anglers. Signs that were erected because many had been caught by surprise, sometimes fatally, too late.

And so the river's quick rise due to the Wilder Dam release was the actual culprit that seized our canoes. As we stood and watched the swelling river gain in fury, a deeper sense of respect came over me.

We had just escaped and survived one of the most dangerous spots on the Connecticut River. We hadn't an inkling of the troubles of those who were here before us. In 1959, only seven years before our arrival Dr. and Mrs. Davidson's turbo boat was upended and damaged on the rocks of the Hartland Rapids, narrowly escaping injury and death.

We also were quite ignorant of how merciless these rapids dealt with Major Rogers and his Rangers, splitting their raft apart at Sumner Falls for the second time en route from St. Francis, Quebec to Fort No. 4 at Charlestown, NH exactly 200 years earlier.

To see water and attempt to respect it is one thing, but to fight it and survive its clutches is quite another. We learned this fact quickly.

With time waiting for no one, our departure was imminent. The trip must move forward. While I was busy with some last minute lunch cleanup details, our long held doubts about these dangerous rapids crumbled somberly a bit more.

Jim, Gene, and Kevin Boulais were situated about 50 feet inland by an embankment. A small portion of the embankment manifests itself as a red sandstone wall. In an arousing discovery they blurted out in unison, "Someone drowned here!"

Most of us bolted up to the weather-beaten wall to verify their claim or our propensity of doubt.

True enough. Still adhering to the wall clung a faded, scrawled message about a young man from Dartmouth College whose life was snatched by the Hartland Rapids years before.

A quiet pall settled among us. Stark reality was taking its stab at us. Now that our ordeal at Hartland was but an hour's worth of history, we could no longer circumvent the reality that any one of our names could have been added to that wall. We were very lucky...and knew it well.

And since life must move on, we raced frivolously back to our canoes shedding the waning pall among us.

And with me in the bow and Steve shoving off again, we joyfully headed downstream leaving the Hartland Rapids to rage behind us.

14 "Sweet Day, Sweet River"

Our departure below the Hartland Rapids was accompanied by exuberant shouts, as the river about us reverberated with our gaiety. Don't misconstrue me. As a group our rambunctiousness was perhaps difficult to top...and we were consistent at it. Ensuring one heck of a good time was the first order of business on most "scouting outings".

But what made these whooping cries different today from previous ones was our zeal for life was inherent in them. Our goal had been met. A goal that had been miscalculated and underrated by insufficient knowledge of the dangers involved. Darting down and over those ruthless rapids was a harrowing experience that drilled home our renewed interest in living!

In retrospect we knew any of us could have easily lost our lives at Sumner Falls and our thankfulness pinnacled that afternoon. Our zest for life was renewed immensely by the fact that we were spared.

Our procession of canoes edged further away from Hartland. Some of us would never be here again; I not being one. Steve and I spread out into our own river space to gauge a comfortable paddler's pace. The muffled roar of the rapids was softening with each stroke. I imagined they were cussing us out in the effort to quench their anger at losing us. Or was it the simplicity of the rocks and water hurling their accusations; each blaming the other for allowing our unorchestrated escape? This was no time to speculate as our minds shifted downstream.

Water conditions from here on down to Bellows Falls would take on a gentle, flat character. Easy goings with that repetitive beautiful scenery. The thirst for adventure hadn't diminished as it lured us on again. Knowing that our canoes wouldn't be tossed about like ping pong balls over some dangerous set of rapids was a comfort.

"Hey, where are we staying tonight?" someone yelled out from behind us, directing the query to Mr. Boulais.

"Sugar River!" he replied, his voice barking across the waters towards us.

"We've still a way's to go. It'll be on the New Hampshire side about 10 miles down," added our fearless leader.

Sugar River instantly stirred up wild ideas in my head as I speculated the origin of its name. Perhaps its water is sweet? I mused. Or how about "...is its bed layered with sugar instead of muck?" Could it be that a sugar factory once sat on its bank? Enough of these foolish and imaginative conjectures and focus on reality. I did.

Suddenly it dawned on me again that it was the Assumption of Mary, a holy day of obligation. Distracted by the evident stress and impending dangers of the Hartland Rapids, the idea of our Mass obligation temporarily went on the back burner. Once again I sensed the duty to remind Mr. Boulais that we had to attend Mass that day. Being early afternoon I concluded there was still ample time to locate a church or at least make the effort. The best bet we had in going was at White River Junction that morning, but apparently it slipped by us due to forgetfulness. Reversing course and going upstream was lunacy and out of the question. Who wanted to face Hartland again in all her ranting fury?

"Hey, Steve, are we going to Mass today?" I asked stupidly, knowing already that he probably possessed as much knowledge as I did.

"I haven't heard a thing yet," he responded lackadaisically.

"Well, we're supposed to be going to Mass today," I quipped, knowing my statement offered nothing new.

"I think we should remind Mr. Boulais again," I replied hoping to win support from Steve.

"Go ahead," Steve countered with stark neutrality. I understood his reluctant feelings. We all knew our scoutmaster was dutifully preoccupied with other matters not the least of which may have been explaining to parents how some of us perished in white water.

Stroking the water and moving on down, I tossed the issue in my mind. I surmised that Mr. Boulais might be a little annoyed with my persistence about Mass obligations but my conscience was getting the better part of me. The idea kept creeping up inside my head to at least ask one more time about Mass. Well, you know me by now that I finally decided to broach the issue once again despite the probability of a negative response.

On we coasted, passing Hart Island lying inconspicuously near the Vermont bank. One easily misses this island if not keenly observing the landscape.

Our scattered canoe confederation once again began to hem in drawing us all closer. Coming within earshot of Joe and Ray they pointed out to the group what they believed to be Mount Ascutney in Vermont. This beautiful and picturesque peak beckoned us at 3,144 feet from the southwest, challenging us to climb her.

"Maybe someday we'll hike it," suggested Mr. Boulais, pausing in

107

his role as river guide.

"Maybe" never came to be. But two years later in August of 1968, he did lead us again on a 70 mile hike along the Appalachian and Long Trails, beginning at Big Bromley Mountain, VT and ending at Mount Greylock in North Adams, MA. During this week long trek we conquered Stratton Mountain at 3,936 feet which put to rest any doubts about overcoming Ascutney at 3,144.

"The Windsor covered bridge is downstream a bit," reported Mr. Boulais, "we'll meet on the New Hampshire shore before we go up and see it," he ordered calmly.

Excitement rose in the ranks. Here was that next chance of ours. We had sublimated our frustration since the Bedell covered bridge was closed to traffic preventing us from running through it.

The Cornish-Windsor bridge was about five miles downstream. Steve and I chattered about the impending bridge just ahead as our canoes gradually dispersed once again.

Here was my chance. Mr. Boulais was still in the canoe with Jim and Gene. Steve and I slowly inched along side them.

"Hey, are we going to make it to Mass today?" I quizzed our scout-master straightforwardly. "It's the Assumption...we're supposed to," I added to my direct question. As if he didn't know already with me around. Mr. Boulais seemed to become visibly rankled with the question but contained himself very well. He stopped paddling and lay his paddle across the gunwales.

"No," he said, being direct to the point, "we're not."

"I don't know of any churches around here and we have to reach Sugar River by suppertime," he answered without looking for my response.

"It's just going to have to be," he chipped in, paddling off with Jim and Gene.

Oh well. I resigned myself to the inevitable that we wouldn't be going to Mass today. I would not press the issue any further although my humble opinion was that we could have exerted greater efforts in this area. It would not be worth it to provoke our leader to anger over this, so I let it die. In all fairness he probably forgot to check beforehand in laying out our itinerary. My reminders no doubt brought out the awareness that the trip would be unduly delayed if we all went church hunting.

Because of my upbringing a small sense of guilt remained with me especially with this being the first time missing Mass on a holy day.

Such was the effect of my unabashed childhood indoctrination.

At home the next week, I shared the story with my Dad. He just chuckled, which surprised me a bit, since he was quite the stickler in these matters. He said we all should have gone to Mass but that it was kind of out of our control under the circumstances. Nevertheless, I confessed it the next time I went to Confession. The priest advised me exactly as my Dad had, and only then did I feel comfortable and at peace.

****

Steve and I began to tire a bit as the sun finally broke through resuming its slow bake on us. Monotony was aching to subdue us when this vast hulk of a bridge caught our attention. She lay there quite obstrusively and seemingly more elongated than the Bedell up in South Newbury. She was. Sixty feet more. The Cornish-Windsor bridge spans 460 feet across the daring Connecticut River. It was a welcome sight and one that would be as you're gazing at the longest wooden covered bridge in the United States.

Our position placed us right smack in the middle of the Connecticut with a couple of canoes ahead of us. Frantically we all paddled in a mad rush to arrive at the bridge first. It was breezy and the head waves

Windsor/Cornish Bridge from the Vermont side. (8/15/66)

109

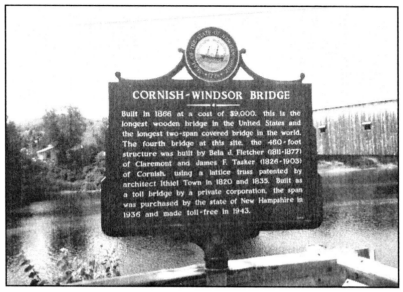

Historical marker in Cornish, NH. (7/99 Photo)

seemed a bit more choppy, lapping the bow at a quickened pace.

We ceased paddling allowing the shifting current to tug us where she liked. During this brief hiatus, we delighted in the cool shade cast by the massive bridge's shadow on the water. She was a masterpiece to behold. We craned our necks peering upward at the conglomeration of chords, bearing blocks, braces and counter-braces, and trusses all synchronized and held intact by wooden treenails (trunnels). A few sparrows darted playfully from joist to joist as the slow current eventually lulled us back into the warm sunlight.

Our canoe crept along the massive stone pier supporting the bridge's midsection. The pier is gently tapered toward upstream to shield it from the abuse of winter ice and log drives of long ago. The other two stone and concrete piers rest on opposite riverbanks, one in Cornish, NH and the other in Windsor, VT. My immediate thoughts focused on how does this baby stay right up there? Well, it's a science and an art but that's for another day for sure.

We pushed for the Cornish pier and beached our canoes on the sandy shore.

This bridge was open to pedestrians as well as vehicular traffic. Its 460 foot span earned it the honor of being the longest wooden bridge in the U.S. and the longest two span bridge in the world. It was first con-

110

structed in 1796 and was destroyed by floods in 1824, 1848, and 1866. So we now were standing before a 100 year old bridge.

"Be careful of the cars," Mr. Boulais advised, "it isn't well lit inside."

Needless to say, we bolted through the portal and into the interior in a frenzy.

"WHOA!" I cried out to the guys around me, stopping in my tracks. The bridge shook slightly when the first car rumbled across its wooden trusses. We all gaped at each other sensing that the bridge would crack and not withstand the strain. But it didn't. It is the crossed spruce trusses that gives this bridge its strength and support. The tin roof and enclosed barnwood sides keep out the elements, preserving the trusses further.

Down the inner wooden sidewalks we ran like frantic nitwits. Darting aimlessly from window to window we bolted. With 18 windows on each side, there were ample openings for each of us to crane our necks out and scream wild unintelligibles into the air. The odor of aged spruce, the cool air and blinding sunlight piercing through from both portals created a unique and rare opportunity for us.

We about had our fill when one in our group discovered a hatchway beneath the wooden walkway at the halfway spot near the middle stone

Cornish Bridge. (8/15/66)
Kevin Boulais in window. L-R, Jim O'Brien, Dennis Riel, Joe O'Brien,
Kevin Sullivan, Steve Kelly, as Pete Boulais looks down.

pier. It was on the north side and allowed us to crawl down and shuffle over to the southern stone pier which supports the midsection. So out we went and sat on the pier's top, gazing down at the 30 foot drop. Ray Roberge was smart enough to click this scene with his camera for posterity's sake. If we went back today the access point would be locked up and has been since the 1998-99 bridge rehabilitation. Looking back I wonder why none of us jumped into the river considering all the other cuckoo things we did.

So rare is a covered bridge that I wouldn't set foot in another one until December 1975 in Woodstock, VT on my honeymoon.

The Cornish-Windsor bridge is the only covered bridge remaining that spans the Connecticut River, since the Bedell was destroyed on Sept. 14, 1979. However, the State of Vermont has more in store for anyone who loves covered bridges. An official Vermont state map will pinpoint over 100 of these structures scattered about its quaint towns and villages. This is just another way Vermont maintains its uniqueness and originality that beckons a constant flow of tourists.

No sooner had we arrived than we departed. It wasn't fair. I paddled away a bit melancholic for I wanted to stay. Feeling possessive, I wished to have that bridge. Wouldn't it be cool to live in town and come here whenever I desired to run through it or coast through on my bike? Most definitely.

"Whadaya keep looking back at?" asked a puzzled Steve Kelly.

"The bridge," I answered, still alternating my paddle strokes with a glance backward.

"Look how small it gets as we move further away," I offered to my sternman.

I continued to be intrigued how quickly this colossal structure diminished as our view narrowed in a few short minutes.

"Oh yeah...I know," said Steve, "pretty soon we'll be squinting just to see a speck."

I took this as an unintended hint and stopped my piddling around. I pushed the paddle down harder and a little faster sensing a need to help my sternman.

As we moved on down the water grew quite choppy as the wind had picked up. Just ahead of us and within sight from the Cornish covered bridge was a rail crossing bridge supported by five concrete hexagon supports. This modern span contrasted greatly with the 100 year old covered bridge we had just scrambled through, but progress is progress.

112

We approach the railroad crossing bridge just south of the Windsor/Cornish Covered Bridge. (8/15/66)

Rippling away from Cornish, NH off our port side is the Saint-Gaudens National Historic Site. This great American sculptor, Augustus Saint-Gaudens, combined naturalism and heroic American spirit into his creations. The Dublin born sculptor, who studied in Paris and Rome eventually settled and lived out his remaining days at Cornish, NH.

Gaudens is famous for his "standing Lincoln" at Lincoln Park, Chicago and Admiral David Farragut in New York. And unbeknownst to us young canoeists at the time was that Springfield, MA's own "The Puritan" was crafted by Gaudens. How many times did I admire this magnificent statue of Deacon Samuel Chapin on the sloping grounds of the Springfield City Library clueless of this masterpiece's creator? Saint-Gauden's mind foresaw this prominent image, renowned in our home city for years. It was here on these Cornish banks that this great work originated. And so we paddled on down, remaining ignorant of this great artist and his works until we matured years later.

The sun chickened out and went back in again.

"Who thinks it'll rain?" Mr. Boulais surprised us from behind with his query.

He had snuck up behind our canoe surreptitiously, still a shipmate at the mercy of Jim and Gene. The question half startled Steve and me who were lost in thought gabbing away about who knows. Realizing now that it was clouding over, we began to worry a bit about rainfall. Luckily it never came. Physically, the day was getting to us. With the stress of the Hartland Rapids episode, the Windsor bridge stop, and paddling in general, needless to say we were tiring.

No one answered Mr. Boulais' question directly about the possible rainfall. We all shrugged giving him the indication that we hardly knew or didn't care.

From our put in below the Hartland Rapids to the Cornish-Windsor covered bridge was about seven miles. From here it would be another five miles or so to the Route 103 bridge at Ascutney. Somewhere below that we would merge with Sugar River.

We scuttled along yearning for the confluence on the New Hampshire side. A twenty mile day was in order if we could make it to Sugar River. The riverbanks here begin to display signs of gradual erosion. The red-winged blackbirds commence a natural integration with the cliff swallows, and get along well.

We skimmed under the riveted, half-rusting beams of the B&M Railroad bridge. No trains or whistles were in sight or ear shot so we moved on down. Mr. Boulais let it be known to us that we would hang a left at the mouth and proceed up the Sugar River seeking a suitable spot to pitch camp for the night.

Finally, as time moved along with our canoes, Sugar River appeared. Steve and I veered strong on the port side. I swept wide with the bow stroke and Steve dragged hard on the J.

Paddling inland and eastward seemed strange. The vast, open expanse of the Connecticut abruptly disappeared. Sugar River is smaller and narrower reaching only about 100 feet across. The Sugar drains Lake Sunapee in New Hampshire and empties her westward into the Connecticut. Its northern and southern banks were thickly lined with trees, many hanging over like willows. A quieter, slower river,...more eerie than the Connecticut, perhaps due to it being inconspicuously tucked away. A romantic river to me. With that perfectly serene, secluded atmosphere begging for a troubadour to court his lady, paddling down this lazy river, singing of his love as they go.

It was lookout time.

"Look out for a decent clearing for camp," Mr. Boulais alerted his exhausted troops. The clouds snuck in thicker, giving the sun no more chances today. The banks here were less inclined than on the

Connecticut allowing us a better view of many fields of tall grass or corn.

We were tired. Racing into my mind came the surreal thought that our canoes must be tired. Can a canoe be tired? I thought. Perhaps. Perhaps, my gray matter was too exhausted to have this protruding idea recurring through it. To me, the canoes were tired simply because we were tired.

Up ahead off the port side canoes were heading towards the northern bank. Finally. A small sandy beach with some sparse hanging trees greeted us. The greensward was knee high. Spots of skunk cabbage here and there fought to dominate the groundcover.

Joe, Ray, and a few others scouted inland about 20-30 yards for a campsite. The slight incline gave rise to a small grassy meadow with a large cornfield behind it. The guys decided on settling right there.

Amid shouts of "Up here!" and gesturing arms, the canoes were unloaded with what provisions would be necessary for the night, and lugged part way up the hill.

Those of us who were scullions were languishing in the throes of hydrating yet another freeze-dried Chuck wagon dinner. Others were busy converting their ponchos into shelters, as the rest were out gallivanting about.

Suddenly, a few of the guys bolted out of the cornfield and across the meadow like bats fleeing Gehenna. There was a farmer in hot pursuit. Needless to say we dropped everything we were doing and gaped big time.

He didn't resemble the picture of happiness. Having dispersed some of our contingent off his property, his focus now shifted to the whole group gathered at the campsite.

"Pack it up!...Get out now!" the man screeched like a lunatic.

"This isn't your land!" he reminded us, continuing his rude and abrupt tirade.

"True," I thought, but gee, there weren't any visible boundaries any of us could see. I hoped this fellow would downshift his emotions without using one of us for the clutch.

"Move out! Right now! Get down the hill by the river!" commanded this overheated agrarian bully. His diatribe scared the pants off us. Thanks be to God he was devoid of a shotgun.

Mr. Boulais treated him with kid gloves, apologizing and telling the old gruff that we were just looking for a place to stay the night. He defused a bit.

Treading lightly, everyone snapped out of their present preoccupation and helped in dragging the camp back down by the shore. The old tiller wasn't satisfied until we relocated "our" site to within 20-25 feet of the shore.

Grumpy did an about face and proceeded back up the hill.

"And stay out of the cornfield!" he snapped indignantly after turning around, shaking his index finger at us. We were grateful it wasn't the middle, you know. He moseyed back up the hill and out of sight. Never saw him again.

He was right though. Somehow we should have inquired or did our homework on camping on the premises of private landowners. Had we not meandered so deeply onto his territory he would in all probability found it difficult to detect us. But detect he did. The group now acquired the additional task of worrying about this irate farmer. No doubt he would calm down but was he out there lurking? Was he secluded and stalking us from afar? I suppose he had every right to if his senses suspected us of trespassing again.

As time passed, we sort of forgot about him even though we had temporarily tucked him in the back of our minds.

"Hey!...where did we get that corn!?" our scoutmaster blurted, as he peered bug-eyed into the pot of seething water.

Everyone looked sheepishly about and of course no one did it. Oh no, no one did it. Like my Dad always said, "it just fell off ear by ear and down the hill it walked, and somehow found this pot of boiling water."

"Ahh... just forget it," Mr. Boulais said, giving up his inquiry before it started.

The rationale was that there was such an abundance of corn along the riverbanks, it wouldn't be missed. For the life of me, I really don't know who confiscated it so stealthily but the operation made the CIA look sick.

"That's not ours. Don't take anymore!" he scolded us, gesticulating with his arms like a conductor.

"And don't bring it back uphill either or that guy will skin us all alive if he sees his corn!" warned our leader glancing uphill towards the cornfield nervously.

It was truly a merciful act of God that the agitated farmer did not catch whomever red-handed pilfering his crop. He would have summoned the local constable in a heartbeat, why with the way he initially lost no love on us.

116

The corn went one up on good. It was butter and sugar and that's hard to beat in mid August. I will not justify the filching of a few ears of corn because it was wrong. But the impetus just may have been going six days on Chuck Wagon food and the reality that we were aching for some fresh produce.

Before you knew it, bedtime had rolled in like it or not. Jim, Gene, Steve and I erected a lean-to out of two or three ponchos to sleep under. Along came Kevin Boulais and Dennis Riel, who asked to sleep under it, also. Well, we said there wasn't enough room while there really was. Subconsciously, we were opening the crack to set up divisions among us, which is something that cannot be allowed on any trip of this nature.

Well, Mr. Boulais got into quite the snit.

"Here then,...take this!" insisted our annoyed scoutmaster, tossing dufflebags and cooking gear under our tarp where obvious room existed.

He had every right to be *"torqued"*. We were being too selective and our leader did not warm-up to the practice of us excluding others, especially with available room under our tarp. We were laying the groundwork for a rift which is never welcome where harmony should exist. Mr. Boulais made us take on the troop gear as a reminder that there was room. He was correct. His role was that of loco parentis and heaven forbid some mishap would occur. The last thing we needed was a sequel to "Lord of the Flies". The bottom line was unity and collegiality had to be preserved however fragile that might be, to maintain a peaceful trip.

Complete darkness edged its way in again assisted by the absence of street lights and illumination from nearby homes. Sugar River lay at our feet. So quiet it flowed; ebbing to and fro without notice. You knew she was there because you paddled her but now no hint of her was manifest save your memory.

We were a bit cramped with the equipment that our scoutmaster had "awarded" us. I preoccupied myself with wriggling and tossing about in my sleeping bag bent on securing that comfortable spot just right for snoozing. What fun. This is an experience that can't really be justifiably described. Only one would know who has ever tried to sleep in one of those manufactured cocoons.

We gassed about the days events until our voices dropped off one by one, alerting the stragglers that sleep was winning out. I lay there, my eyes groping for a twinkling lonesome star. I found none as the clouds did their job of shielding them well. Entertaining snores as

117

responses I quickly realized that my conversation was going solo again.

My thoughts shifted to the days events again. We never did make it to Mass for the Assumption I pondered. I took it for granted that most of our parents went to Mass back home that day. Without doubt their prayers were for us.

Funny thing. Musing years later, I came to realize that the Virgin Mother is known among other titles as the "Star of the Sea". Indeed, all those in any vessel on any body of water are inclusive of her protection. Was she not with us that day, her day, the Assumption, as we dared the channels of the notorious Hartland Rapids like bloody fools? She was.

A gracious favor it was...Mary guiding us safely over the falls under her mantle. Funny thing again. Yesterday we had stopped at Our Lady Queen of Peace to attend Mass. And the Queen of Peace did not forget that we paused in our trip to honor her Son, Jesus. And all was peaceful now.

Wrestling sleep for the final time, I reflected on the unfortunate young man who drowned at the Hartland Rapids and whose name remains etched on the rock wall. The name could have been any of ours. Lying supine in the night's silence I prayed three Hail Mary's for his soul. And that was all I remembered for that day...and night.

✐15 "Duped"

Voices aroused me as the morning greeted us in its usual state; misty and foggy. The fog, dampness, and thick mist would loiter until later on when rays of sunlight would descend upon them, dispelling them in minutes. A few of the guys had risen and Mr. Boulais was up and about. Without commands and like clock work the rest of us rose, rolled up our sleeping bags, repacked our personal gear and loaded the canoes in a habit-like trance while rubbing sleep from our eyes.

Lining up for breakfast I clearly recollect reincarnated hot dried fruit mix and pancakes filling our aluminum plates and cups. Even the pancake syrup started out as powder and became functional only by adding boiled water.

"Bless us O Lord, and these Thy gifts which we are about to receive from Thy bounty through Christ Our Lord, Amen," someone led the group in the traditional Catholic grace before meals. At each meal it would be someone else's turn to lead the group in prayer.

Here was a practice that commenced that year when many of us in the troop began working towards the *Ad Altare Dei* Award. This is the religious award for Catholic Boy Scouts, a three part program where a scout must "Know Christ, Love Christ, and Serve Christ."

John Mathisen was our instructor that year, a young man in his twenties who took on the inane task of teaching and guiding about 15 scouts through this challenging ordeal in faith. John must have expunged all of his sins with the penance he endured just putting up with us. A modern day Job in patience, he graced his class with a love for teaching and an amusing sense of humor. We squirmed in our fold up metal chairs during the one hour class each week, wearing scout uniforms no less and taking notes.

John insisted we do our work...and we did.

On July 18, 1966, merely one month before the canoe trip he signed my *Ad Altare Dei* card on requirement two of part three which is "...give evidence of reciting grace before and after meals at home or camp for 30 days." This was on your parents word and your scout's honor. Funny thing, scouting. That Catholic award requirement was the seed which sprouted the habit of table grace at our family dinner each evening. It also spawned the same practice at all of the camping trip

119

meals. I have never displaced it with anything else. To this day, my own family prays grace before every meal that is shared. Funny thing scouting...sometimes it changes you without it ever trying. It just offers you the challenge that you either live up to or not.

And so with the habit set, we continued the practice at every meal, with heads bowed, on the big river banks or little river banks. Or we didn't eat.

Returning westward down the Sugar River would place us back at the Connecticut. The morning seemed to mirror yesterday's weather paddling in at supper time; overcast, dismal and cloudy. The type of weather that makes it difficult to discern whether it's morning or evening...minus a clock. We were on our way out and knew we could never look back upstream whence we reached the Connecticut River confluence. For a while I thought about the seclusion of this river. So quiet and tucked away. A smaller and slower river flow. I preferred this as a boy's special hiding place. So sequestered that one wanted it for their very own, to get away from the world. Its hidden nature captivated me but our stay was purely ephemeral.

This tributary would terminate momentarily since a few hundred yards ahead awaited the Connecticut. Moving southerly this maternal river drew the Sugar unto herself, embraced her and carried her, enduring the ride to Long Island Sound.

Our entourage merged onto the Connecticut without incident. Veering gradually to the port side, our canoes quickly turned and headed downstream on a southerly course. One last look inland granted us a farewell view of Sugar River...then she vanished from us. We would have to be enthralled with her in our minds from here on in. And so we left our "little haven for a little while." In my mind it would imaginatively remain known only to ourselves and that vexed farmer.

Today, Tuesday August 16 is the half way point on the trip, with three days behind us and three to go. The fog was being gobbled up quickly. About a mile or so down from Sugar River the brilliant sun began to warm us up. Blue skies and puffy white clouds dominated. Temperatures would not elevate too high today. The Bellows Falls station recorded a high of 66°F and a low of 62°F for the day. Vernon station had recorded a high of 65°F and a low of 60°F. The sun's warmth kept the cool breeze at bay as we paddled on in search of something new.

Once again the serpentine river revealed new countryside to us, beautiful as ever. Here one begins to lure the senses inland. What cap-

120

tivates us and fulfills one's nature up here? Farmland. Rural Vermont's unplanned plan for a picturesque river seems to be its own Vermont farmer. For miles, the crops, fields, and open meadows preserve the land. New Hampshire contributes also, but it seems farmland is more prevalent on the Vermont side.

I feel good for the farmer as I paddle and am able to identify with him and his love for the land. With their interest in vegetable crops or livestock the farmer is in love with the land. He needs and cherishes the quiet, open space. Upon vast tracts of land he erects only a house, a barn, and perhaps a silo. His trees line the river banks. His fields, whether filled with corn, tomatoes or squash or pumpkins, preserve thousands of acres from development. And so with the farmer's simple way of life the river and environs are somewhat preserved.

With the absence of industry, homes, and shopping centers, one continues to enjoy the majestic and serene landscape along the Connecticut.

"Hey!" I blurted out to Steve in realization, "it's my Dad's birthday today."

"I guess you won't be making the party," replied Steve nonchalantly.

"Yeah," I responded, pulling another bow stroke while staring into the water and reflecting on home birthday parties. This is the first time that I would be absent from home on Dad's birthday, I thought. Jim and Joe wouldn't make it either.

In those days I couldn't even tell someone how old my Dad was if they asked me. It was trivia back then. There were too many other things on our minds as kids. Besides, it was hard to figure out because I didn't even know what year he was born. It wasn't important for thirteen year old's to know so it didn't faze me. Well, ""ole Joe" was 42 that day, meaning his birth occurred in 1924 if my math's correct. That is eight years younger than my 50 years now! And I thought he was old then. Some things will never change. Think about it.

We slowly crept on past Jarvis Island which hugs the Vermont shore patiently anticipating the scenario just past the 90° elbow turn up ahead. Here the river cuts sharply eastward and then abruptly drops south. This morning Steve and I are trailing the canoe confederation and not thinking much of it. We hadn't a clue that we were dead last until we negotiated that sharp elbow waiting for us...Weathersfield Bow.

As we clear the sharp bow and focus downstream we are greeted

121

with the piercing sounds of hooping and hollering. Well, what the heck is this? I thought. Steve and I painfully discover that we're the last canoe on the scene.

"Hey...no fair," I barked defensively, hoping someone would care.

Are you kidding? They were all having a grandiose time and they're supposed to listen to me? My remark was lost to the wind. After all, the early bird gets the worm.

The scenario was none other than a great big tree that sprawled out over the river. It was equipped with a tarzan swing attached high on a limb, and was swarming with scouts below ready to scramble up and brave the plunge from the sky.

My brother Jim was perched warily on some flimsy boards nailed to a branch awaiting the rope's return. He snared the rope from its pendulum swing just in time and clung to it with a vise grip. Jumping up enough to clear the branch and with tucked knees at his chest, Jim bravely lunged outward. Descending quickly and accompanied by wind blown hair, he screamed "Geronimo!!" the entire route down.

With the rope taut at its pinnacle, Jim finally released his vise grip of the radius and plunged from a 10 foot height into the cool, murky Connecticut.

What thrills. Rather what lunatics?

Steve and I brought our canoe to shore quickly for I assumed we wanted to try this also. I felt cheated. How long had these guys been here?! I asked myself. I guess that is the price one pays for dillydallying and bringing up the rear in a canoe caravan. We knew that we were coming up short on this once in a lifetime chance for fun when Mr. Boulais yelled out to the group, "One more jump!"

"Oh man," I concluded forcefully, "we gotta get up there!" telling Steve in a rush.

"I don't wanna go," Steve offered plainly.

"OK," I replied, while I tumbled out of the canoe and made straight for the tree ladder, nailed to the bark. Before I knew it I had reached the wood planks and was eagerly waiting my turn, looking down over the water. Soon the rope was coming at me and I grabbed it so as to not look foolish. Now I perceived myself to be more elevated than I had previously thought. Yikes!

Below a couple of canoes were heading out already and moving downstream. "Hey, wait up!" I yelled to no avail.

"It's now or never," I coached myself nervously.

My hands clenched the rope and then I took a leap of faith. I stepped out and allowed my wobbly legs to dangle in thin air.

"WHOA!" I screamed, wondering just how this situation might terminate, and hoping that I wouldn't.

The toes of my right foot tried to stay in contact with the damp wooden planks but they just bid them good-bye. Gravity brought me down.

"Gee," I wondered. "How deep is this water?" along with "What the heck is below the surface anyway?" Kind of late now I'd say. Well, everyone else's safe resurfacing made my situation seem less dubious, I suppose. But was it? The water was a brownish tan and murky from all the turbulence of us jumping in one after another.

I closed my eyes the instant my feet hit the surface. Down I plunged with my eyes shut, struggling as I kicked and pulled to regain the surface. I never did touch the bottom.

Coming up unscathed, I saw everyone bantering about my performance. Joe was drifting aimlessly along the shore with Ray in their canoe, as he warned me, "The sea monsters!" looking for my reaction. Leave it to Joe for calculated foolishness.

Upon hearing this phrase, I swam the short distance to shore like crazy hoping never to get snatched by large fish, submerged lanky trees, or sunken automobiles. Wading ashore in ankle deep water I finally reached my canoe. Steve was still in it raring to go after having watched my spectacle with humor. I steadied it, crouched over and clambered in. We shoved off.

Being in the shade while soaking wet doesn't help one keep warm. Goose bumps blanketed me as I stayed cold. Moments later we reentered the sun's rays and warmed up in a jiffy. This whole episode spanned ten minutes, tops. The feeling was ecstatic on that tarzan swing even if only for once. Had we dillydallied more so, my chance might have been lost altogether.

The warm sunshine working with a cool, dry breeze dried us river rats off in no time. Jim and Gene tagged along side Steve and me. We chitchatted back and forth about our brave feats on the tarzan swing. Our two canoes befriended each other as we traveled downstream maintaining a safe distance from the pack yet we were still in first place at lagging behind.

Bye and bye, a few miles passed when the appearance of a queer island made its presence known. Our paddling veered us close to the New Hampshire side. Had our position been at midstream or the Vermont side this island would have eluded us outright. There had been a few islets along the river but this one was quite large. Unbeknownst to us by name at the time was Hubbard Island. This island clings to the New Hampshire shore so snugly that its western bank seems to blend with the Claremont, NH mainland itself.

Happening upon the Hubbard lent itself to a unique challenge. At its northern tip, Jim and Gene had stopped churning and coasted inland toward the eastern bank of the island. Steve and I also stopped and drifted in with the waves, listening to the cadence of the lapping waves against our canoe's sides. Our craft tilted towards the outside of Hubbard Island... its western bank trying to hold back the Connecticut.

"Look how far down that stream goes," said Gene anxiously, eyeing the narrow channel slipping by the New Hampshire shore.

"Hey, we're going this way," insisted Jim, letting his intentions be known to everyone.

Gene never offered a word of resistance which meant he seconded the motion.

"Let's see who comes out first," I replied, offering them an equal challenge.

We would paddle the Connecticut and they the rivulet along the Hubbard's inner bank.

"Let's go," countered Gene to Jim, sealing the challenge in the affirmative by plunging his paddle down deeply which lurched his bowman backwards.

He didn't even wait for a "ready, set, go!" They were gone before they were off. Their resolve was evident as their paddling quickened into a ferocious frenzy. Sporadically they glanced off their starboard side to check on our progress, and to ridicule our efforts with a good, hearty laugh.

Steve and I had already launched our counter attack in this sophomoric duel as we dipped and yanked our paddles frantically.

"We'll beatcha!" Steve yelled over to our rivals almost now out of earshot.

Jim and Gene then disappeared down the narrow channel pumping away between the muddy banks off their port and starboard sides. Steve and I lost sight of them and then attempted to "guesstimate" how long the island actually was.

"Can you see the end of it?" asked my determined sternman.

"Nope," I answered, huffing and puffing, paddling like mad.

"It's way downstream," I offered, taking a stab at guessing, since I couldn't discern where the island ended.

124

The two conditions of the island's close proximity to the shore and our point being too far from the island's end created the impossibility for us to demarcate anything.

"Just keep paddling," Steve encouraged me from the rear. "I am!" I bellowed.

Dipping and churning we clipped away like never before. It was our first challenge since the trip began. Actually, I can't recall any of us racing before today. Thus far, the trip was one of enjoyment dedicated to preserving our energy, and for that we all paced ourselves pretty moderately to slow.

The sprint seemed like hours but obviously was not. It really was more in tune with a middle distance race such as the 880 rather than a sprint. But the more we paddled the sooner we realized that our bodies told us it was going to be more long distance than anything else.

Hubbard Island is 240 rods long and 40 rods wide, according to Eliphalet and Phinehas Merrill in 1817 as published in **The Gazetteer of the State of New Hampshire**. Regardless, that stretch converts to 3960 feet long and 660 feet wide. That's 23 feet more than a kilometer; or six tenths of a mile. It seems longer with a challenge and an attempted sprint no doubt.

Steve and I worked the paddles hard. He coordinated and synchronized his dip exactly when my paddle sunk down. The island was too wide to see across, yet our intermittent glances inland were prompted by the hope of locating our opponents which would verify whether we were trailing or leading. We assumed that they were high-tailing it like we were. But no such luck came our way in pinpointing their whereabouts.

My thoughts focused on obstacles they might encounter which would briefly detain them and give us the advantage to win. Perhaps low water level might lodge them in the muck. A massive strainer such as a fallen tree would create some delay. Or maybe their discovery of yet a second tarzan swing would tempt them to stop paddling and give us the victory? Who knows?

We skimmed along, bolting past trees and shrubs. Small poplars waved their triangular hands at us in the breeze. They seemed to be cheering us on. A few ducks swam back ashore under cover, stopped and gawked our way wondering what the excitement was all about.

Suddenly the end was now in sight which was good because our "sprint" was getting the best of us. Sheer exhaustion slowed us down as the Hubbard's southern tip and jutted inland appeared. The rivulet's opening at this southern end emerged somewhat wider than its northern counterpart where our race began. The brief respite was welcome. In our minds, we had won this hectic jaunt simply because Jim and Gene were nowhere in sight.

"Do you think they finished first and are downstream?" Steve asked with a puzzled look.

"That's impossible!" I shot back. "We would see them just ahead of us and no one is around here," was my rationalization.

We reasoned that Jim and Gene were way behind fooling around somewhere so our paddling was reduced to a snail's pace. The idea was that when they exited their side of the island we would be there to greet them due to our dawdling. Time went by. We floundered about for a good 15 or 20 minutes craning our necks hoping to spot those slackers when they emerged from the channel. Nothing coming...nothing doing.

Steve and I became puzzled and concerned. Perhaps these guys were staging a ruse. We both thought they would get tired of playing hide and seek and eventually manifest themselves. An eerie feeling hovered about us. It was that quiet "quiet" kind of quiet.

"This is kinda weird," Steve shared in a hushed tone.

"Yeah...this is like the Twilight Zone," I commented, referring to Rod Serling's 1960's show about strange unexplained happenings.

Straining our eyes we peered back up the rivulet from our position and detected no movement whatsoever.

Were we looking at a mirage? Were they back there but we failed to see them? These two questions were inclusive of many that Steve and I queried ourselves with.

"Maybe their route was a small stream that goes inland and they don't even know it," deduced Steve with wonder.

"Man, maybe they're lost and don't even know it," I worried out loud.

Steve and I then laughed ourselves silly for a few moments, but inside this somber situation began to take a serious hold on us.

"What are we going to tell Mr. Boulais?" asked Steve with a grave expression.

"I don't know," I replied awkwardly, not wanting to reflect on his reaction and our possible consequences.

We should have stuck together yet no one could have foreseen this separation. Our split was purely inadvertent. We would just have to tell it the way it was when the group gathered again.

"Let's go," Steve advised, "maybe we can catch up to the group and

126

tell them about Jim and Gene."

"OK," I agreed, as we began our steady paddle downstream. The ride south couldn't have been more pensive and nerve wracking as we worried and pondered both their elusive location and fate.

****

The emotional haul was long and arduous. I don't know about Steve but I was worried near sick about our lost opponents. Late morning finally showed up accompanied by lunch time pangs when Steve and I closed the gap on our group and edged in toward the first canoe in sight.

"Hey, you guys!...did Jim and Gene come by yet?" I hollered over to Ed McGrath and Kevin Sullivan, who sat drifting about a hundred feet away.

"Not yet," returned Ed, glancing back at Kevin for any up to date newscasts on Jim and Gene.

"They're probably back on the tarzan swing," Kevin opined with a chuckle, "knowing those guys."

"We lost sight of them back at that big island right after a race we had," Steve explained wearing a semi-concerned look.

"They'll show up...don't worry," Ed McGrath assured us in his usual quiet positive manner.

Our two canoes pressed on which turned out to be short-lived. Up ahead the remaining canoes had been ushered to shore by their hungry crews.

The stretch covered that morning had us pass the mouth of Little Sugar River and Glidden Island. As Steve and I coasted slowly past Glidden Island we peered closely to see if Jim and Gene were hiding out. Nothing there. She wasn't a particularly large island by any means but she was there. We would never set eyes on her again. By 1990 the **Complete Boating Guide to the Connecticut River** put out by the Connecticut River Watershed Council (CRWC) stated that "Glidden Island isn't much more than a blip on the screen of water." By 1999 the Connecticut River Joint Commissions' **Boating on the Connecticut River** stated "Glidden Island has now completely eroded away, some say as a result of heavy use by water-skiers." Nature with man's "help" will take its course. Believable. We had yet to venture as far south as the Chesire Toll Bridge but could see it in the distance. Our tired limbs had churned out about 11 miles with an equal amount to go to reach

Bellows Falls.

Lounging about waiting for lunch one notices the river spread wider as the distance stretches further to the opposite bank. Geographically, the river does in fact grow wider from the Chesire Bridge on down to Bellows Falls.

"Where's Jim and Gene?" Mr. Boulais queried the group searching for something in his pack.

Steve and I just stared at each other with raised eyebrows, speechless.

"They were right behind us for a while," I answered, choosing my words carefully to avoid unintended alarm.

"They should have stayed with the group," our Scoutmaster quipped with mild concern, peering upstream.

"Yeah, they should have," Steve agreed, trying to keep the mood as calm as possible.

"How about Kevin and Dennis?" Mr. Boulais continued.

Blank stares department revisited. Nobody knew their whereabouts either.

The subject was dropped momentarily as lunch and other immediate shenanigans consumed our time.

Steve and I instinctively surmised that with time passing and their absence the situation would escalate portentously. Secretively we avoided telling Mr. Boulais about the incident but revealed it to Joe and Ray, our senior leaders. They weren't too concerned yet, reminding Steve and me that every time the whole group stopped canoeing for a break someone had to come in last. True, I thought, as my worried concerns were briefly allayed by their confident remarks. Yet, despite this nonchalance of Joe and Ray's it drove me crazy with worry as to why they were still aberrant. They couldn't see the whole picture like Steve and I so why would they worry. I hoped and prayed their situation wouldn't turn woeful.

"Hey, is that them out there?" Ray alerted the group, minus an air of excitement.

He was an "in control" guy who didn't relish hollering and yelling over much of anything. A true leader, I always supposed. I, for my part had jumped up to observe the potential duo out in their craft.

"Yeah, it is!" most of us reverberated, answering Ray in the affirmative.

"That's gotta be Dennis and Kevin along side of them," said Joe, peering across the water.

128

Boy was I relieved as all heck. Steve gazed at me, frowning slightly, and said in a rhetorical fashion, "Where the heck did they go?" I simply shrugged my shoulders ignorantly. The ivory canoe grew larger and larger with each stroke of their paddles. All doubt about their identities evaporated as soon as we detected Gene's red Robin Hood hat. Who could argue now? Our group settled back partaking of lunch while awaiting the landing of both canoes. We didn't pay too much attention to them even amidst Jim's persistent hollering. His verbiage was unintelligible as the distance created difficult comprehension.

"What the heck is he squawking about?" Mr. Boulais wondered aloud, squinting out across the water.

We all shrugged and resumed eating our lunch. Closing in now at about 150 feet off shore, Jim bawled out with yet another screech, but this time in a clearly audible tone, "We got goats! We got goats!"

The entire group freaked out and sprang up leaving their food aside as they bolted to the muddy shore.

Gene DeGrandpre confers with his goat. (8/16/66)

Gene supported his trademark grin from ear to ear. Without waiting for them to beach their canoe the guys waded right out in the water to see...the goats? Sure enough. There they stood; two kid goats. Light brown and white, fidgeting to death. One in each canoe. Dennis and Kevin had the female while Jim and Gene had the male. They started to shake like crazy not knowing much of what to do or where to go. Four little bluish gray beady eyes bulging out at us with fright. They were wedged in by the personal gear which didn't afford them much leg room.

"We found 'em, we found 'em! They're ours!" Jim insisted with determination, stopping short of defiance.

"Calm down," advised Mr. Boulais, "calm down."

"Who found them?" continued our leader, who was frowning at the spectacle.

"I did," answered Dennis, matter of factly.

"What the heck are we going to do with goats?!" barked Mr. Boulais with annoyance.

"Take 'em along for the ride," countered Dennis, with an air of confidence.

"What!? Who's going to clean up after them?" questioned the Scoutmaster.

"No one needs to," persisted Dennis.

Mr. Boulais was getting nowhere with Dennis and so shifted his inquiry elsewhere.

"Where and how did you get them?" he continued.

Dennis Riel chats with a goat while Kevin Boulais opens a candy.
(8/16/66)

Dennis responded, "Well, you see, Kevin and I were paddling along the inside of that big island back there, going pretty slow when we heard some rustling in the bushes. So we went on shore to look and there was this female goat just standing there so I took her and put her in our canoe. Just then the male began bleating loudly in the underbrush. So we went back in to get him and then Jim and Gene pulled up in their canoe to see what Kevin and I were doing. Gene asked the same thing, 'What are we going to do with two goats?' I told him we were taking them so I tossed the male in Gene's canoe and then we left. I really thought they were lost."

"Yup...,we got 'em," said Gene in a convincing tone, stepping out of his canoe.

"Hey! Get him!!" Gene screamed, holding one goat back as the other darted out in an attempted escape. Kevin Boulais apprehended him before it fled.

"We need rope," pleaded Jim, hoping someone might like the idea.

When the rope was harnessed around their necks, they wriggled and tussled to no avail. But it was necessary to prevent the certainty of their escape otherwise. In a few moments, when the commotion over the goats subsided a bit, Mr. Boulais interjected some uncomfortable information amidst the hubbub.

Gerry O'Brien holds the reins.

131

"You guys probably don't know this, but farmers up here put goats on these islands so they'll eat everything to fatten them up," he addressed Jim, Gene, Dennis and Kevin specifically in the presence of all.

We all looked at Mr. Boulais with semi-jutted jaws.

"Really? You're kidding," said Joe, who seemed as puzzled as everyone else. None of us had the acumen to foresee that.

"It's too late now," Gene snickered, "they're ours."

"Don't you understand? You guys probably took some farmer's goats! He'll be going crazy looking for them in a week or so when he goes back there," Mr. Boulais paraphrased frankly.

"No one can prove they're his goats," protested Jim. "If we bring them back and leave them, they might die!" continued Jim, escalating his defense defiantly.

"From what?" asked our confused Scoutmaster.

"I don't know," replied Jim, plain as day.

"We can't go back now," Dennis piped in, "it's too far."

Mr. Boulais knew that. Besides, the whole group had already taken a serious fancy to these two critters meaning that the whole lot of us would be outright disappointed if we returned the goats. He knew we would drive him mad with complaining for the trip's duration if we lost our two little friends.

And so empathy won out.

Besides, deep down I don't think Mr. Boulais relished the notion of back tracking upstream and losing valuable canoeing time either.

"OK, we'll take them along," decided our leader, halfheartedly after a brief pause. "But they have to be separated, one in each canoe. And on land, they have to be kept tied up so they can't take off," he continued reasoning to the group.

"No problem. We'll take 'em!" boasted Gene, in an upbeat mood while leading the male about.

Finishing up lunch, Steve and I moseyed on over to Jim and Gene for a chat and an update.

"Boy, we thought you guys were lost back there or in some big trouble," Steve whispered to the prodigal canoeists.

"We waited so long for you to come out of that channel that it seemed like "The Twilight Zone", I added, hoping for them to show some excitement.

No way. Not a thing. They were too engrossed in their new role as the caretakers of two goats to be even fazed by our remarks of concern.

132

The confiscation was viewed as a compassionate act and not one of malice or stealing which made our whole group more at ease. Needless to say, Steve and I returned to the river that afternoon paddle in hand, at peace and thankful to heaven that our "race mystery" had been solved. We weren't so much concerned that we had won competitively but that we had won doubly when our prayers were answered by being spared of disaster.

As for Jim and Gene, they undoubtedly had called a time out and confounded us big time with their canoe.

⚔16 Bellows Falls

Resuming the canoe trip after lunch was fairly undramatic. The Chesire Bridge to Bellows Falls, VT stretch was about ten plus miles. Monotony was knocking on our doors again, yet the "two goats in a boat" definitely abated the situation.

As expected, a few of the canoes and guys huddled aside the "goat boat" for the first few miles simply because they wanted a piece of the action. It was comical just to watch these creatures coasting along scared as heck, bleating and observing everything in sight.

Then some short lived fun began. Taking my paddle with two hands and swinging it lightly enough onto the water's surface, I produced a small splash and spray directly at the goats. This provocation caused them to bleat to the high heavens. The situation ended quickly because Jim and Gene didn't fancy having their gear soaked in the process.

"Hey!...knock it off! The gear's getting wet you jerk!" Gene shouted, getting pretty fired up.

And I was a jerk, but it was fun.

Backing off a bit, Steve and I discovered that the spray could be calculated to land precisely just outside the canoe. Steve joined in the assault. This spray was also sufficient to prompt the goats into bleating again while keeping the gear dry. It was great fun for the moment but ended soon so as to prevent these goats from going "over the edge" - no pun intended.

We moved on down. The goats, which we never really named, gradually became acclimated with their new situation.

And again unbeknownst to us was the fact that Augustus Saint-Gaudens, his niece Marie, and son Homer had their own goat named "Seasick" by their pool side in 1892. Gee, Cornish is only a few miles upstream from Hubbard Island. Could it be that these two goats were actual descendants of "Seasick"? Only a DNA test could tell, but you never know. Regardless, in the thick of it all these two goats would certainly be on their way to being "seasick" by the time this trek was over.

They must have sensed no harm would befall them through us, as their bleating eventually diminished. The two would cavort and frolic about when not busy with filling their bellies with riverside vegetation. It was critical to tie them to the canoe or tree when grounded or they'd bolt in a flash.

The afternoon sun garnished an atmosphere of laziness on the river. Our jabbering ricocheted from canoe to canoe. The stark reality of the inevitable question as to who would take these two goats home finally surfaced.

"Hey, who's gonna take these two guys home when the trip's over?" inquired Gene with a puzzled look about him.

"You," murmured Jim with the utmost confidence.

Gene snickered and scoffed back, "No sir!" "We can't have goats where I live," referring to the housing project where he resided. He then stared at Jim with a whimsical look.

Jim read his face and said outright, "Forget it. My Dad hates cats...so he ain't gonna let us have goats!"

With Jim and Gene absolving themselves of this post-trip responsibility the goats would seemingly transform into homeless critters at the trip's duration.

For all of us, the issue lie too far ahead to be concerned right now. Yet in three days someone would be the lucky or un-lucky one to adopt two goats and head for home. I knew it wouldn't be at our house...ipso facto.

The current meandered along at a snail's pace from Chesire Bridge on down to Bellows Falls. As always our efforts had to ensure setting a steady pace. Ten miles had to be covered, so dawdling was out.

A few miles downstream off the port side we were slightly distracted by a re-creation of the old Fort #4 on the Charlestown shore. The original was built in 1745 and was the most northern British settlement on the Connecticut River. Strategically, it was an important outpost during the French and Indian Wars. Major Rogers and his Rangers managed a few daring runs from St. Francis, Quebec to this Fort. Why it never struck an interest with us I'll never know because we cruised right on by.

With Mr. Boulais being the sole adult leader, we naturally found ourselves isolated from him on most days since he obviously couldn't be at the front, middle, or rear of the pack. He put much faith in us. Looking back there were no doubt a few prayers tossed in there for our protection. Usually, two canoes "latched" on to each for companionship, bonding, and tomfoolery. As a group, our flotilla was pretty haphazard. Each pair of guys needed their freedom and space to canoe unimpeded and this was the unwritten rule that guaranteed a fun time for all. Despite apparent risks and the dangers of river canoeing on our own, it was far better than hanging onto Mr. Boulais' apron strings. We might have mutinied if our canoeing freedom was absent. It was necessary to experience the river and its environs on our own or we would have gone loco. In retrospect, I believe Mr. Boulais knew we all had it in us and to a degree I'm glad he left us on our own. It was the only way to discover if we were at least half mature. Inside we already knew we were half crazy. After all, we were 13 to 16 year olds and "Live Free or Die" was the New Hampshire motto directly off port side.

Were we lucky or not to have canoed with a single leader? Who knows? It's too late to speculate but it's darn for sure that the memories just never would have been the same. The BSA two person adult rule didn't have any teeth until 1985 so we could have attempted the trip for another 19 years under the same conditions. Go wonder.

We stopped for rest quite infrequently, perhaps once in the morning and likewise in the afternoon. This afternoon we were tiring around three o'clock when someone got a hankering for a break heading for New Hampshire. My biased perception and well kept notion of a clean, clear Connecticut River up here in these remote parts was shattered on this hiatus ashore. I had paddled for three days viewing the river as a fairly clean, unsullied and uncontaminated waterway yet not quite perfectly pristine. I regarded the White River stench as the lone eyesore on an otherwise clean river. The ripples of each wave gleaned with sparkling sunshine resonating vitality. It was evident I hadn't a high school chemistry course under my belt as my perception might have differed especially in water analysis. Steve and I eventually beached our canoe on the shore looking forward to a quick break. The grassy bank seemed unspoiled. The shore supported a small tract of sand blending with a bluish-black stone shoal under three or four inches of water. Being a true bowman, I hopped out preparing to tug the canoe inland a few feet while Steve exited the stern and poised himself also.

"AUGHH!!" I gasped, glancing down between my feet, which were soaking in four inches of river, shoulder width apart.

"What's the matter?!" Steve snapped back with a disturbed look, for I had half scared him out of his pants.

"AHH! A rat!!" I blared, cringing backwards, repulsed at the sight. The willies had already gone twice through me.

"Where?" Steve inquired, not half believing me. "Here!...Where else?!" I answered exasperated. And there he was. A six or seven inch Norway brownie. Stone cold dead. He was doing the back float, lodged neatly in a little slate crevice filled with water. His little nose perpendicular to the blue August sky. Similarly, both his front and hind legs pointed straight up into the air, like toothpicks in a stick of butter. He swayed to and fro gently rocking with each wave, as if he couldn't decide if he was coming or going. His six inch tail swayed with all the fluidity of a piece of over cooked spaghetti. He was dead but had done his job well and that was to frighten all the buttons off of me, boy.

Despite all this, I garnered sufficient courage to poke him in the side with a small dry stick. Why he was stiffer than stiff. Without taking my gaze off Mr. Rat, I heard Steve say, "I think he's dead."

"I think you're right," was my response, seconding his opinion, making our quorum of two valid.

Then we cracked up, releasing our tension with a good hearty laugh. Was this Stuart Little? or Little Stuart? I pondered the whereabouts of his family in this vast river, or on land for that matter. I felt a bit guilty because I had poked him in the side with a dry stick testing his mortality. My act reminded me of the Roman soldier who had pierced Our Lord in His side to see if He was dead also. I didn't share these thoughts with Steve but kept them confined within me not wanting to be ridiculed for them.

Our respite was brief. After exploring the shore for a few minutes we headed out again. Heading on down towards Bellows Falls, I began to think that the rat should not have been there. "What is a rat doing up here? Why this is the 'country'," I ruminated. Nice river. Beautiful meadows and no city around. My image of where rats should be was crumbling. To me, without question, rats stayed in cities, under filthy, squalid conditions.

I looked at the river long and hard as I paddled.

"This water just ain't the same," I conveyed to Steve, as I paddled on.

"Why?" Steve asked with a puzzled tone from behind.

"That rat's been in it!" I said with diluted disgust.

"There's probably more in here, too," Steve replied, continuing my education.

"Great," I deadpanned, "I'll keep a lookout." And on we paddled to Bellows Falls.

****

I didn't encounter another river rat for the rest of the trip although they loomed all right. If there's a creature come down off "the ark" that was adaptable it was the rat. Is there any city on the globe that has eradicated this guy? Nope. Control yes, but not removed. If the local DPW jackhammer is out of commission just get any mature rat and he'll gnaw through concrete for you. It's peaceful coexistence like it or not.

The wildlife along the river was edifying to see and certainly the order and serenity of groomed pastures soothed our restless spirits. Both shared a treasured comportment which assured a certain paradise for us floating by.

Yet under this panoramic, majestic view was a daunting dichotomy slowly unraveling. Despite the wonderful array of wildlife enveloping us along the way, there was one species on the back burner. The peregrine falcon. He was pretty hard to pick out simply because he wasn't around. Perhaps unknown to our much revered and respected farmer who no doubt had the best of intentions for maximum food production, was the enormous power-packed punch of his DDT pesticide program. It may have eliminated squadrons of nasty insects ready to devour food crops but the flip side was the utter disregard on this fast flier.

*Two Muscovy ducks share our space a long way from their
native Mexico.*

Once dubbed the "Duck Hawk" this falcon easily took out ducks in midair being clocked at 275 MPH on a nose dive. Yet despite it being regarded as one of the fastest fliers in the world, it could not escape quick enough when it came face to face with DDT. It was too late even when conservationists called a "pass interference", at least in the eastern United States. The pesticide used by farmers caused these falcons to produce eggs with shells too thin to ensure viability.

None of these aviators were in the skies east of the Mississippi River in 1966, the year of our canoe trip. In fact, I never saw one except in a textbook no doubt due to the effects of DDT. It took until 1999 to remove their name from the Federal Endangered Species list. The comeback has located about 200 pair of peregrine in Western Massachusetts. Even Springfield, MA has a high rise tower supporting a brave couple's nest.

****

"I knew we were tired but not that tired," I thought peering ahead, squinting my eyes for a more focused view.

Paddling along uneventfully I sensed my first mirage in all my born days. Our flotilla was situated just above South Charlestown, NH somewhere below the confluence of Commissary Brook flowing in from the west. Route 12 runs adjacent to the river, sandwiched by the Boston and Maine Railroad and the river itself.

Each time I squinted and refocused again onto Route 12, NH the same scenario returned. After three attempts to refocus my eyes, I gave up. It was the blue-gray Ford Window van of Mr. D's, the one with the shift on the column, sitting pretty by the guardrail. As our canoe moved closer, I made out Mr. and Mrs. DeGrandpre, and their daughter Ann. They began to wave.

"Hey," I quickly yelled out to Dennis Riel and Kevin Boulais. "It's Mr. D and his family over there!"

"Oh, sure," Dennis replied, doubtfully.

I looked again.

"It is!" I insisted with half a chuckle.

Momentarily everyone became alerted to all the commotion, placed a salute above their eyebrows to shield the sun and looked for Mr. D.

"It is, too!" shouted Jim, "that's the blue van!" Approaching closer, it appeared the whole family was now waving to us from the river bank.

"Well, I'll be," said Mr. Boulais, cracking a big smile. Once the group recognized the DeGrandpre's, they raced inland without delay screaming like nincompoops, for we couldn't arrive fast enough.

We beached our canoes on a very rough graveled bank a few feet from the guard rail. As if it wasn't enough just to discover someone from back home. Mrs. D had quite a surprise in store for us. Holding a brown A&P grocery bag in front of her, she reached down into it and pulled out two Wonderbread bags filled with peanut butter and grape jelly sandwiches. Oh, man alive! Did she know what we wanted or what? She knew. Fresh white bread with PB&J. Oh. Ohh! Real food. Someone on the trip had obviously said a prayer and this had to be the answer. We devoured. The sandwiches were gone before the bag was open...at least in our minds.

"Thank God," murmured Dennis Riel.

The connection with home was heartening to say the least. Gene had surmised correctly as his dad chuckled when someone asked him if he could keep the goats. "Sorry," was the reply and pretty much the end of the story. Mr. Boulais engaged in quite the chat with Mr. D. He had our daily itinerary and actually took an educated guess as to our where-abouts hitting it off just right.

Mr. DeGrandpre was one indispensable guy who over time wore every hat in Troop 40 except for scoutmaster and served the troop longer than anyone else in my memory. From 1963 on he was there. He carted more guys to campouts, klondike derbys, summer camps, cam-porees and paper drives than one really wants to calculate. He remained with the troop long after his two sons Ernie and Gene left scouting. He served on the troop committee for years with my Dad, always stopping by our house in his van to talk scouts with him. He became a Troop 40 Boy Scout Camp Trustee and was always up at camp maintaining something. And then one weekend a Boy Scout troop that came to rent out the camp found Mr. D "at rest" in the troop cabin. The place that he gladly spent so much time at and loved so much was the place he would leave this world from. He had epitomized the scout slogan, "Do A Good Turn Daily." That was Mr. D, always there when you needed him. Or didn't need him. But he was there. Mr. Troop 40 himself.

Our rendezvous lasted all of twenty to thirty minutes for we were "booking" it to Bellows Falls before night fall. Before long we said our reluctant good-byes and were paddling away. Steve and I looked back waving and yelling like everyone else as we savored the PB&J sand-wiches. How they lingered on our palates. I paddled along thinking about the transition back to Bolton Biscuits for the next few days. We appreciated home a lot more in our minds but could not admit it out-wardly.

"I'll bet he knew he was coming up here today last Saturday but he never said a thing," Steve commented, referring to Mr. D, who assisted us with our gear and shoving off in South Newbury.

"I guess," I responded weakly, still engrossed with the events of the last half hour.

The surprise was profound, catching us all off guard, and is forever with me.

The haul into Bellows Falls was near completion. Still water sits idle for about three miles above her dam causing us to labor a bit more on the pushdown with our paddles. We were closing in on the 55 gallon drum necklace warning us to back away early enough so the dam draw wouldn't pull us over the top.

Bellows Fall Dam (7/99 Photo)

This 643 foot concrete gravity dam stretches the Connecticut between Bellows Falls, VT and North Walpole, NH and contains the water necessary to produce electrical power. She creates a 2,804 acre pond. A timber dam was first constructed here in 1792 creating the United States first navigational canal. To make this power, river water is rerouted from the pond around the falls, through the canal and to the present power station. The water drops 62 feet, churning into motion three giant water wheels which bring to life the generators so some-

141

where someone can flip a switch to illuminate their kitchen.

The canal was rebuilt in 1926 and checks in at 100 feet wide, 29 feet deep, and 1540 feet long. It would be another 18 years before a fish ladder would operate here in 1984, an integral part of the Connecticut River Salmon Restoration Program.

Edging downstream a mile or so from the town, I quickly understood where my friend the rat may have migrated from. Bellows Falls exuded a sense of congestion and exhaustion. She seemed tired and droopy. Her buildings shouted out with an ache and a desire to collapse and tumble into the river. They did not.

It became overcast and cloudy, the sun evading us again. I felt it was playing a game with us as I failed to decipher her time of vanishing again.

We edged closer to the stark necklace of drums linked before the dam. She sent out her vivid warning that needed no further explanation, "KEEP OUT AND KEEP BACK." We heeded.

Our fleet glided effortlessly the final footage toward the New Hampshire shore where our portage commenced. The warm presence of a weathered, red brick building summoned us in to rest. It sat upon a grassy slope with a sandy apron running to the shore at the end of Pine Street, in North Walpole, NH.

Without doubt we were tired and after resting a spell Mr. Boulais grouped us in.

"This is a longer portage than Wilder," he informed us with that smile that always read, "...sure you can do it."

"How long?" someone barked out.

"I don't know exactly but it's longer," he repeated. He wasn't about to commit that error and reveal the portage length for he probably feared our moaning and groaning which he didn't need...believe me. Bellows Falls portage is one of the longest due to the canal and gorge combined.

Well, Egad! It's a mile and a half. And for the life of me I don't know how we did it. Well actually, I do. We did it slowly, that's how we did it.

And taking our sweet time this entourage moved eastward on Pine Street then hung a sharp right onto Church Street. What a scene. Jim and Gene loved it. With their goat tied up to the thwarts and sitting in the canoe going for a ride. As if the canoe wasn't heavy enough as it was. It was the usual grunting and groaning, lugging and tugging. Suddenly Jim and Gene stopped abruptly ahead of Steve and me. The goat hopped out.

"You are walking!" Jim commanded semi-irritated, pointing his index finger at his loving animal of God. The logic was simple: If I can walk then you can walk, especially if you've got four legs my little goat friend.

"Watch out!" Gene warned Jim, who had almost tripped over the rope tied to Kevin and Dennis' meandering goat.

We all moved out. The street was graced with ample shade bearing trees. Small houses, kept and unkempt ones, alternated down the street to our right. Uneven concrete sidewalks and black asphalt sections kept our eyes glued to the pavement. Bulging tree roots set their booby trap tentacles out to trip us up.

We took many a rest. Church Street intersects at the junction of Route 12 NH and the Bellows Falls bridge at Route 5. To our left Route 12 headed east then curved south. Off to our right was Main Street which spans the dam into Bellows Falls, VT. We bided our time for the traffic at the end of Main Street in North Walpole, NH not realizing that we were only at the half way point.

On we trudged as there was no easy way. Shoulder lug. Hip lug. Either way you transported your canoe, languishing bravely and then pooping right out. Hugging the shoulder on Route 12, our portage was shrinking with each step. Racing frantically to beat a possible shower or erupting thunderstorm, our eyes darted from roadway to sky, avoiding a trip beneath us and watching for rain above. There was scant room to walk with a galvanized guard rail to our right preventing us from spilling down the bluff. To our left cars zoomed by four or five feet away. Between rests we toiled and struggled gracefully.

The end was in sight. Up ahead, part of our group finally reached the hairpin turn cutting sharply to the right and descending an old asphalt road to the river bank. It seemed like an overused boat ramp; the crumbly asphalt blending gradually into the sandy bank. We lugged our canoes past the weathered road and into a small copse that offered some protection from the elements. It was predominantly filled with poplars but shared the scene with some black willows. Copious skunk cabbage overstated its dominance. The copse's seclusion was sufficient, sheltering us also from the busy traffic of Route 12, yet if rain developed we most likely would enjoy only a partial reprieve from it.

We plopped down and rested our weary selves. I felt like napping but we couldn't. Exhausted and spent the assigned crew prepared supper while I assisted in securing deadwood for the supper and breakfast cooking fires and the evening campfire, going in for the kill while it was dry.

Supper was no less than "Chicken a la 'Phoenix'"(?) bringing forth itself from the tomb of the plastic bag to life again in a pot of boiling water.

The rain never came while conditions remained cloudy and overcast. Dusk crept in.

After supper we moped about looking for something constructive to do and didn't find much at that. Across the river lie Bellows Falls tempting our curiosity and beckoning us inwardly. Our scoutmaster must have sensed that.

"How about scouting out the town?" Mr. Boulais offered us, as he had no doubt sensed our restlessness.

"Yeah, let's go!" responded most of the group, eager for something more tangible than canoeing and campsites.

A few of us ran and grabbed flashlights while the others determined to do without them, then headed for town as a group, retracing the steps of our long and arduous portage minus our cumbersome canoes.

****

The group scooted out and then settled for a slow amble up the Route 12 incline. We hugged the shoulder cautiously remaining wary of the swift oncoming cars. The Vilas Bridge Road greeted us at the top of the hill as we hung a left. The structure of this bridge issued an unsure feeling as the aged concrete prompted me to question its support base. The pale dim yellow lights seemed to garnish its image with uncertainty. This site marked the first ever bridge to span the Connecticut River in 1784. Thankfully this one wasn't the original.

We crossed over the Vilas Bridge into Bellows Falls instead of heading straight on Route 12 leading to the Route 5 bridge. The long summer days which allowed us ample canoeing time were now shortening. The July sun went to bed about 8:12 PM whereas the August sun in the third week was turning in at 7:51 PM. I felt that Autumn wanted to sneak in the back door early with the bridge lights on and the veil of dusk creeping in rapidly. Inwardly I became defiant and said "No!" as that dreaded word "school" was knocking on that same back door.

"Hey, this place doesn't smell," Joe announced to us, after conducting his olfactory experiment via his scientific nose.

"Yeah," some of us agreed, drawing a longer sniff up our own

144

snouts.

Joe was making the comparison to White River Junction which offered some choice fumes due to pollution and raw sewage in its waterways. Despite its worn down and tired appearance Bellows Falls offered you a breath of fresh air as they had their waste water treatment plant up and running in 1962, sixteen years before White River Junction's.

Rambling into Bellows Falls was marked with unsure feelings as this was the first town we had stopped to venture into and explore. None of us knew a soul.

We shuffled along in two groups staying close to each other for security in the event something troublesome might arise. The town seemed tired wherever we roamed. A laundromat and a bar seemed to be the only business open, one of which we didn't want, the other we couldn't get in anyway. Dusk was pushing her weight around even more so as additional dim yellow lights came on similar to those on the Vilas Bridge.

Curiosity lured us down another street in the business district only to discover closed shops and storefronts. Our moms would have been proud as we excelled at window shopping. It wouldn't have mattered anyhow as money was not to be found in my pocket. As darkness grew denser the yellow lights dimmed dimmer. It didn't take long to figure that our visit would be brief.

Enroute back to the Vilas Bridge townsfolk cast cold, unwelcome stares our way. No one approached us to engage in friendly conversation. Some teenagers afar off watched us like hawks yet said nothing. Perhaps we should have expected as much, being strangers. No one knew us and what was up our sleeves was hard to tell. Watching the townsfolk cautiously it was apparent they were doing just that...watching us cautiously. We seemed outcasts. Even outcasts had to belong to a group or town before being cast out. But we had never really belonged here. Were we ostracizing ourselves, blind to our image? Did we portray two tough gangs of which people would be leery? That wasn't our agenda but only we knew that. I left town and felt no real animosity toward these people but was struck with a keener awareness of what ignorance on both sides can do.

On the return, crossing the Vilas Bridge I sensed relief. A murky enigma settled within me as I walked away from this dimly lit town. I wasn't about to figure it out. Perhaps somewhere down life's road it would reveal itself to me.

145

Walking back down Route 12 in North Walpole to our sandy bivouac emboldened my love for home. To miss home is one thing but to compare it with an unfamiliar town where one is unknown and unwelcome, presents a teacher like no other.

The dew dampened us as the cool air made for some nice sized goose bumps on my arms. Cars whizzing by briefly shifted my thoughts back to town. Were some people following us, I imagined? Did they want to find out where we were located for the night? "No" seemed to suffice for an answer because the cars zoomed down the long highway failing to decelerate or stop, their lonesome red tail lights fading until gone.

My kooky imagination ceased as our group went zany. I was nearly the last one again to realize everyone bolting downhill along the guard rail with their hearts set on reaching camp first. I failed to hear the initial challenge lost in the commotion which most likely was a definite, "Last one there's a rotten egg!" Screaming, yelling, and running ensued. There were only a few flashlights with yet fewer street lights so you had to watch carefully in running along at top speed to prevent impalement on a curb or guard rail. We all arrived injury free as we hit the sandy bank entering our copse of trees called home.

With three or four guys insisting on building the evening campfire no doubt it was roaring in no time. Typically, everyone tossed in wood to fuel it and keep it blazing. Mr. Boulais had to warn a few of us to stop the onslaught of wood because there wouldn't be enough left for the breakfast cooking fire. He didn't want a bonfire either which might grant us an unwanted visit from the local fire department.

"Hey, isn't Bellows Falls the place where the 'witch of Wall St.' lived?" Joe quizzed the group, matter of factly.

No one seemed to know. I for one had never even heard of her, whoever she was, but Joe was right. He was referring to Hetty Green who was dubbed by that phrase. Apparently she was loaded with money and had lived in Bellows Falls until her death in 1916, fifty years prior to our arrival. This woman inherited quite the sum from dear old dad and managed to invest her finances cleverly. Rumor has it that she waited so long to seek out the cheapest medical care for her son Ned's leg that it had to be amputated. Ned supposedly got the $100 million that Hetty left in 1916 but I've reason to suspect he would have opted for his leg instead. Boy, too bad some of that $100 million couldn't go for sprucing up this town right now.

We huddled closer around the campfire as the camaraderie warmed

146

us as well. The only connection to back home was ourselves and our families. I sensed we basked in and cherished the memories of our homes and backyards without a peep from any of us. We overlooked any faults and defects among us in deference of more important matters such as arriving home safely in one piece.

A few lingering, hardy yellow flames fought valiantly, resisting the urge to transform into red-orange embers, knowing they would eventually succumb to ashes. Across the river some street lights flickered atop their lamp posts and stayed alive reproducing their effects upon the small rippling river waves, stretching their luminous fingers to our shore.

We were tired and exhausted but still sang "Day is Done" to the somber tune of "Taps", and then turned in.

****

The night's chill descended on us as the fire burned out. The shore line was a good hundred feet away allowing us to peer through the copse in the dark to see the small ripples on the water. The hissing was growing faint from the water sprinkled on the dying campfire and scalding rocks as we watched the rising smoke and steam slither through the trees in silence.

No one had erected any type of tarp, lean-to or protection from the elements. Rather than scatter ourselves about for sleeping arrangements we formed a simple line and bedded down adjacent to each other similar to railroad ties on a track. Whose idea it was I don't know but the formation was snug, shoulder to shoulder. With only the best of luck I got butted out and just plain ended up isolated on one end with Jim on my right and not a soul to my left.

The conversation was typical lunacy encompassing some talking, shouting, rude outbursts, scant listening, sporadic laughing, peppered with the usual pushing and poking, and elbowing the next guy. Pure bilge.

As I jostled about to obtain some degree of civilized comfort, the quiet grabbed my attention. It had come in quite swiftly signaling to me that the guys were dead tired. I squirmed again silently to locate the right spot for sleep, hoping not to disturb anyone. My task wasn't easy since our beds were a mix of sand and packed dirt. We were after all sleeping at a public boat ramp.

I gazed heavenward at a few intermittent twinkling stars that tried

147

to evade the clouds for some valuable show time. The poplar leaves jiggled left and right in the breeze far overhead. The street lights chucked their rays through the thin trees. I shifted back to the glimmering stars and became infatuated with them wondering if they would win out over the clouds.

Thinking got a hold of my mind.

"Was it yesterday that the river diverged and we paddled down Sugar River?" I wondered doubtfully.

It was. But it seemed like two weeks ago. "That tarzan swing. Was it today?" I thought incredulously. Gee, it seemed like four days ago!

"Get 'em! Get 'em!" screamed Dennis Riel way down the end of the row of sleeping bags.

He scared the heart and soul out of me with his shout.

"He was right up near my face!" he shouted again.

Minor pandemonium broke out down at the other end of the row as a few river rats stealthily were attempting to get into Dennis Riel's pack. Dennis and Jim ran down and got a canoe paddle each, but by the time they came back the rats had scurried away.

"We'll get those suckers if they ever come back!" Dennis proclaimed from his sleeping bag.

Dennis and Jim searched a bit in the underbrush, hoping to wallop a few river rats but they apparently hid well enough.

"Wait quietly and they'll be back," advised Sparky McGrath. I shuffled and tossed to find that comfortable position for the ninth time. Oh, what's this sand doing in my puss? I thought. Only for the love of the great outdoors. The rats waited and so did we. It grew quiet as the guys had dozed off.

Slumber then wrestled me down, put me in a chickenwing, and held me for two seconds or more, with sleep winning the match once again.

I must have slept for a while but it wasn't enough. I wished to have slept straight through to the morning because it was so difficult for me to fall back again. The silence made me uneasy and I didn't relish it. Glancing slowly to my right, Jim was asleep crumbled up in his sleeping bag. "Good heavens," I mused, "how he could sleep like that I'll never know." It drove me crazy. Did he have a vent pipe somewhere?

Peering further down the row of sleepers not a stir was evident. Two muffled snores were barely audible yet their cadence was exact with one kicking in right when the other one droned off. I couldn't decipher who emitted them.

I was the only one awake...or so I perceived. It had to be late since only a few lone cars buzzed by puncturing the silence for a brief interlude.

Then I heard it...whatever "it" was! Off to my left about fifteen or twenty feet away rustling commenced among some dead leaves and underbrush. What was it? The goats were tied up with the canoes by the shore so that eliminated them. "It" delayed as if to stalk me. Crawling and creeping its sound seemed louder in the dead night silence.

Roaming about my imagination did nothing to alleviate things and actually fueled the situation, escalating my notions. I hadn't even the slightest glimpse of the river rats by Dennis and Jim earlier that night but now I began to wonder.

"Isn't anyone up but me?" I hoped diligently. No luck there.

"Thanks guys," I reflected. "A scout is helpful."

What was "it"? I didn't want to look. Yes, I did, but was fearful of what lurked out there. I wouldn't budge in a calculated effort to prevent agitating this intruder to anger. I considered my flashlight. That's it! Sure...it was in my pack and out of reach.

"You stupid you," I admitted regrettably.

It shuffled and crept closer.

Then, oh! I simply had to conjure up remnants of that river rat that Steve and I came upon just today! No! Oh no! To bring up river rats at a time like this was both agonizing and emotional suicide. Not only did I picture that river rat doing the elementary dead float near the shore, but my mind foolishly jolted back to my Mom. Mom!? Yes. Dear old Mom would recount stories to us about the "huge" river rats in the East Providence River back in Rhode Island that were the size of large cats!

"Wonderful," I speculated further. These stories were indispensable to me now. "Please stay down at Dennis' pack," I wished.

I groped further and concluded this had to be "it". To me, Bellows Falls was a definite river rat town, certified in every way just by its presumable image. My mind refused to purchase any other product. Again! Yes again, it is slithering amongst the leaves, rustling them nicely and tormenting me. Someone arise and make this creature(?) monster... scat! A quick head turn found my comrades still dreaming as I asked forlornly, "Where are you guys when I need you?"

Deciding now in desperation to awaken someone, I paused and then backed off. Sabotaged by shame, the notion to awaken someone to rescue me would be too humiliating. The guys would simply laugh silly at me and my lack of courage, berating me asunder about my failure to execute the tenth part of the scout law, "A scout is brave."

I tried to quiet my mind. "Oh tremulous emotions quiet your-selves!" issued my command. Nothing doing.

And so I screamed. In my mind that is. "What is out there? Will it attack me?" AUGGH!! It crept closer and closer edging its way in towards my personal space. I jelled with fright. Nearer to my bag it trod on. Raccoon? Oppossum? Squirrel? No. My mind kept flashing in neon, "the river rat was out to get me." I gave up and decided to go inside. Inside? The sleeping bag that is.

Tucking my head inside the bag, I would wait for the inevitable. If it touched me I would kick him good and sound the alarm hoping the others would surely awake.

It was stifling inside the bag as I thought, "This is the real 'shake and bake'." How could Jim ever sleep like this?! "I'm outta here." I poked my head back outside and gave thanks for fresh air.

But the rustling. The crawling. The creeping. Nearer and nearer it came. Was it circling? I had nothing to throw at it. Here I was defend-ing against what? Some river rat? My fear more likely. The goats were still secured as I had suspected. The sounds drove me. Light snores, my heartbeat, slithering intruder, flapping poplar leaves, a distant auto coming and going. I despised this cacophony's nerve-wracking instru-ments.

"Help!" I screamed to myself...,"Help!" echoed in my skull. Retreating into the sleeping bag I awaited the inevitable.

I heard the sand moving outside my bag, and sensed "it" was quiv-ering also along with myself. Well, here goes, I thought.

Opening my eyes, I felt great relief and joy. It was morning. Joe was walking around the camp. Boy, was I glad to see him and sat upright quickly. Half the guys were still asleep. I checked out the dead leaves that carpeted the ground beneath the skunk cabbage while sitting up in my bag. Nothing there.

Phew! Thank God, I thought. The tied up goats confirmed my sus-picion that it wasn't them. "It" was gone, whatever "it" was. It felt odd that I took it for granted that this creature "river rat" would get me when it was my fear that had gotten a hold of me.

But God was good to me, as usual. So I unzipped my bag and wel-comed in day four.

17 "Living the Outdoor Code"

"Hey, what are ya looking for?" Sparky McGrath inquired half dazed, sitting upright in his sleeping bag.

"Uh...sure," I mumbled, looking slightly embarrassed, as I meticulously scoured the vicinity for traces of that imaginary river rat.

Before I made a complete fool of myself, I sauntered back toward the breakfast campfire, feigning my actions.

"Did anyone hear some creature in the brush last night?" I quizzed the guys, hoping someone might recount a similar tale. The dead silence response put me back on the spot.

"Well, I woke up and something like a river rat was crawling around over there in the bushes," I began to explain.

"Bigfoot!" blurted Dennis Riel while munching on his breakfast evoking much laughter from the group.

"You did a bad dream," Kevin Boulais inserted amidst the snickering.

Oh well, now I felt qualified as a certified bonehead. My hope was that the laughter would take the heat off me momentarily but my self-induced ridicule lingered more than I desired.

Gazing into my cup of dehydrated mixed fruit I noticed that prunes were in the vast majority of this tepid cocktail accompanied with some sparse bloated grapes. The ratio always seemed that way and presently my desire for this choice delicacy hovered around minus four on a scale of one to ten.

I felt compelled to continue my description of the elusive nocturnal critter but also regretted having opened my big trap in the first place as the guys made sport of my comments.

"Gentlemen, today we've got to find a spot for that conservation project because we've only got two and a half days left to do it," Mr. Boulais made clear to us.

A few grunts and groans peppered with huffs and moans rose up from the ranks but I for my part felt relief. I was saved by the bell. If Mr. Boulais hadn't changed the subject, sure as sugar I would be standing before the guys trying to weasel my way out of being a laughing stock for my tales. Surely I would have brought dishonor upon myself if I even remotely portrayed myself as being afraid of something unknown.

"Clean up so we can move out," ordered Ray Roberge in his straightforward manner.

Breaking camp and cleaning up went far quicker and smoother here than on ordinary campouts since the canoe trip was a novelty. Each day presented us with a new section of river along with the urge to explore and discover new adventure. This made cleanup go without a hitch. And so it did. Finally, the inspected camp area met Mr. Boulais' satisfaction which wasn't easily come by since he was mighty finicky about policing the area and ridding it of microscopic trash.

"Head out," he said in a soft spoken tone, as he gestured us toward the river. We were already loitering about our canoes awaiting his approval anyway. Steve and I shoved our canoe out onto the aqua turnpike as did the other guys eagerly embracing day four of paddling. Churning our paddles to midstream, the Bellows Falls Dam flanked our starboard side, falling water bubbling into foam at its base. It exuded the same anger the Hartland Rapids had when we escaped its reach and fury. We pivoted our canoe to the port side pointing her nose southerly. Looking back inland we caught sight of Jim and Gene in a tussel with the goats, trying to keep one on board while forcing the other to get in. They finally accomplished their mission, embarked on the river and furiously began a hot pursuit of the fleeing flotilla.

****

Mercury for today August 17, 1966 would only escalate to 76°F, ten degrees warmer than yesterday. The skies were still once over lightly with silver-gray clouds. The National Weather Bureau recorded a "trace" of rain which amounts to less than 0.1 of an inch. Where it was measured didn't matter because it never sprinkled on us. We lucked out again weather wise. Back upstream in South Newbury, our departure point, it poured almost a full inch of rain with side shows of thunder and lightning.

Seventy five miles of paddling and portaging trailed us, with another fifty eight just ahead. The question or doubt about quitting never presented itself to us. After all, we were young teenagers and nothing could stop us save death by drowning or a hot lightning bolt. At Sumner Falls, the Hartland Rapids episode embedded itself deeply into our craniums but it ceased to faze us anymore. Yet our spirits readied themselves for whatever came. That is faith, I suppose, and we had it. Others would

152

label it craziness if they were around at the time...but they weren't.

"Hey, what are ya taking next week at summer camp for merit badges?" Steve wondered inquisitively, startling me and popping me out of an early morning daydream. I was re-living last night's scene with that elusive, terrifying river rat I had conjured up. Whatever it was got the absolute best of me.

"Gee, Joe and I haf ta finish Lifesaving Merit Badge. We finished most of it when we passed Red Cross Junior Lifesaving in June at Trinity Pool," I informed Steve proudly.

"I got Camping Merit Badge all done except for that requirement about one week of summer camp. I'll get the badge just by going to Woronoak next week," I continued.

"Oh yeah," Steve replied. "The troop committee let us go on this trip even with that five day requirement undone because summer camp is the day after the canoe trip," he explained back to me what I already knew.

There were a few of us who benefited from this gesture provided that all other Camping Merit Badge requirements were completed.

"My paperwork is all done for Forestry Merit Badge so all I need to do is the field work. And I'm definitely going to try Rowing and Canoeing," I finalized with conviction.

"Yeah, I can't believe we still don't have the Canoeing Merit Badge," retorted Steve in amazement. "We should be experts by now," he chuckled.

"I'll be going for Canoeing also cuz if we don't know the stuff by then, we never will," Steve added.

"My Dad says that my brothers and I should try out for the Mile Swim Award," I chipped in, continuing to paddle. "I'd like to try it. I think the lifeguards make everyone swim laps around the waterfront dock," I described with some seriousness.

"That's gotta be hard," Steve offered doubtfully.

"The bad part is when you're halfway through and you look over to see someone trying to make you laugh," I revealed.

"Oh great!" Steve replied, "you could drown by laughing if you're over your head. That's real bad...to laugh as you're dying. I don't know if I'll try that," he mused lightly.

Within the hour overcast skies dissipated. The sun broke through and it felt good upon us.

On the horizon loomed the Route 123 bridge linking Walpole, NH and Westminister Station, VT. Historically, Westminister is the birthplace of "New Connecticut" which was later named Vermont, being declared a state on January 16, 1777.

The scenery then reverted back to the serenity and beauty of the upper Vermont and New Hampshire shores. Rural conditions, open meadows and tranquil farmland grew more vivid. We all initially had our eyes peeled for that conservation project site in order to fulfill the 50 Miler Afoot-Afloat Award. Yet as time rolled on we instinctively assumed that Mr. Boulais would actually decide where to stop so we more or less gave up looking.

The river banks gradually steepen along this stretch of water from the Route 123 bridge on down towards Putney, VT. The terrain adopts a more barren face supporting wrinkles and rifts of erosion especially up on the steeper banks. The bank swallows tend to increase in the region perhaps due to the increased accessibility of desolate banks in which to build nests. Or was it the cliff swallow we saw more of? Perhaps both as they compete for habitat and insects alike.

We had already passed the confluences of the Cold River in New Hampshire and the Saxton River of Vermont without much of a bother. Here the Connecticut becomes shallower on the New Hampshire side which naturally steered us over toward the Vermont shore seeking deeper waters.

No one had the desire to race around any islands today as we all kept to the starboard shores of both the Dunshee and Spencer Islands. We paddled lazily along still shy of Putney and a bit below Spencer Island when our group took out for lunch. Nearby was a red stone ledge with some scary looking dangling trees slouched down near the water's edge. Crooked, old, peeling grapevines wrapped themselves about the tree limbs seeming to burden it further by sapping the life from it. Bittersweet clung to the bark posing well as arteries and veins supplying the tree's life blood. Our location was in the vicinity of the Great Putney Meadows, a spectacular haven for birds.

At lunch, it was decided that our conservation project would most likely be erosion control or prevention since numerous banks were more pitched and erosion was in the early stages.

"Gentlemen, we've got to get the conservation requirement done today since time is running short," Mr. Boulais reminded us again.

"Ten hours have to be put into this project. The scout office will let each scout put an hour towards it and that should do it because there are ten scouts here," he spelled out for us.

We were quite relieved. Originally most of us had understood the requirement to mean "ten hours per scout." That formula of ten hours each would no doubt have set us back a bit. Two hours a day for five days would have taken ten hours of paddling from us. A day or two would definitely need to be added to compensate the difference in lost paddling time.

Lunch was a shorty. How'd you guess we had Bolton Biscuits? We put back in and kept the "canoe congregation" a bit more snug than usual. Joe and Ray suggested this tactic to avoid our drifting too far ahead out of earshot. The last thing we needed was half the guys too far ahead oblivious that the other half was upstream working on a conservation project.

Mr. Boulais, Joe and Ray were a few hundred feet ahead of Steve and me. Their canoe floundered about while the three pointed and gestured inland toward New Hampshire.

"This is it, bring it in!" Mr. Boulais turned and bellowed out to the rest of us. The site was just below Partridge Brook, NH and still above Putney. Despite Mr. Boulais' commands, Joe and Ray summoned us in, near and far.

The idea of a conservation project was a simple one. As scouts we had learned the Outdoor Code early on and were expected to adhere to it for life. You professed as a scout, I will:

- Be clean in my outdoor manners;
- Be careful with fire;
- Be conservation-minded;
- Be considerate in the outdoors.

So we were carrying out the third part of the Code. As a rule, whenever our troop or patrol went on a hike we were indoctrinated with taking out trash we found along the trail. That assured us a cleaner forest than when we went in. It's a great mind-set that everyone should acquire, not just scouts. In earning an award, National B.S.A. aims to impress upon scouts that canoe trips and 50 mile hikes were not solely for fun. There is a serious side and a responsibility on our part toward the environment we were enjoying.

And so without a doubt, we shifted our frame of reference to be "conservation-minded" like the code advises, to help stem the tide of rampant soil erosion on this steep New Hampshire embankment.

"Who ever has the hand saw, axe, and Army shovel better get them. We'll need them over here," Ray respectfully advised. We congregated at the slope's base and looked up to face an incline of about 50°-55° over a distance of about 40 feet. Both sides of the hill supported scant vegetation cleaving on its fringes, consisting mainly of weeds and a few bushes. The slope's center had three or four jagged gullies funneling into one main furrow with crevices about six inches deep exposing hundreds of loose stones. It was plain to surmise that each rainfall or thunderstorm was eroding valuable topsoil downhill on to the shore and eventually into the river. Sand, pebbles and gravel had a one way ticket also.

Yet there was "hope for this slope." It was necessary for us to erect a barricade about one third the distance up from the base. This barricade or "erosion wall" would delay the tumbling sand and soil flowing downhill. Over time, the soil and sand would accumulate and back up further and further. In the interim, between storms and heavy rains, weeds, grass, and small vegetation would germinate, take root and stave off further erosion. Yes, there was hope for this slope.

I was assigned to the search for long, dry solid timbers which needed to be about 3-4 inches in diameter and 10-12 feet long if possible. Kevin Boulais and Dennis Riel alternated their excavation skills by digging three holes about three feet deep and six feet apart, running across the hill adjacent to each with one hole on either end and the third one in the middle.

The timbers were not particularly difficult to locate since along the river bank an accumulated variety of debris, natural and unnatural lies strewn about. One just needs to be intent on finding them. Spring rains and a swollen river brings down winter kill and weak limbs that would have otherwise remained upstream. As the water line settles this wood is left ashore.

Joe and Ray supervised Kevin and Dennis with the digging. Steve and I assisted Jim, Gene, Sully and Ed with the wood hunt, dragging it back to the site. None of us were lackadaisical with our task as Mr. Boulais had assured us that we had to put in one hour to build this structure and if we slacked off we'd have to stay put until the job's completion. Obviously we ventured only as far as necessary in securing these poles since no one relished dragging them any further than need be.

Three sturdy limbs were selected, about 6-7 feet high, and each was sunk into one of the three holes leaving 3-4 feet exposed. Everyone tossed in the dirt and gravel, tamping it down, stabilizing them intact. With three firm supports now secure we placed the longer narrow timbers behind them. The shorter timbers that we gathered were positioned only behind two posts in a log cabin style wall, log upon log. It was necessary to lash some of these timbers to the upright posts to prevent collapse.

When the holding wall was complete everyone spread out to gather thinner sticks, grass, twigs, and large rocks. We dropped the rocks and let them tumble downhill settling into place where they may. The thin sticks and twigs were tossed in behind the wall also. We stamped and trampled these asunder lowering them to the slope's contour.

"It looks pretty good," Mr. Boulais analyzed, as he stepped back towards the river admiring the project.

He then tested it by throwing his weight against it in hopes of finding a weak spot. Nothing gave. He pushed in. Nothing gave.

"Well, all we need is a good rain to see our work put to use," he stated in an anticipatory tone. Instinctively we knew the unreality of awaiting a rainstorm. Simply put, quality control would have to wait.

"Moving out, gentlemen?" he continued with a question. We answered non-verbally scattering about towards our canoes.

"Keep the paddling at a steady pace," he commanded, as we shoved off again. "We can't dilly dally because we've got to make up the lost hour," our captain shouted out to his five ships as we eagerly slipped downstream.

Steve and I pressed the paddles down hard hoping not to become the trail canoe again, exhorting each other to speed it up. I gave up this hot pursuit again because I didn't want to work too hard and make this a drag. I wanted to enjoy the canoeing and not force it. As I slowed down I reflected on the mechanics of the bow stroke. This motion could be done in my sleep I thought.

Drifting away, I glanced back pensively as I grew protective of the wall we had just constructed.

"I hope no one wrecks it," I confided to Steve.

"They won't," he answered, as sure as ever.

"Do you think it'll stop the erosion?" I quizzed my confident sternman.

"Sure," he offered with ease. "Why not?" was his challenge to me.

"I think it will hold too. I just don't want some kids to knock it down," I remarked seriously.

"It'll be fine," Steve reassured me, "Don't worry."

As I resumed a more serious paddle stroke I contemplated the ferocious attacks of late summer thunderstorms upon "our wall." I so hoped the rushing, gurgling rain water descending towards our wall would be horrified that a new obstacle would challenge their potent eroding properties. Without doubt, I concluded, this raging torrent of rainwater would have to be intimidated and skirt past the rocks, timbers and sticks, leaving its mud, gravel and soil behind in our newly constructed "sieve." Our wall would be relentless in keeping at bay the "aqua siege" thrust upon it. Just like Cliff's cliff. I snapped out of it.

Abandoning now my unbridled imagination, I bid a final farewell to the wall and relinquished it to posterity. Coming around to a more positive outlook, I shared with Steve,

"Maybe someone will fix it if they find it broken."

"Maybe."

And we moved on down.

****

It became the usual again...paddling and talking, and talking and paddling. Time did not allow us the luxury of stopping at Putney, VT for exploration. Aside from Santa's Land and Basketville there isn't too much more here. My Mom talked about Basketville often but it wasn't until years later that I ventured into it with my wife, Eva. Not only was it a great store but it was like going on a field trip from a child's perspective. I hadn't realized the myriad of creations that encompassed "basketry". Eva had searched high and low for a large laundry basket to no avail. Putney didn't have it but the Sturbridge, MA Basketville outlet store offered one for sale. We picked it up and have it to this day.

The goats continued to hold everyone's fascination, slaking our thirst for humor. They seemed to enjoy each canoe ride down the river. Mischievousness was getting hold of them while they waited and watched us build our "conservation barricade."

Lying before us was the day's homestretch. Being mid to late afternoon, five or six miles awaited the passing of our canoes. Our location crept deeper into the southern most recesses of Vermont and New Hampshire. A distance of only about fifteen or sixteen miles south would thrust us into our home state of Massachusetts. From there on down, dual river banks would both lie in Massachusetts.

Presently, there is no bridge between Putney, VT and Westmoreland, NH but we were paddling right over the now submerged "Elephant Bridge" which was the last bridge that linked these two towns in 1820, according to the History of Putney. It was dubbed the "Elephant Bridge" because a reluctant elephant was forced to cross it at

158

the point of a pronged stick from its keeper. The traveling circus was almost to the New Hampshire side when the bridge collapsed. The terrified elephant screamed as he hung by its trunk on a bridge brace. It eventually fell and later died from a broken back. Its keeper was killed in the fall also. The submerged bridge slept soundly for 181 years until the mother-and-daughter team of Annette and Christine Spaulding and Royal Mounted Police Officer Patrick Madden discovered it while scuba diving on Nov. 4, 2001. The top of the structure was 20 feet below the surface in a river depth of 39 feet. It's too bad the circus folks didn't listen to that elephant, because they all may have lived a bit longer, I suppose.

About supper hour we terminated the days paddling in the vicinity of Catsbane Brook, which joins the Connecticut from the New Hampshire side. There is a public access ramp with a large grassy area located here. Twenty two miles had been covered again today and needless to say we were bushed. The soft grass presented a welcome change to the usual sandy river bank and underbrush. Ritually we took it upon ourselves to spend the night here. Much to our dismay, meteorologic conditions changed again with clouds invading the atmosphere right after supper.

With a few hours of daylight remaining, Mr. Boulais allowed us to frolic about. We were elated. Here the river is flat and quick yet lacking a substantial class II, III, or IV current. Grateful that the skies hadn't opened up with rain, we set out to explore the river and the opposite Vermont shore.

"Hey, look at Gene," Steve pointed out to me.

Mr. Boulais had let us try "the gladiator" with the canoes if we wanted to. Jim was watching from the shore since "gladiator" is a one man show. This was great fun and a true challenge that requires skill, balance and smarts.

To execute "the gladiator" correctly one paddles out onto the open water alone operating from the canoe's stern. Being a good distance from shore, the canoe is pivoted and faced inland. Putting your paddle on the floor, your next move is to shift from the kneeling position to a crouch; positioning both hands on the gunwales. From here you proceed to place one foot at a time on each rear gunwale attempting a precarious stand. Here you are truly lucky if you maintain your static balance and fail to topple into the water. Now the more advanced skill.

Here the competitor bends both knees and thrusts downward through the feet and into the gunwales. This is best described as an

159

Kevin Boulais beats Kevin Sullivan to shore in "gladiator."
(8/19/66)

exaggerated deep knee bend. The downward force on the rear gunwales lifts the canoe's bow upward, causing the canoe to gravitate and traverse forward. The idea is to generate a rhythm as strong and as fast as possible without losing your balance of course.

As to be expected, one falls off and into the "drink" quite often attempting to master this feat. We had dubbed it "the gladiator" at summer camp because the act usually took place with two canoes facing off with each other about 100 feet away. As each man moved his canoe towards the other, waves would be produced that were intended to knock the other "gladiator" from his canoe into the water. It was a great challenge besides the fun of toppling your opponent into the water.

Gene lost his balance and inevitably spilled into the river, providing ample entertainment for us all.

Steve and I started back to shore, hashing over the idea of one of us doing "gladiator". The notion was temporarily put on hold as we were distracted by some grotesque form of "marine" life.

"AUGHH," Steve moaned, sporting a contorted face while peering off the port side.

"What's that?" I queried, simultaneously asking and realizing what it was in the same breath.

"A dead fish...what else?!" Steve retorted, amazed that I didn't know.

"I couldn't see him that well," I replied, defending my ignorance.

Here we became acquainted with our first large dead fish. This guy was belly up and shone that pearly white belly to the heavens. All stretching aside, this fish had to be 18 inches long. I can say that as I am not a fisherman. We poked him with our paddles, our nudges moving him along like a little stiff log, maneuvering side to side.

"Turn him over," I said.

"You," Steve countered, without even raising his eyebrows. I rolled him top up with the paddle and then released him. He rolled back like a tumbler and bellied up again.

Joe and Ray paddled along side us to check things out.

"It looks like a big carp," said Ray, with Joe piping in his agreement.

Momentarily, a fisherman came by in a small houseboat, reducing his engine to a putter. He verified the species as a carp.

"This river is filled with carp around here," he said. "They thrive in polluted water but I think that one got a little too much!" expounded the man, laughing at his own joke. Before I glanced at Joe, he already had his eyes rolled towards the clouds.

The fisherman slowly chugged away upstream waving to us as he trolled a line in hope of a good catch.

Joe and Ray paddled off as Steve and I headed ashore toward camp with the sinking red, salmon sun behind us.

"Hey Gerry, you wanna try 'gladiator' now?" Steve asked, reverting to our original discussion.

"Not really," I answered, "after seeing that dead carp."

"Me either," Steve added, as we paddled in for the night, leaving *carpio genus* behind to drift downstream in the cool dark waters of the night.

18 Yucky Water & Vernon Dam

The disorientation of waking up in unfamiliar surroundings was absent on Friday the 18th. Once again, the nocturnal clouds the night before withheld what rain they contained, if any. Today's recorded rainfall was .00 inches with a high of 80°F and a low of 59°F, a.k.a. "a perfect day."

Dew usually found a way to annoy us as our ponchos and the fringes of our sleeping bags were saturated come morning. At this point in the week we were ready to barter our sleeping bags in exchange for our warm beds back home. Not one morning offered ample time to air out our bags as is the ordinary ritual on camp outs. On this number five morning I'll leave it to your imaginative skills to guess what our bags may have smelled like.

"I can't wait to sleep in a real bed," Gene murmured to himself as he rolled up his bag, brushing off dead grass and sand, knee walking as he went along.

"This dew makes the dead grass brush off easier," he continued sardonically while slapping his bag.

The public boat area was pretty dormant and quiet. A couple of squawking gulls pierced the solitude, one chasing the other perhaps over a morsel of stolen food. Moments later, a lone boater slowly emerged at about midstream with his throttle so low that its stalling out seemed imminent. He did not, but edged northward at his sleepy pace.

I do not recall the actual breakfast repast but without doubt it was either oatmeal, pancakes, or scrambled eggs.

"Hey, who wants some fried carp for breakfast?" asked Kevin Sullivan with a snickering smile, eventually laughing, knowing full well he had grossed us out.

"Sure," some of the guys responded like half-wits. Then my mind started to fade again.

"Just where is that dead carp by now?" I thought. He had to be way the heck downstream compliments of the river's all night drift. Gee, he could be staking it out at Vernon Dam waiting for us to begin our next portage.

I glanced out across the river's surface and bemused myself with doubts about the Connecticut's pristine appearance. It didn't seem quite deteriorated enough to kill a fish. But what about that dead river rat back there? Perhaps he died in a typical bar room brawl where the local rodents hang out.

"Hey, that's it," I realized, "it was an old carp and they gotta die sometime." How about that for rationalization?

Actually it was difficult to cull an exact cause of death for *carpio genus* from the miniscule menu of options available to me. My new found role as self-proclaimed "freshwater game fish medical examiner" didn't help matters a darned bit either.

Well, despite my limited surface vision it seemed hard to accept the inevitable sense that something lurked in that great looking river that was causing valuable fish to take a fatal swim down some one-way sewer. What was it?

Our efforts to be conservation-minded was indeed positive but still the river was dirty and a coordinated campaign to protect its wildlife and to clean up this sewer was desperately needed. The 1972 Clean Water Act was still six years away.

Gee, we just didn't particularly care at the time about what killed *carpio genus* on the Connecticut, but there was something quite serious transpiring in all major rivers back in the sixties.

That boater last night had poked a little humorous jab at us about excess pollution causing carpio to turn and belly up. Conditions had to be pretty bad as the carp is an Asian import well known for thriving in polluted waters.

The Federal Clean Water Act of 1972 finally put some teeth into a grave national scourge: our rivers and waterways were dying. However, the New England Interstate Water Pollution Control Commission (NEIWPCC) had been diligently working on its own long before 1972. Since 1949, the Commission sponsored 23 research projects and published 11 valuable reports on waste treatment and disposal.

The University of Rhode Island and Wesleyan University combined to produce 17 studies from 1950-1961 studying textile and industrial wastes. Cotton and wool production, synthetic fibers, dairy wastes, tannery wastes, pollution reduction by chemicals, copper, sewage and sludge, and extended aeration were all studied in the lab.

In October 1959, the N.E. Commission had a Classification and Standards of Quality for Interstate Waters in place. In the "dissolved oxygen category" Class A and B had a limit of "not less than 75 percent saturation." Class A is described as, "suitable for any water use." Class B is "suitable for bathing and recreation, irrigation and agriculture use, good fish habitat (carpio!?), acceptable for public water supply with filtration and disinfection." Class C is "suitable for recreational boating (that's us!), irrigation of crops not used for consumption without cooking; habitat for wildlife and common food, and game fish indigenous to the region." A Class C dissolved oxygen level could not be less than 5 ppm (parts per million). Class D was "suitable for transportation of sewage and industrial wastes without nuisance, for power, navigation and certain industrial uses."

In the coliform bacteria department (hold the nose), the standards were set by state and lacked a New England or regional criteria.

On September 14, 1966, three weeks after our canoe trip, the NEIWPCC revised water standards again.

The "dissolved oxygen" standards for Class A and B remained intact at "not less than 75 percent saturation". Class C waters were upgraded from "not less than 5 ppm" to "not less than 5 mg/l". Class D waters could not have less than 2 mg/l.

Coliform bacteria standards were now set by NE regional criteria rather than by state. Class A had a limit not in excess of 100 ml, Class B not over 1000 ml, and Class C and D having none in each that would impair the usages of their classes.

In 1966, a new pH category was added. Class A was 6.5-7.5, Class B was 6.5-8.0, Class C was 6.0-8.5, and Class D was 6.0-9.0. Water had to be free of sludge deposits, solid refuse, floating solids, oils and grease, scum, color and turbidity. Gee, who'd want it anyway?

It's noble to sit at meetings and set standards which no doubt has to be done, but quite nobler yet to enforce them. Alas the problem.

Little did I know that a 1963 Wesleyan University study of "white water" wastes from paper mills would introduce me to a second definition of the term. Sure, we had survived the white water of the Hartland Rapids but this "white water" is "water that has been separated in a paper mill from pulp or paper stock and carries short fibers, fillers and soluble materials."

This study confirmed for the second time that starch was a major BOD (Biological Oxygen Demand) source as a major pollutant as had been previously indicated studying cotton mill wastes. It solidified the evidence (no pun intended) that carbohydrates in general are the greatest BOD source in our nation's streams. They are emitted in the pulping, paper, cotton, canning, milk, laundry, starch, brewing, fermentation, sugar, candy, soda bottling, and other industries. That covers some ground. The Wesleyan Study recommended further study of the effects

164

of starch in these industries.

Three years after our trip, a 1969 study of the Connecticut River from the U.S.-Canadian border to the Comerford Dam showed that waste discharges from the Groveton Paper Co. on the Upper Ammonoosuc River, severely degraded the water quality of the river for many miles downstream.

Dissolved oxygen levels were drastically reduced at the confluence of the Upper Ammonoosuc River and the Connecticut River as well as downstream. A slight improvement in the oxygen content was recovered along the next 25 miles to the Moore Reservoir. Yet since the Moore and Comerford Reservoirs hold back water flow, water quality was greatly reduced. Oxygen deficiency existed at both reservoirs with sections of the Moore Reservoir lacking oxygen outright. Scant fish life and almost no game fish inhabited Moore Reservoir in 1956.

High hydrogen sulfide levels were also found at the mouth of the Upper Ammonoosuc River and downstream. Concentrations greater than 1.0 mg/l kill fish and other aquatic life. The pH values changed from alkaline to acidic at the Upper Ammonoosuc and downstream also.

The study concluded the obvious: that only pollution tolerant organisms, plankton and benthic, could survive in the waters affected by the Groveton and Georgia-Pacific Paper Mills, and exposed numerous violations of the Classification Order of the Upper Connecticut River in the counties of Caledonia, Essex, Orange and Windsor by the Vermont Water Board dated February 9, 1968.

This was a first in a series of published Water Quality Surveillance Reports. Well, you can imagine that if Groveton and Georgia-Pacific were doing that damage then other mills and industries along the 410 mile waterway performed pretty near identically. Water conditions were none other than "yuck" and a good guesstimate of how our genus carpio, that pollution resistant species, perished.

****

OK, OK, I hear you. Let's get out of this here "hydro-chemistry lab". I agree, as my Holyoke Community College Chem. 101 class required a repeat due to my superb efforts in achieving a "D". There just never was a passionate love for chemistry in my life the way it took hold for my brother Joe. B.S. Chemistry; '72 UMass. Special love affair with polymers also...or illness if you will. Wow. Majoring in that stuff?

165

But I did enjoy Botany and Zoology. Labored with pleasure in a 22 greenhouse business also. I do love the creatures important to Saint Francis of Assisi which encompasses all that descended Noah's plank to dry land.

Aside from the water pollution woes, there exists little rare creatures trying hard to survive amidst their fragile river habitats.

The Nature Conservancy and the U.S. Fish and Wildlife Service have identified the highest concentration of globally rare species in Vermont and New Hampshire occurring on the Connecticut River from White River Junction to South of Walpole. Nine sites serve as habitats for 28 rare species: Johnston Island, Burnaps Island, Evarts Station, Sumner Falls, Silverweed Seep, Chase Island, Hart Island, Hartland Ledges and Rivershore, Dunshee/Great Island and Walpole Island.

One of our stops was at the rocky outcrops of Sumner Falls on the New Hampshire side, the Hartland Rapids, for lunch after surviving our harrowing ride. The advice for this area is: "Please do not walk on the vegetation to avoid trampling in particular Jesup's milk-vetch." This is a legume with bluish-purple flowers blooming in late May or early June. Jesup grows in the bedrock crevices or at the high-water mark along the river bank. It's indigenous to only one sixteenth of a mile along the Connecticut River at this Hartland stretch.

Well, leave it to us to play the role of "greatest threat" which is people crushing rare plants as they walk on by innocently and ignorantly. That was us. Back in '66 we hadn't even heard of the milk-vetch but could very well have ruined a few. Sorry.

For most of these nine sites the advice is: "do not disturb the cobbles, collect plants, build fires (oh boy) and avoid walking in designated areas". Well, I'd say we built a few fires to say the least.

Cobble shores, including Sumner Falls, are home sweet home to the cobblestone tiger beetle. There are only six river sites worldwide that harbor this beetle. This species hadn't been discovered in the Connecticut River until 1977 by two entomologists. The Connecticut is the only Northeast home for this creature who measures only 0.5 inch long. The tiger beetle larvae must grow over 22 months and survive two winters before growing into adulthood. He lives at six island locations and we may very well have walked on him and his relatives in 1966. Sorry again, but the only endangered species we even heard of back then was the pink lady slipper.

We also hadn't a clue about Eurasian and exotic milfoil. These weeds cling to boat bottoms, motors and propellers and are transferred to other waterways principally by unsuspecting boaters. Those conditions didn't apply to us.

So, we reduced the magnitude of our guilt simply by means of our ignorance. Yes, I hear you, we should have done our homework more thoroughly. But we didn't did we? This was supposed to be a fun trip laced with a bit of seriousness, not a painstaking and meticulous National Geographic expedition. And thank heavens for that, for half of us probably would have stayed home.

After breakfast when our gear was packed and ready, by nature everyone gravitated towards the campfire. This occurs not solely to watch breakfast or supper being cooked but for belonging and bonding. The temperature was only 59°F at 8:00 AM and the dampness refused to budge. The fire took care of that. Yet day or night campfires attract because they offer so much. Fire is a respected element from God. As scouts we had learned to begin a campfire or cooking fire, contain it, and sustain it. Without any philosophical discussion, instinctively we were aware that the campfire was good for our mental and emotional health. We were all linked to the same fire, gathered around it, each of us drawing warmth from it, stepping back or drawing towards it, as each felt the need.

The campfire was the center of sharing among us. Jokes, anecdotes, songs, skits, fears, expectations, hopes and dreams, frustrations...all emerged at the campfire. Everyone had the chance to speak and be heard at a campfire. I loved the listening too. There was much to learn from our scout buddies. I don't remember a fight or quarrel around the campfire. The beauty, comfort, and peacefulness of a campfire calmed those who hovered around it. The campfire replaced the living room or kitchen table back home where families would talk and discuss. The campfire atmosphere helped one to vent feelings that otherwise might be suppressed at home also.

There is nothing quite like a good campfire being shared by good people on a starlit night. Try it sometime if you haven't already. Be focused on offering good talk and listening intently, for the campfire is based mainly on the goodwill and sincerity of those gathered about her.

****

Before long we were manhandling our canoes and dipping the bows back in the river. The fog eventually burned off the water's surface and from the atmosphere, consumed by the morning sun. The 59°F would not last as the mercury escalated at the Vernon Weather Station in Windham County to a beautiful 80°F. Clear, sunny skies shared the day with that 80 degrees.

And the river took us down.

Conditions were pretty near perfect for canoeing. The sun had done its job on us earlier in the week. Most of us were tanning after our initial sunburn. Sunscreen? In '66? Never heard of it. The bake on us didn't seem too bad.

The landscape on both shores continued to permeate my senses with picturesque beauty. It mattered little to me that any town or village along the 133 miles could have easily qualified as Podunk, U.S.A. That's what helped maintain the serenity of the area anyhow. It was difficult for me to surmise how that dead river rat and last night's "carp carrion" became involved with such a captivating river. Obviously, my naivete was shining through. Oh, I had heard of pollution in seventh grade science class as well as in the Boy Scouts but my mind had placed it in or near the big city. And the rural, beautiful countryside devoid of it. I knew so much!

Not being a biochemist, environmentalist, or water quality control specialist definitely helped to preserve the fun of the trip.

This is the point Dr. Joseph Davidson made in 1959 while collecting water samples from the northernmost point on the Connecticut River and at intermittent spots along the 410 mile waterway and in southern Connecticut. The river was more polluted downstream whether one observed it or not. I, like the general public saw only the surface water and scenery but failed to think about the actual chemical content of the water. Despite the Federal Clean Water Act on the horizon there was a colossal undertaking to be tackled in restoring this waterway.

****

Mr. Boulais had discussed our final portage at breakfast. The Vernon Dam was approximately ten miles downstream and it would be awaiting us around lunch time, our projected arrival time. I hadn't heard or rather maybe hadn't listened well enough about the portage at breakfast. Surprising?

An hour or so of paddling had gone by when the scuttlebutt going canoe to canoe had reached us. The next portage was to be a short one. Most of the guys had concrete doubts from the start given the torturous trek at Bellows Falls.

"I'll believe it when I walk it!" I convinced myself, out of sheer experience.

We trudged on.

I was beginning to think that this was more water than I'd ever seen in my entire thirteen years. Our senses were literally drowning from the ubiquitous fluid hemming us in from everywhere. My mind darted again as I dug up an age old issue and tossed it at Steve. It was the "water cycle".

"Hey, did ya ever think that this water in the river is the same water that was around with Noah and the flood?" I asked Steve calmly.

"What!?" Steve exploded, unaware of my thoughts.

"You know," I conjectured in sequences, "this river goes to the ocean, then the ocean evaporates. The evaporated water goes up into the clouds. Then the winds move the clouds up north and it rains again. So the rainwater falls into the river and here it is."

"I know," Steve affirmed in a deadpan. "But I don't think scientists really know how much of the original water has hung around," he continued, qualifying his opinions.

"I think most of it has to be here," I remarked, trying to convince him.

"Whadaya thinking of that for?" Steve wondered aloud.

"I don't know?...just thinking about all this water and where it goes I guess," I offered in explanation.

"Well, some day we'll have to ask God," he finalized,"he'll know."

Towards late morning Joe and Ray scooted by us laughing about something.

"Hey, it's not too far ahead," Joe barked out his report, in reference to the Vernon Dam.

"Mr. Boulais says we're only a few miles away," Ray piped in, as the two kept on at their steady clip.

As Joe and Ray buzzed by I began to wonder if Steve and I had been lollygagging again. Perhaps chewing too much fat again.

****

The Route 119 bridge loomed on the horizon, linking to Route 9 in Brattleboro, VT. Our contingent was now descending upon Brattleboro but did not stop in an effort to reach Vernon by lunch time.

How little did we know once again and much less appreciate that the world renowned English author Rudyard Kipling had immigrated to Brattleboro and made his home there. Dummerston to be exact. Here Kipling built "Naumkeg" his beautiful home with a majestic eastern view to Mt. Monadnock from his window. Rudyard was so captivated by this river valley that it inspired him to pen *Captains Courageous*, *The Jungle Book*, and *The Naulahka* all while a resident here.

Unfortunately, family difficulties forced him to return to England where he lived until his death in 1936. Having won the Nobel Prize for Literature in 1907, Kipling was added to the list of numerous artists, authors, sculptors, and statesmen who truly loved and appreciated the magnificence of the Connecticut River Valley.

I paddled on ignorant of this bit of trivia only to have my appreciation of it awakened in later days.

****

Jim and Gene were now adjacent to our canoe, some twenty five yards off and were paddling hard. As sternman, Gene had the better view of the goats since they sat at mid-canoe. The goats for their part just sat pretty every day, took in the surroundings, and enjoyed the ride, with an occasional bleat.

"They must have to paddle a little harder with those goats," Steve quipped, alluding to Jim and Gene.

"I guess," came my unenthusiastic response. It was a true "African Queen" remake with Jim and Gene supplanting Captain Charlie Allnutt (Humphrey Bogart) laboring day after day to transport Rose Sayer (Katherine Hepburn) down an African river to the sea. Our two goats obviously took Rose's seat onboard.

Bye and bye, the last hurdle presented itself on our 133 mile journey. Identical in warning systems to Wilder and Bellows Falls the Vernon Dam's log boom bobbed on the horizon. We would take out off the starboard side as the portage trail meandered the Vermont shore. The meadows just above the dam lie peacefully serene devoid of any hint of further development. Little could we foresee that in 1968 construction would commence here.

The Nuclear Power Corporation, Vermont Yankee would be completed and opened by 1972 kicking its nuclear reactors and cooling towers into nonstop operation. River use and landscape would transform quickly here in only a few short years after our departure.

Vermont side of the Vernon Dam. (7/99 Photo)

Moving on down, we tempered our strokes with Steve pulling a quarter sweep while I employed a diagonal draw. Our craft progressively pivoted, pointing its bow toward the Vermont bank, as we paddled in towards the beckoning shoreline. Most of the group had beached their canoes ahead of us, as Steve and I kept up our consistent pattern. The sun beat down on us from directly overhead as we listened to portage instructions for the third and final time.

"This is a short one," Mr. Boulais reiterated. "We'll go up around the brick building, along the guardrail about fifty yards and then back down the portage trail," he continued speaking as if he had been there before.

You could hear the mumbling and grumbling abuzz in the ranks before the poor man was done speaking. His pitch wasn't cogent enough for most of us.

We started out.

"It better be a short one," was the mantra we chanted shambling along the trail, hoping to avoid a disastrous trip of the feet.

It was.

To our delight this portage seemed to be shorter than the Wilder Dam hike which was about a half mile long. Perhaps we were becoming more adept at portaging? After all, this was our third portage in five days with the same canoe, weighted gear, and staggering partner. We should have had the kinks ironed out by portage number three. Heavens! Much to my dismay, nowadays one can just dial a phone number and reserve a vehicle-assisted portage in advance for their canoe trip. The word for that: WIMPS.

Bellows Falls was a killer portage...one and a half miles. Moses in the desert for forty years was slightly longer, I'll have to admit. Here at Vernon, upon ascending the incline to the guardrail, a direct view is afforded down the trail's balance to the put in spot. An obscured view to the river's edge is absent due to a lack of pines and deciduous hardwoods. A sandy and grassy slope offered us a clear calculation of just how far we needed to descend. With our exact put in point a few hundred feet visibly below us the portage seemed a mere jaunt.

We rambled the descent with more adroitness than at Wilder and Bellows Falls. We were getting a bit cocky, pure and simple. It was quiet below the 1909 dam. Presently, there was no water release to foment the Connecticut's calm waters. Our put in spot was a couple hundred yards south of the dam pretty much clearing us of any imminent danger of water release turbulence.

At the put in spot, Mr. Boulais approached the group with his trademark Chesire cat grin, seeking immediate feedback.

"Whadja think?" he threw at us. "Better than Bellows Falls?" he persisted.

"Definitely," a few of us affirmed. "Definitely." The distance: a quarter mile. Alleluia.

19 The Good Man

Ten miles had been covered that morning inclusive of the Vernon Dam. As usual, Joe, Ray and Mr. Boulais were conferring again. The trio decided that our group would log in a few more arduous miles before lunch break. We put back in no sooner than we arrived...or so it seemed. We didn't seem to mind. It became the instinct, the ability to push oneself harder. It always appeared excessively tedious paddling when the finish line was so obscure...so remote...so distant.

The river, the water, the monotony...mesmerized us. Dipping a paddle down under and pulling it behind you likened itself to pulling on your pants. None of us thought much about it anymore especially on the flat open water.

To break up some of the drudgery we devised a simple challenge. The bowman would take his paddle and upon dipping it into the water for the traditional bow stroke would thrust it right down under water, release it and wait. The paddle would disappear on this aquatic descent and the idea was to grab hold of the paddle as it shot back up straight out of the water.

Since the paddle was naturally buoyant it would often eject airborne like a geyser. The trouble was you never knew what angle it would emerge at, often finding its way up at 45° angles. Sometimes it would be completely out of reach and the sternman would have to extend his reach in order to retrieve it. Other times it remained submerged a bit too long and with the canoe gliding on course even the sternman was out of reach of the recurring paddle.

The practice became no fun when both paddlers missed the aberrant paddle causing the sternman to back paddle the canoe in retrieval of it.

The ritual evolved into quite the challenge to one's timing and eye-hand coordination. With repetitive attempts, one became adept at employing the precise force in order to coincide with hand plucking the paddle at the exact moment of its launch from the depths. A jolting thud alarmed us into thinking about the dire consequences of a direct hit to the canoe's bottom. Luckily, and I mean luckily, the paddle's grip did not puncture the canoe's bottom on its ascent, for a puncture would almost certainly have terminated the trip for the occupants.

Approximately one half mile or so below the dam, the "great bow" appears in the river. The bow abruptly juts eastward, then shoots back up northward, sidestepping east again until progressing south again. Right smack in the middle of the river is Stebbins Island. This site was strategically important for the Waumponoag tribal Chief King Philip and his Indian cohorts during the French and Indian Wars. When I was a youngster, a few summers found our family visiting Historic Old Deerfield Village following a jaunt up Mount Sugarloaf in neighboring Sunderland, MA.

Slowly chugging down "The Street" at Old Deerfield one is literally thrust into a time warp within this seventeenth century village. We could hardly wait to see the Indian House door split open with a still intact tomahawk, standing erect in Memorial Hall. This event came to life at the Deerfield Massacre of 1704. The infamous Bloody Brook Massacre in 1676 occurred here also.

The "great bow" served as King Philip's secluded headquarters. Numerous assaults on the Connecticut River Valley settlements of Deerfield in 1675 and the burning of Springfield in the same year were spawned here.

I'm glad Philip's ancestors weren't lingering in the "bows" vicinity that August day. Or were they? No doubt they would have provided one heck of an "Indian War Relay", in a frantic hot pursuit of our canoes.

****

We pressed on.

The Massachusetts line is fixed six miles south of Vernon Dam waiting to be pierced by our five aluminum bows. In a mile or so our lunch stop by Upper Island would be our final interlude on either the Vermont or New Hampshire shores. The backdrop was shrinking. Taller mountains subtly faded as their foothills sprawled into wider, calm meadows. The Green and White Mountains were forced to watch our backs after viewing our flanks for five days. Massachusetts and Connecticut lie ahead with their abundance of municipalities and industries. Now "the Nation's best landscaped sewer" as it was once dubbed would more aptly live up to that name amidst the murkier waters of Southern New England.

Calculations were never made pertaining to the exact number of strokes each of us paddled per mile on this here "little trip". Whatever

174

that digit was could have been multiplied by 133 to derive our product for the trip's duration.

"Hey, how many times do you think we paddled a stroke?" Steve asked me with chuckle, obviously in reference to the question's inanity.

"Hey, come on...who's gonna add that up?" I volleyed back at Steve, flubbing my chance at a guesstimate.

"It's easily got to be in the thousands," Steve projected confidently.

"For sure," I agreed, "but it's kinda late now to count, don'tcha think?"

"I know," said Steve toning acquiescence. "Just wondering."

****

Our canoes gravitated towards the New Hampshire shore. The imperceptible turbulence of the Ashuelot River was so slight that we nearly missed it. Despite this condition her pollution was profound adding considerably to the sluggish and deteriorating Connecticut. We beached our canoes and reclined for lunch. Somehow we managed to continue partaking of the Bolton biscuits. We hadn't ditched them by now simply because there was nothing left to eat in their absence.

"Too bad we haven't got those peanut butter and jelly sandwiches now," Gene reminded us.

"You think they would have lasted til now?" Sparky McGrath replied with amazement.

Gene glanced up with a droll, obviously knowing full well that they never would have escaped consumption to this point.

Most of us just plain relaxed for a while basking in the sun. At lunch we learned that we were a bit ahead of schedule and that time would allow for some swimming. And so we did. For the next half hour or so we dove in and swam about. The water isn't very deep here which provided for a safer swim. That we were in fact swimming in a murkier river due to the Ashuelot didn't faze us simply because we didn't even know at the time. It looked clean and didn't smell too bad to a bunch of teenagers, so what of it.

"You know, we've canoed over 100 miles so far," Mr. Boulais announced, so all could hear. No response.

"Actually, we hit about 100 miles right around the campsite last night, but I forgot to let everyone know," he continued, hoping to ignite conversation.

There was little clamor if any on having traversed 100 miles plus of paddling. We were perhaps so dogged tired that we could care less at this point. Another mile is another mile. Are there odometers for canoes? Who knows? Don't tell me.

Prior to our post lunch launch, Gene noted the lack of actual fishing that we had failed to do in our spare time. I think he just realized that the time just spent on swimming could have been used for fishing. Good heavens, I thought, what spare time? This trip was a ten hour plus operation a day. Upon beaching for the evening, cooking supper, and securing dry wood for cooking and campfires, scant time was available for fishing. We had chosen to explore the vicinity or horse around after supper before turning in.

I had gradually lost my desire to fish anyway. As a youngster Joe, Jim and I had yanked bounteous harvests of bullhead and pumpkin seed fish from nearby Long Pond in Indian Orchard. We managed to eat some of the big ones after frying them in margarine on Mom's stove...a project of ours that she virtually despised. She was particularly adverse to fish and even stuck her nose up to open cans of tuna fish. My pursuit of trout is woefully dismal. Of all the annual treks to Lake Lorraine in Indian Orchard with my brothers on Opening Day each April, I only took home one trophy! (trout). Before giving up one morning in April 1965, my resolve convinced me to cast out my six pound line one last time. Wow! It worked! My red and white bobber plunged beneath the surface and I reeled in a 12 inch rainbow trout. You talk about proud. Sure I brought it home and ate it. Besides I had to prove I caught it because with my track record no one would have believed any story coming from my lips. My fishing pole retired after that incident because I simply lost the "fire in my belly" to fish thereafter. Besides, it seemed an excellent point of departure "quitting while I was ahead."

"Any fishing has to be done tonight," our Scoutmaster informed us, as he helped shove off his canoe. "There's no time left now."

And on we slithered.

****

The canoes inched their way out and about like an octopus slowly projecting its tentacles. In a day the trip would cease. Ours was a pretty affable group, no doubt, but regardless we paddled on errant as ever.

Agreeable weather kept us company. From Upper Island on down to the railroad bridge numerous gravel bars threatened our canoe bottoms as a natural paint remover.

This was a challenging obstacle course and once or twice each canoe ran aground. We took turns laughing at each other as we hopped out into ankle deep water to push our way off of a sand or gravel bar, freeing us for deeper water.

The Boston and Maine Railroad Bridge loomed ahead as we finally focused upon her. Instinctively, this iron hulk reminded me of the railroad trestle bridge back home which spanned the Chicopee River just off Indian Leap Street. As kids we would walk from Indian Orchard to Ludlow via this trestle. Occasionally, the train's whistle would ripple a shudder down our spines as we sauntered along. This thirty second goal was to figure out if you had ample time and speed to get across the bridge and...well, live. Once we had to stop and cling to the outer iron trusses as the train edged by. What Mom never saw.

As we floated beneath the Boston and Maine it seemed a duplicate of the one back home causing me to think that perhaps it was built by the same company.

The river lulled us again. Steve and I ruminated briefly about who might possibly show up the next day in the parents department in order to cart us all back home from Turner's Falls. It was purely speculative but one certainty agreed upon was that if anyone showed Cliff Dumas was a shoo in because he had the round-trip task of lugging the canoes back to Camp Woronoak on that airborne trailer of his.

"These canoes have to be back to Woronoak by Sunday," said Steve assuredly.

"Well, what are they using this week for canoes?" I wondered, cognizant that we had five camp canoes.

"Whatever's left, I guess," countered Steve, without a care.

"Gee," I thought that was pretty good that Camp Woronoak let us borrow five canoes for our trip, but no doubt some campers were probably lingering all week just in hopes of getting a canoe. Hopefully our troop wasn't getting a bad rap back at camp on account of a canoe shortage. I never thought about it again.

Amidst our daydreaming, absorption of the fields and unspoiled scenery, enjoyment of the delightful bird twitterings along the river banks, and our general air-headedness we slipped unobtrusively over the state line into Massachusetts. Quietly and uneventful Vermont and New Hampshire watched us slip away as a mother bids her son off to war incapable of ascertaining his long-awaited return.

The peaceful, flat and slow moving waters upon entering Northfield, MA truly mask the fury of a bygone destructive river. Following years of wooden bridges succumbing to the elements of nature, the Northfield Bridge linking this town with Boston was rebuilt as a steel structure in 1901. Yet as a river flows it has not the time nor cares to decipher whether the obstacles or structures in its path consist of wood, stone or steel. And so it did flow as the steel bridge tried in vain to hold back water so high that ice chunks could not pass under its lower chord. And with no pun intended, come hell or high water the steel bridge collapsed after a fitful duel with the spring ice floes, stone piers included.

University of Massachusetts biology professor Ed Klekowski and his team of graduate students researching the river's bottom by scuba diving discovered this wreckage in 1996. Ed's crew discovered the sleeping remnants beginning at twenty feet below the surface lying severed into three segments with its twisted and mangled beams, girders and trusses strewn about. The stone pier blocks lie dormant savagely tossed downstream a bit. Otherwise, curious fish swim in and out of this artificial reef finning their way to obscure aquatic destinations unimpeded.

The afternoon served a beautiful buffet weather-wise. Here the river retains its serpentine character, ambling in and out through the lush green fields and meadows. The serenity possessed a celestial aura that prompted this teenager to think and ask himself, "Can't we stay here to live?" I knew we couldn't and somehow felt cheated.

Rushing to beat the clock wasn't necessary as we were apparently right on time almost paddling in slow motion. But the clock ticked right along as our shadow, and dueled us as if in a long-distance run. The sun was dipping lower than we wanted it to on the western horizon. "What's this?" I thought peering up ahead to see our other canoes banking it on the eastern shore. "Suppertime, already?" I mulled. The afternoon was ditching out on us. The evening seemed to show up too brusquely and was about as welcome as some uninvited distant in-laws at your favorite barbecue. Well, we couldn't do much knowing that no one has held back time as we knew it.

The take out point for our final nocturnal bivouac was along a particularly rich, emerald green meadow happily married to an abrupt, clean sandy shore in Northfield, MA. The exact location was somewhere south of Pauchaug Brook.

The meadow's grass rolled neatly eastward a few hundred feet and

178

humbly met a great thick wall of towering pine trees. Tucked snugly into the far northeast corner of the meadow was a small shack, the color of avocado pulp with a white trim, and reminded me of a lonely house on a Monopoly board.

In our search for firewood, we spread out slowly in our gun-shy attitude. Could you blame us for being a bit leery following our episode at Sugar River? We just didn't know who lived in that little shack, and friend or foe only time would tell. We were on the defensive and ready for another raving maniac like the one plodding through his corn field along Sugar River ordering us to scat.

The door of the small abode swung open swiftly and onto the floor of the tiny porch stepped a man who seemed in his fifties or early sixties. We all froze as he looked us over in a millisecond. With one hand he sent us a hardy wave while the other held a smoking tobacco pipe from which he puffed. Then came that shedding smile. Shedding smile? Yes, shedding because with it we all shed our fears, doubts, and worries about this guy. Those two hands and smile spoke more wisdom, love and goodwill than any published volume of psychology text the world over.

We gravitated to him in peace. He seemed happy to see us and told us he loved to fish. A gregarious soul was he.

"You want to camp here? Go right ahead," he said answering his own question before we could, obviously reading our minds.

A sense of security and belonging befell us. Thank God this wasn't Sugar River revisited.

I don't recall his name but it doesn't matter. Mr. Boulais chewed the fat with him while the rest of us collected wood and prepared supper.

****

In the wake of our evening repast, the daylight hours rapidly converted into minutes remaining. Over the last six days the sun was setting a minute or two earlier each night. Tonight, Thursday, the sun would retire somewhere after 7:30 PM. Instinctively, we knew it was becoming darker earlier so we scrambled to pass those "minimal moments meaningfully!"

I had chosen to explore the vicinity, searching for anything new that came my way which included a one of a kind night time fishing party.

Jim, Gene, Kevin and Dennis were off meeting the challenge of fishing without proper gear. The raiment of darkness was dropping quickly but how they persisted. Someone had a safety pin and another found some string lying about which I believe was enough. Their woes could be heard off in the distance... ##Q!!@$!#@! ... No bait. Coaxing fish to bite without bait? Yup, you bet. Not to mention that shad, trout, and salmon had departed or died off years before. Their flashlight beams stabbed the murky knee deep water with rays of hope aching to spot some fish. Oh brother. Anyone watching this production sensed that this endeavor would unravel soon because the only species that was biting was the mosquito. Fine cussing erupted intermittently as their ears and napes of their necks were bitten unmercifully by those small flying hummers. That did it...fishing was over. Putting up with fish that won't bite is one thing but combined with annoying mosquitoes was enough. And why they never asked the man in the shack for some bait I'll never know. But the fishing was done.

All of us gradually migrated back from wherever we had frolicked, to a small crackling campfire as naturally as bees returning to a hive.

The lonely shack tucked snugly in the northeast corner of the meadow emanated a glow of pale green as the front porch light bulb illumined its gold array into the twilight.

The evening was beautiful and would be our first and only one where Massachusetts sandwiched the river. Directly across from us on the western bank lie the town of Bernardston. Only moments ago the sun readied itself for slumber, pulling its salmon and burnt orange quilt over the days end. In its place emerged a navy blue blanket studded with twinkling stars that danced gracefully in the boundless heavens.

This spectacular celestial backdrop dispelled any ambitious rain clouds with any notion of dampening our final evening of the trip.

The heavens in these parts devoid of city lights put my senses in overdrive. Gazing upward, one can find a whole lesson in theology. This stupendous display of heavens cried out and thundered in silence, "I AM." God was using this whole vast array of heavens as an edict of His creative power. This thought is carried with me throughout life. At times, I wonder about the thought processes of those who gaze heavenward and cannot find Him. Perhaps it's best to let Him do the work as He reveals Himself to us.

Did I say "nocturnal activities" back there? Sure did. Well, everyone alive has "nocturnal activities" and for us no less. Big time plans this evening were attempts to fish, fleeting explorations, a communal campfire, and sleep. Wow!

A novel situation on Saturday past inevitably began to adopt a

180

mundane character tonight.

In less than twenty four hours our canoe trip would grind to a halt not for lack of steam on our part but for time. I briefly juggled the notion of canoeing beyond the Turner's Falls Dam but realistically our calendar was satiated. Our troop was scheduled to show up at the Horace A. Moses Scout Reservation in Russell, MA for a week of summer camp. The check-in time was 1:00 PM sharp on Sunday. This was the time that individual physicals commenced for each camper and if you were late it was too bad and get to the back of the line if you could ever find it.

To venture on in a canoe simply meant your absence from summer camp, and that idea was out. A week of summer camp offered too much fun and adventure to miss out on. Besides, merit badges had to be earned there that normally couldn't be earned elsewhere.

Ritually, we sat and stared at the camp fire, gazing into and through the flames as campers do the world over. The orange, white, and blue tinged flames crackled and danced for us. Coming to life from the dying bed of amber coals, flames shot up and overcame the dry wood tossed in at random when we became bored. The burning bark lost its brief attempt to protect the inner wood of each stick of pine. Thick, white smoke poured from the holes that some long gone woodpecker had left. Flames darting in and out, up and away into the sky were being chased by a few fading sparks and embers.

Things were quiet. Thinking quiet. We were wrapped in thought similar to the flames wrapped around the burning wood. Each of us staring into that circle of warmth perhaps dreaming of a week's worth of escapades gone by and having a difficult time of letting them go.

I reflected on what awaited us back in the "Orchard". Camp...Home...School...Life. My frenetic desires had no effect on the clock and reduced my powers to only a wish that the end wasn't tomorrow. None of us outwardly expressed a desire to see this trip terminate. There had been no grousing or discord all week or it was hidden quite well.

The river's scenery was idyllic and lured us to remain. Could we not identify with Huck Finn, and his friend Jim in the *Adventures of Huckleberry Finn*? We could.

Samuel Clemens, pen named Mark Twain, authored his two great masterpieces, *The Adventures of Huckleberry Finn* in 1884, and *The Adventures of Tom Sawyer* in 1876 while residing along the banks of this Connecticut River in Hartford, CT.

181

In 1870, Sam reminisced to a Hannibal classmate: "The old life has swept before me like a panorama; the old days have trooped by in their glory again; the old faces have looked out of the mists of the past; old footsteps have sounded in my listening ears; old hands have clasped mine; old voices have greeted me...." Twain was longing for the good old days. He verbalized that perhaps a boy's most memorable and fun-filled days are those of his childhood. For us it was no less.

As Huck and runaway slave Jim jumped from their raft in the night fog rather than be bowled over by an oncoming steamboat, they realized fast that risks accompanied the fun and adventure of "life on the Mississippi".

Our shenanigans adopted a similarity of "canoeing without a clue" of what lie ahead especially at the Hartland Rapids.

The embers deteriorated into an orange and black casserole which longed for bed also. We lie dead tired within our damp covered, warm sleeping bags. The lingering, dilute smoke made its way to my nostrils. A billion stars overhead would be our nightlight.

Before losing the battle to sleep, I mused about the great times we had over the past five days. What seemed to be mundane now was really not. It was not as long as unexplored and unchartered river adventure awaited us the next day. Even this final nocturnal event could not dispel our eagerness for tomorrow. Despite only a half day of canoeing ahead of us, we were raring to get on with it.

I reflected on the situation back home. There were kids my age hanging about the streets of cities and towns. They were bored perhaps and even on the brink of trouble for a lack of something to do.

We were one lucky bunch of guys and like Huck and Jim enjoying their adventure, I hoped it would go on forever.

$\stackrel{\times}{\Longleftrightarrow}20$ Over the Abyss

The magnificent night yielded and embraced yet another magnificent day. The habitual scenario of early morning fog presented itself again only to be wooed out by the scorching, August sun. Despite the mercury escalating to 88°F this day, it was our preference to be out on the river rather than wimping it out ashore in the cool shade of some deciduous tree. With ubiquitous water, a slight breeze was prevalent most of the day anyway providing more bearable conditions. No doubt the U-V rays would add richness to our come along tans, peacefully coexisting with an increased risk of melanoma. At the time we cared little if at all about health issues and maintained the status quo regarding typical teenage apathy.

The scuttlebutt at breakfast was about breakfast itself. Man alive! Our final Chuck Wagon meal was before us. We had eaten out of a bag for six days and the situation had given all of us a chance to evolve into connoisseurs of the dehydrated meal.

As a cook, we discovered that disaster meant adding too much water to the meal, but that adding water slowly in the cooking process presented an easy safety net: just gradually add water until the right consistency formed. The complaints against the cook were few and far between since everyone had to play the role at some point and didn't want to endure similar criticism when their stint surfaced.

A few, small cheers went up as the last plastic bag from the dehydrated food melted and sizzled away on the hot coals beneath the breakfast fire. We didn't help the air quality that week by the burning of plastic Chuck Wagon food bags, but rather added to the cause that passed the Clean Air Act years later.

"This is the day, gentlemen," Mr. Boulais announced, redirecting our attention his way.

"We're scheduled to meet the parents at Turner's Falls. They're supposed to meet us at the public boat ramp," he informed his charges before embarking for the last time.

"We won't be stopping for lunch until we get there because the rumor is there may be a cookout waiting for us," he hinted further.

This pretty much psyched us further for a "real meal". "Hamburgers? Hot Dogs?" I thought. Oh. Oh. Oh!! How did you guess our appetites to be voracious? Well, needless to say, that Chuck Wagon line helped a bit. Man, real food was imminent.

"There's only about eleven or so miles left, so we've got plenty of time to canoe all morning," coached our leader.

"What about the French King Rock?" Joe inquired seriously, with a tone that rang hazardous.

"Stay away from it," commanded Mr. Boulais, in a voice that spilled over with warning, "and canoe near the shore to be safe. The water is turbulent around it and its deep water below."

No sooner were those words said when off in my head sprang the notion of "...now which canoe is going to deviate from that order and head straight for that rock?" I'll concede and allow you to speculate.

Without another word or delay, we launched our canoes one final time, sinking our feet into the slimy, shoreline muck. We then hung them over the gunwale and washed off the goo in the cool river water.

As the sun inched higher, it sucked up the fog ravenously, completing its dissipation in minutes.

Paddling away from shore, I turned and looked back to see the small, pale green house dwindle in size. It suddenly dawned on me that none of us had bade farewell to the good man who lent us his property last night. There was no going back now to say good-bye as things were in motion and no one would back track either.

"Hey, what are you looking for now?" Steve startled me with a question.

"I was just wondering where that man is who let us use his land," I answered pensively.

"He's probably sound asleep," Steve guessed.

I pivoted to refocus on my paddling without responding to Steve. We set a slow and steady pace and headed into the freshly painted canvas of morning. The brief, lingering cool morning breezes hit our faces and darted away, fleeing madly from the army of rushing warmer air. We heeded the advice not to push it and glided graciously downstream. Ambivalent feelings had already taken hold of me.

"You know, it'll be nice to sleep in my own bed," Steve thought out loud.

"Yeah," I responded, adding wryly, "then in two days we'll be sleeping in those bunks at Accomsick," referring to our troop's waterfront base at Camp Woronoak.

The sun beat us good.

Naturally, missing the comforts of home wasn't too difficult for us as scouts. It was this idea that we desired the best of both worlds...having our cake and eating it too. The adventure hooked us. The exuberance of adventure and our new found freedom if only for a brief respite was liberating. Such a trip, if we had to traverse or were forced to make would no doubt have been tedious by now. It was not...simply because every one of us had desired to be there.

Come late morning and we had surpassed the confluences of Roaring Brook and Bennett Brook with Kidds Island off our port side. Canoeing this section of the river one continues to bask in the awesome and picturesque farm lands and meadows. It took the Massachusetts legislature until November 2000 to designate the Connecticut River Scenic Farm Byway. This stretch commences at the New Hampshire border in the town of Northfield, MA at Route 63 and Route 10 and reaches south ending by Route 47 at the Hadley town line. My senses were right on target about the beauty of this area and the state house only needed 34 years to second the motion.

Ray Roberge catches Pete Boulais napping and Joe paddling.
(8/19/66)

Although no white water rapids developed, the water upgraded into a swifter current. Soon the water's depth increased and appeared deeper than I would have liked.

Ray Roberge captures Joe O'Brien and Pete Boulais paddling out of the French King Gorge. The French King Bridge is behind them. (8/19/66)

About a mile and a half on the horizon, the French King Bridge caught my eye and beckoned me. From our location here the lowlands, farms, and meadows yield graciously to the rising promontories of the French King Gorge peaking out with 250 foot walls on both sides of the river. As we slowly paddled towards the bridge a slight sense of claustrophobia tried to edge its way over me. Had the gorge been narrower this sense may have escalated but it died out. Here one easily wonders why the abrupt change in landscape occurs and rightfully so. This river section is the exact spot of the Eastern Border Fault which was formed when Pangea split millions of years ago. The river marks this split well with the older Paleozoic metamorphic rock on the more elevated eastern side of the gorge and younger Mesozoic sedimentary rock on the slanted west side. Both sides support abundant growth of mountain laurel from its crevices.

About one half mile north of the bridge sits the famous French King Rock. This glacial conglomerate is humongous and was dubbed for the French King Louis XV in the 1700's by one of His loyal canoeists. The bridge takes its name from this rock. This arch type steel and concrete bridge rises 110 feet above the river's surface and employs both sides of the gorge as skewbacks. At 130 feet above the water Route 2 scoots across her linking Interstate 91 westward and Old Beantown to the east.

Onward we churned as the rock and bridge grew larger and more focused with each stroke. Now prior to our trip, we had been made aware of the legend or myth of this French King Rock, by simple hearsay. Although never verified by historical record, supposedly this rock was the site of a hand to hand duel between two crazy guys, a local Indian and an English soldier. The story claims the two fought to the death during King Philip's War, but doesn't identify the victor. It's difficult to visualize how the two made it out to the rock because prior to the 1916 construction of the Turner's Falls Dam the river here was a raging torrent of deadly rapids dashing against many a jagged rock. I suppose there was a way back then if there was a will, no doubt. The account doesn't go into what followed this duel as the duo's allies and enemies both watched in suspense from opposite shores. Whether it truly occurred didn't matter but in our juvenile minds it was fact...it happened!

With the sun directly overhead and glistening the ripples off the dark, green blue water, this leviathan rock without doubt lured us on.

"Stay close to shore!" Mr. Boulais yelled out, hoping to coax us inland. Not much compliance.

As usual, when some intriguing object attracts people, listening to reason often doesn't take the upper hand. Mr. Boulais may have had better luck with us by ordering everyone straight for the rock simply because as smart aleck teenagers we might have ignored him and cruised off.

Yet we all paddled as if in a temporary trance with our crafts gravitating directly for the French King Rock. Whatever happened to listening? Well, we were listening allright...to ourselves that is. Like the Seirenes luring Jason in *The Odyssey* this rock enticed us wonderfully yet terribly. It did the trick by its mere overwhelming presence. Why did we move towards it? Because it was there. Simply put, it invited exploration and close observation. We were so smart.

In the vicinity of about one hundred feet or less from the rock the cudgel of common sense smacked me in the forehead or elsewhere on my cranium. A distant or not so distant soul had stormed heaven with prayer and my guardian angel kept up the consistency of his work.

"Hey...we better move over," I urged Steve, coming to my senses.

"I think so," came the agreement from the rear.

Before Steve could respond, I was already sweeping wide off the starboard side with my bow stroke. He must have pulled hard on his J-stroke because we quickly veered to the port side almost on the dime. We chopped away with our paddles at a 45° angle which gradually positioned our canoe about 50 feet off the port side of this massive hulk. Now this rock seemed a little too ominous to tangle with and a relief came over me.

My relief lasted about a second and a half when my peripheral vision snagged who else but Jim and Gene in a beeline for the French King Rock. On top of this, they were chuckling. Mr. Boulais' screams mimicked the incoherent cries of a madman trying to call them off. I froze with fear and my hearing along with it. Joe and Ray were paddling with Mr. Boulais in the middle. I glanced quickly to Joe who watched helplessly, not saying a word. His face said it all, "fools".

Just what they were thinking we didn't know. Looking back, I don't think they were thinking. Perhaps they wanted to add a little more macho to their machismo? Perhaps to them this rock was some prehistoric kiosk in the middle of this gorge. Or Neptune's bald spot? Whatever, my friend, the two were in dangerous waters and they were fixated on the rock and not on the teeming, turbulent surface.

Jim and Gene were tempting fate by paddling closer and closer to the rock...no more, no less.

I over heard Jim boasting to Gene that "...he was gonna get up on that rock."

In an instant, their canoe pivoted broad side and broached into the French King Rock. The swelling waters played with the canoe as it tried to mosey away but could not. Gene was laughing and the goats were bleating frantically, as Jim reached over the gunwales to grab the rock. His hands kept slipping for lack of a place to grasp the smooth, rounded surface. The agitated water presented a deadly situation that neither could see. Thanks be to God the water was too quick and forceful for Gene to steady their canoe with just his paddle. Jim backed off his plan to climb the rock and at the last moment they both shoved off this bolder with their paddles and headed downstream.

Needless to say, everyone was relieved. I never said a word to Steve about this episode but immediately fast-forwarded my mind to the scenario of Jim and Gene capsizing at the French King Rock. With the swift current, who knows what direction the two would have drifted off to. Would their canoe have resurfaced in time for them to hang onto if it capsized? Your guess. The rest of us would no doubt have paddled over to assist them but would they still be acting silly upon being rescued? Go for it. How about the notion that both of them might be panic-stricken and might desperately try to climb into a canoe rather than just holding on. Oh joy, now a second canoe might be perilously on the brink of going asunder! Then, heaven forbid that the under current at this gargantuan rock might keep both of them under water despite their good swimmer status. Again I say it, and mean it well, there were guardian angels on heightened alert that day and other angels besides, sitting on the bridge waiting to assist us. And not the least of which was the angel of death, who by God's good grace, put their dispatch among us in abeyance.

****

Mr. Boulais had his words with Jim and Gene, but Steve and I didn't hang around to tune in. The steady, swift current kept us moving and before we knew it the half mile from the French King Rock to the bridge was about to lapse. The massive French King bridge looked down upon us. We craned our necks back to gaze upward in awe for she was higher up than any other bridge we had slipped under. She stretched out 783 feet long from shore to shore and towered 139 feet above the river's surface. The McClintock-Marshall Corporation created her for $375,000.00 and Governor Ely dedicated her on September 10, 1932. The American Institute of Steel Construction for their part awarded this bridge the "most beautiful bridge in North America" in 1932.

"Please do not come down upon us," I mused nervously. My thoughts skipped back six days to the Newbury Crossing Bridge with its rusty iron beams spanning a quieter, softer river.

We paddled with the impression that nothing could happen to us, that danger was past us now because we were so close to the end. Yet little did we know at the time that we were coasting over perhaps one of the most dangerous sections of the river. For one thing, if Jim or Gene or anyone of us for that matter had gone under at the French King Rock we would have been in for a surprise. The depth to the base of this rock ranges from 25 to 30 feet depending on seasonal river conditions. The turbulence here would have made things a little challenging to say the least in our efforts to resurface if we had been dragged down under.

The Turner's Falls Dam performed well in providing flood control and hydroelectric power but it likewise erased the majesty of a roaring river, steep precipices, and torrents rushing through a forgotten gulch. In 1966, the dam was 50 years old and there had to be folks still around who recalled the river scenario prior to construction. Regardless, we hadn't done our geologic or historical homework about the river, so as usual we were clueless. We hadn't done much of any homework come to think of it.

The French King Rock played the role of the "tip of the geologic iceberg" which marked the beginning of a narrow stretch of rapids known as the "Horse Race." This section of the river had so many bulging and protruding boulders that as the waters inundated this stretch it resembled horses racing frantically towards their finish line 1.7 miles downstream. Again off our port side nothing was particularly exciting except for Northfield Mountain. In a few short years the water carrying us along would play an additional role as a lower reservoir. How so? In 1968, the Northfield Mountain Project commenced as the first of its kind in the world. Northeast Utilities, a regional power company set out to create a hydroelectric project that would simultaneously store the water potential to produce electricity as well as generate it.

Northfield Mountain provides the ideal metamorphic rock which insured stability vital to the water intake tunnels. Engineers drilled a tailrace tunnel from the river by the French King Rock inland to a powerhouse deep inside the mountain. An access tunnel to reach the powerhouse and a ventilation shaft were also drilled. From the powerhouse which operated the water pumps, another pressure shaft was drilled up to the Northfield Mountain summit. Here a man-made reservoir held water pumped up to it from the river. The trick is to run water back down the tunnel through the pumps which now serve as generators producing 1 million kilowatts. And the trick works.

This mammoth project was completed in 1972 and has dealt no adverse effect upon the river. Thus the Connecticut river is the lower reservoir and Northfield Mountain is the upper, all the same water. Pretty ingenious. Visitors still come the world over to view this marvel so if you're in the area, stop in and check out the tour schedule if you haven't done so.

And so with the river guides advising canoeists to steer clear of the "rock" and stay close to shore, we didn't, and survived, and moved on down.

****

It wasn't as if we were suffering from a lack of objects or events off our port side but coasting on down the river and right below the French King Bridge, the confluence of the Millers River greeted us from the east. Local river guides warn that in medium or high water this confluence may become rough. I never noticed it or perhaps the water level hadn't risen to that depth to make a difference. Either way, the Turner's Falls Dam no doubt eclipsed the fury created when the Millers went head to head with the Connecticut prior to 1916.

Those of you in the category of "ye of little faith" regarding this, best believe that the area was treacherous with rapids because a few poor souls perished there. On April 24, 1725 a canoe with six men overturned just below the Millers River confluence, leaving three survivors. The others, Simon Pomeroy, Thomas Alexander, and Noah Allen all drowned. I don't know whose idea it was to begin the trip downstream but it was fairly ill-conceived.

At the time, none of us knew we had commenced floating above the "Horse Race" route beginning at the French King Rock. We hadn't started our own race yet to reach the finish in Barton's Cove and were conserving energy for this sprint. Whenever one in our group decided the time to be ripe and close enough to Barton's Cove the challenge to race to the finish might be shouted out. Or perhaps those guys ahead of the rest might try to quietly charge ahead and beat everyone else lagging behind.

Immediately following the confluence, the Connecticut makes a sharp turn and flows westerly searching for the Turner's Falls Dam. The paddling and the water grew calmer for the next half mile or so as we neared the end of the Horse Race. We had no clue what we were passing over and I doubt anyone else did. Had any of us gone under at the French King Rock or at any point along this Horse Race and drowned, there was a good chance we may never had been recovered. Why?

Ed Klekowski found out why in the autumn of 1997 while boating along this section of the river with some grad research students from the UMass/Amherst Biology Dept. Professor Klekowski and his students were shooting a video to promote Franklin County when student Sean Werle noticed the sonar depth finder acting wacky. It went from 20-30 feet to 120 feet and then back up to 20 feet. Fortunately they were traveling slow or they may have never detected the huge discrepancy. Ed has dubbed the find "King Philip's Abyss" and says it's likely "the last environment in Massachusetts whose biota is unknown."

The abyss is about 20 feet below the river's surface and less than

60 feet from shore, with a pure rock cliff that plummets 110 feet to the bottom.

Without a doubt, endless days of risky dives and research await this team as two challenging questions remain: just "...What the heck is it?" and "...Where did it come from?"

Professor Ed doesn't want to speculate but does give the most likely educated guess regarding its origin as a part of the chaos created with the Pangea split. The bottom of the abyss is devoid of any sediment and looks as if moving water has swept it clean. An ancient waterfall may have carved out the abyss or when Lake Hitchcock violently drained off in the Connecticut Valley, it did a little reconstruction work.

The Turner's Falls Dam, similar to so many others provided the green light for us to venture here. Before the dams, canoeing this river demanded frequent portages to say the least. Stretches like the "horse race" were just too perilous to negotiate in any craft. Any attempt might be labelled suicidal.

And so our perception of the Connecticut at the time was slanted, vague, and power-packed with ignorance. Identical to a book that one usually judges by its cover, this river's surface concealed well what our minds failed to imagine.

In 1999, after learning of the abyss and the "horse race" an eerie feeling briefly came over me. For any of us to have capsized near the French King Bridge would have been calamitous enough. But not to have one's body recovered after drowning and being holed up in an abyss 120 feet deep provided some distressing and woeful thoughts.

Dillydallying along this final few miles, most of us assumed the water's depth to be perhaps between ten to thirty feet but never the actual depth of the abyss. My brother Joe would have endured grandiose shivers up his spine if upon capsizing he had known the waters depth plunged to 130 feet. Mercy!...his imagined sea monster that pursued him from the abyss would have made the creature from the Black Lagoon pale in comparison. Oh well, if the physical world doesn't destroy you, our minds and imaginations lie in wait to do the job at full throttle.

As with any trip, especially with youngsters, destinations seem forever remote. Any parent can attest to this by the number of "...are we there yets?" carved on the dashboard of the family car. Likewise, the return trip home seems shorter perhaps only because we now know the two end points of our trip.

Steve and I paddled on in this vein, sensing that we were closing in on our destination but going wacky over, "How much further?" Before we realized it, we had been gradually marooned to the rear of the pack again. However, it was our doing as we paddled minus the resolve of America's Cup Race.

We coasted out of the Horse Race and past the small jutting peninsula called the Doctors. An aerial view of this protruding land mass portrays a homeless uvula seeking out a barren soft palate. Off our starboard side is the southeast side of Barton's Cove, our destination and we were ignorant of its location as we floated by. Had we beached there and run up the hill and down the other side we would have run into our parents awaiting us. A hairpin course lie ahead of us and we were clueless.

The river flows southwesterly but because of the dam about one mile downstream a wide cove or bay stretches out here to about 2500 feet in an area known as the Deep Hole. This land mass off our starboard side is known as the Lily Pond Barrier. Prior to dam construction in the 1800's the river ran headlong into this sandstone barrier with erosion occurring strictly south of it. Yet enough river water made its way over this barrier in two locations creating two waterfalls. These waterfalls formed deep plunge pools at the bottom of a ravine where a lily pond did thrive. In time the river finally cut through this barrier and the waterfalls dissipated.

According to Prof. Richard Little of Greenfield Community College at the end of the Lily Pond Barrier a third waterfall may have been but is perhaps eroded away.

Regardless, the 2500 foot wide cove south of the barrier "narrows" drastically at its end to only 400 feet wide. This may not seem that narrow but as we paddled around the bend in this hairpin turn and into the expanse of Barton's Cove the comparison became evident. It is precisely this abrupt change in the river's width that this section is dubbed "The Narrows".

And then no sooner had we come onto Barton's Cove then we were greeted by a flurry of motorboats with and without water skiers. Our paddling directed us northeasterly as we made out our buddies and brothers about half a mile ahead. They were heading in and beaching their canoes at the public boat ramp which was the flip side of the Lily Pond Barrier.

We plowed ahead urged on with new found excitement and quickly realized that we were in the tail section...again. We paddled slower now bracing ourselves for the large motorboat wakes, that would toss us about, oscillating our canoe from high to low, until the soft, dying lapping waves against our craft were rendered indiscernible. I was so grateful that we weren't toppled over by these wakes in front of the parents awaiting us no less. How embarrassing that would have been.

Our paddling was routine but my feelings were ambivalent. I watched the waves from the motorboat gradually fade away and head into shore. In a few moments, their once powerful size and force would lose steam, die and absorb into the sandy and pebbly beach. Our beloved canoe trip would do the same in no less time.

21 The End and Beyond

There was a little tussle of feelings and moods attempting to garner my heart as Steve and I paddled onto the shore of Barton's Cove. With six days and 133 miles behind us, a great sense of accomplishment prevailed. It felt good to have licked the challenge. The gauntlet had been cast down. We picked it up, met it face to face and won.

Sadness showed up as the urge to repeat the trip was tempered by reality in that I knew we wouldn't. At least not anytime soon. Familiarity with the folks from back home was gaining the upper hand, for as we paddled in to beach our canoes parents and siblings awaiting us grew more vivid and real.

Mr. Dumas was waiting in the shade by his pink Rambler and attached trailer to begin the job of loading and securing the canoes for the trip home.

Mr. Sullivan was there also accompanied by his daughter, Maureen.

There were a few more awaiting us but they are lodged into my forgotten memory bank.

Instantly I felt as if I'd fallen out of a good book. Wasn't I enjoying this chapter here? You bet I was. Enjoying myself then PLOP! I was thrust back into...reality? Perhaps.

"Hey!" I didn't like this one bit, I resisted in thought. For six days we had cut loose the strings of home if only in a physical way. It seemed a long time but really wasn't. You could have honestly fooled me though. Gone were six days of pure fun, adventure, shenanigans, solitude, peace, quiet, low risk, high risk, exploration, fake food?, eleven clueless guys, fears, joys, good weather, learning, luck, and unbridled faith. I wanted to prolong the trip in the worst way but the feasibility factor was absent and I knew it. I had to let go.

Steve and I ceased paddling and coasted inland, waiting for the first sound of stone, pebbles or sand to apply friction and scrap our canoe's bottom. It came and out I hopped. I grabbed the bow thwart with two hands and yanked our craft further ashore, stirring up some peaceful and dormant mud, seaweed and algae. Together we tugged and lugged our canoe onto dry land one last time when I noticed Sully's sister, Maureen.

This cute Irish-American lass was preoccupied with leaping from

195

rock to rock interchanging her static and dynamic balance. We watched her romp about as we settled the canoe between two protruding rocks for a well deserved rest.

The tantalizing aroma of sizzling beef diverted my attention not in a small way. It was at least two to three weeks since my olfactory nerve had picked up a whiff of barbecue. As I walked towards a smoking hibachi, I thought about Mr. Boulais' prophetic rumor...there was a cookout.

We headed straight for the smoking grill and were almost tripped up by "Mo" Sullivan as she bounded out of nowhere and landed on a large rock set before us. She blushed and smiled bashfully at us for a split second and then was off as fast as she arrived headed for another rock.

It was surreal mingling with the parents and re-acclimating into our real world. My efforts to adequately describe the trip to Cliff Dumas was cumbersome at best. Putting your heart, soul and feeling into someone else doesn't do justice to a great trip or spectacular event. It couldn't be done the way you'd want it to be done, simply because experience has to be experienced. It was futile to expect anyone to have the same enthusiasm and excitement over the trip the way we did. I wanted everyone to enjoy our thrills in the worst way but it just couldn't be done.

Just when I thought events were pretty much being put under wraps, I glanced out onto the cove to see Kevin Sullivan and Kevin Boulais flaunting their prowess at "the gladiator". They were about 30-40 yards out giving it their all pumping the canoe up and down, standing and riding the rear gunwales. They were good at it but before long both of them fell into the drink.

I scrambled back into our emptied canoe, solo paddled out onto the cove waters and executed this ritualistic feat again for one last fling. I fell into the water too but didn't care since its coolness felt refreshing.

The time rolled around to go home and if I got into the car any slower it would have been a clamber. The entourage made its way out to Route 2 and eventually down Interstate 91 for home. I can't recall it though because my head was way back upstream. My longing to go back took me there mentally since physically there wasn't an option.

After our one day hiatus it was back to the grind, shifting gears transiting into summer camp in a heartbeat.

The canoe trip was over.

Whatever we lugged around as baggage emotionally and psycho-

196

logically was our concern but the trip was over. Speaking of baggage, it was none other than Dennis Riel who was awarded the two goats. Norm Riel, Dennis' dad, proved to be so good hearted when he couldn't say "no" to his son's request, that the goats were no longer homeless. It didn't last though. The two nibbled and ate every blade of grass and leaf which rendered Norm's yard barren. When Mr. Riel could endure no more, he located a permanent home for them on a nearby farm in Agawam, MA.

****

Well, with the trip in the history books there emerged three scant vestiges associated with it.

The very next week at summer camp found Mr. Boulais proudly recalling the canoe trip tales to just about everyone he ran into. This included the Arts and Crafts director, Bob Achen, who was evidently an accomplished illustrator. Mr. Boulais employed his career skills in salesmanship to cajole Bob into painting a 2 ft. by 6 ft. section of plywood with oils of the trip. It gave the troop something to hang onto and it sits propped up against the wall at the Troop 40 Trustees Camp to this day.

School began, and two weeks after the trip I found myself in the brand spanking new John F. Kennedy Jr. High School. Mrs. Lucy, my eighth grade English teacher was seeking oral accounts of summer adventure from the class. I jumped at the chance and rendered the best two minute recap to the class that I could muster. As I commenced my story a girl in the next row, down about three or four seats pivoted in her seat and faced me with a Cheshire cat grin. It was none other than Maureen Sullivan. Boy, there wasn't anything new to reveal to her. Kevin, her brother, no doubt had told tale after tale of the canoe trip inside out. It was good to see "Mo" identifying with my tales as her face lit up at each event.

And finally during September's last week, all of us except Dennis Riel, who was away at school, were the stars of "Tom Colton's Highlights", a local 15 minute show put on by WWLP, Channel 22. Decked out in our full uniforms complete with red berets, we sat in front of the camera as Mr. Boulais retold that story again. After the show we posed proud as peacocks for a photo shoot which would add to the few souvenirs of the trip.

So there. You have it. For all it's worth.

****

The weeks blended well with the months and likewise the months meshed with the years. Canoe trip tales were told and retold on future campouts and hikes whatever that number may have been. We drifted out of scouting in a few years to high school, to college, to girls, to jobs, to wives, to careers, to life. But the memories survived to a different time. A different time indeed.

In August 1998, I discovered that I was taken back in time and the memories were increasingly clear and vivid.

And where was I? In my family's 1989 Green and Gray Chevy Window Van returning from a vacation on the Vermont shore of Lake Champlain. My wife Eva was with me along with Erin and Moira, our two daughters. We had just come off of Interstate Route 89 South and were merging onto Interstate Route 91, in the townships of Hartford and White River Junction, when the landscape enthralled me. Enthralled? Yes.

Bombing along the highway, I noticed the increased panoramic view of this valley since 91 South is more elevated that 91 North. A bird's eye view if you will. Below to my left, trickling slowly along the valley floor is the Connecticut River. The mountains of Windsor County, VT and neighboring cross river towns of Lebanon, Hartland, and Plainfield, NH were sparkling emerald as emerald could be. The setting western salmon sun blanketed those peaks and valleys with a rich beauty so hard to describe.

The beckoning and passing of the White River Junction sign tumbled open my buried trunk of dusty memories, clearing up shrouded events, escapades and itineraries of the past. Joe's suggested title, "The Canoe Trip" by everyone who went on it challenged me, yet embarrassed me, simply because we put the canoe trip on idle for 32 years. Mr. Boulais had passed on to his reward and no one that I knew of had recorded the event. Well, Dad was correct again, procrastination was in vogue, but I would try. It was 32 years to the week, I thought, but my resolve surfaced. Undaunted, I began to write. I'm glad I did.

****

The backyard became more alluring in August and September of 1998 as I found myself gravitating toward the family "park bench" on

198

our old brick patio. With clipboard, paper, pencil and a steady mug of tea, I sat beneath the silver maples and began to write. Most events came back clear as I pondered the seriousness of such a narrative. Big deal, I thought, there were myriad canoe trips on the Connecticut since Lake Hitchcock commenced its drainage 9,000 years ago. So what.

I reflected on the number of trips that went unrecorded and concurred with myself that the number must be high. I determined that our trip wouldn't be part of the count. Still I felt compelled to write and I did. Voraciously. At times, I couldn't stop and was reminded of my drive when Eva yelled three times that supper was ready. Sporadically, there were times when I couldn't start. But, I scribbled away anyway. My desire to write was quite strong, intense, and free flowing. Now it was something to enjoy and I did.

Mrs. Hinckle came into my mind. As I bade farewell to Holyoke Community College in January 1973, my blond Western Literature professor from Oklahoma sat before me analyzing my final essays.

"Gerard, you're good." "You're the best." "Really...you can do it," she soothed my ego with her encouraging words. I surmised she was real heady and off in the clouds somewhere, or she was simply trying to make me feel good. In a few years I realized she was neither, but was being down right honest and genuine. It was hard to believe her then because I didn't fully know myself and had no real working knowledge of what "good writing" was. Sorry...I was nineteen. I informed Mrs. Hinckle that my intended major was to be special physical education at the University of Massachusetts at Amherst. Her reaction seemed to portray slight disappointment because I sensed she would rather have me take up the pen. But I didn't take up the pen and kept to my own road in life. Yet her words and demeanor always followed me to this day and I have failed to shake her. Perhaps it's because she was the only professor who took me aside and encouraged my abilities. I left Holyoke Community with ambivalent feelings. I had to do what I had to do but I also felt I let Mrs. Hinckle down. She had done wonders for my self confidence and then I sort of burst her bubble. Perhaps I had read more into it but that's how I felt.

Regardless, it was a crucial time for me to write and now I could identify with my professor's words. Not the part about being a good writer but the "you can do it" part.

But as I wrote, different and deeper meanings emerged and came to mind about this canoe trip.

The river, the trip, the obstacles, the challenges, the risks, the rewards, the water, the everything...all seemed symbolic of hidden meanings. As I pushed the pencil, the trip and all of its affects upon me became more focused and seemed part of a much larger silver screen. There was much to absorb from the canoe trip and I came to realize that the digestion of many lessons came over time. A larger picture loomed before us that I failed to see back then but one that should have come into view as life went on.

The river, did it not represent life itself? Surely. From its source at the Fourth Connecticut Lake on the Canada/U.S. border, winding its path slowly but surely, steadily edging towards Long Island Sound 410 miles downstream, like life it moves along at an even clip, lazily "getting there". Our days move as such do they not?

How about those serpentine banks and curves along the river? Don't they seem to be analogous to the twilight each evening? Twilight?! Yeah. How many of us can really foretell what tomorrow will bring as the sun goes down and the evening shadows move in? No one. Oh, we may very well have our consistent forecasts of tomorrow based on events of days gone by. Yet more often than not the good Lord sends us a different plate of vegetables on any given day which makes a better day or one more overbearing than we would like. Likewise, as we paddled none of us could see what was "up around the bend". We just took it as it came.

So too the rate at which the river flows is synonymous with our seemingly mundane lives. This rate of our lives is equal to the river flow being too slow and placid at times. We become frustrated when life grinds almost to a standstill. And then clutching our paddles, the current transforms into a swift and furious clip so much so that it's a wonder if we'll ever make it through at this pace. But we do. And looking back we realize that some things in our lives had to be accomplished quickly, decisively, and at a quick pace without giving any quarter to dillydallying.

What about that which lies beneath the river's surface? Logs, old cars, deep abysses, fast currents, submerged bridge debris, anything to tangle one up...just to name a few, along with the dark unknown. These all weigh in as our daily events only minutes and hours ahead of us. Potential accidents and unfortunate events await all of us on the brightest, sun shiniest of days. But the hand of Providence stays most of these events does it not? It does. And the troubles and strife we encounter are usually more often the result of us foolishly meddling with the unknown in the first place.

How about our canoeing buddies? Similar to our friends, spouses, family members, or what have you, cooperation is imperative. Teamwork is essential in life or what you start keeps puttering until it dies. So, in life getting along with others makes life more bearable does it not? It does.

Likewise, on the river as in life, major obstacles were thrown into our paths. More formidable ones we encountered were the Wilder Dam, the Bellows Falls Dam, the Vernon Dam and the infamous Hartland Rapids. Do these not represent major changes or obstacles in our own lives? Adolescence? College? Careers? Illness? Beliefs? Marriage? Divorce? Pain? Death? You name them. Often the barriers or hurdles before us seem so insurmountable that we label them ominous. Yet each obstacle like those dams or rapids have a way around them or right through them. Time and experience may have produced two portage routes with one being the more preferred but everyone must decide the best route for themselves. Similarly, the most turbulent events in life like the rapids must be an occasion for one not to cower but to delve right into. We all have major obstacles in life, but the mature, courageous response is to face them. Not to face them is our weakness or fear. To stop at the dam and evade the portage is defeat. Likewise, our failure to face life's great obstacles or responsibilities is to quit. For the result is the same as on a river. You really cannot renege and paddle back upstream. And one cannot retreat in life. One stagnates and remains dormant at a particular stage, floundering in immaturity until they become ready to move on.

All rivers flow to the sea or an ocean for that matter. An ocean or sea here can be none other than the heavens that await us. Each river or life as it moves usually cannot physically set eyes upon its destination. Our faith reveals to us that there is One greater than us ready to receive us. Do rivers sense as they weave in and out, inching toward the sea that they possess the greatest power? Yet when it meets headlong with the sea at its mouth, a river becomes both overwhelmed and humbled. No river can match the sea and so submits itself without resistance giving up its life waters to join the greater life waters of the sea. When one gazes upon the ocean for the first time and perhaps every time, it is usually with awe. The amount of water, the powerful waves, the teeming marine life therein, moves one's soul to respect the power before them. Oceans and seas represent that endless power and grace and life of heaven which is God Himself.

Yes, our canoe trip on the Connecticut River held symbolism for all of us...our life from beginning to end, with all the joys, pains, surprises, tricks, and challenges along the way. Through it all we must somehow discover that He is with us along every stretch of the way. Despite the rough parts, when life is as fast as the rushing rapids amidst the immovable boulders, when we are afraid of what might be in the turmoil of life...He is there.

After capsizing, Kevin Boulais clung to the rocks in the surging waters of the Hartland Rapids, waiting frantically for Kevin Sullivan's outstretched arm and paddle to reach him and so bring him to safety. Was this not similar to God the Father reaching with His two fingers to touch Adam's hand and so bring him to life in "The Creation" as shown on the Sistine Chapel ceiling? You bet it was.

He works in subtle and gentle ways and often through the efforts of good people, and many times through us who have made many a blundering mistake.

And His Providence was there every nautical inch, foot, and mile of those 133 miles we churned. All of us paddling like a bunch of knuckleheads unaware of the impending dangers ahead and donned without life-jackets but trusting all the while.

And so as we terminated our canoe trip on Friday, August 19, 1966, we stepped out into the larger canoe trip of life, with all the lessons it had to offer.

And we moved on down, into "the water still ahead".